Lineberger Memorial
Library

Lenoir Rhyne University

Lutheran Theological
Southern Seminary

4201 North Main Street, Columbia, SC 29203

DISCUSSION AS A WAY OF TEACHING

Tools and Techniques for Democratic Classrooms

Second Edition

Stephen D. Brookfield

Stephen Preskill

JOSSEY-BASS
A Wiley Imprint
www.josseybass.com

Published by Jossey-Bass
A Wiley Imprint
989 Market Street, San Francisco, CA 94103-1741   www.josseybass.com

Jossey-Bass books and products are available through most bookstores. To contact Jossey-Bass directly
call our Customer Care Department within the U.S. at 800-956-7739, outside the U.S. at 317-572-3986,
or fax 317-572-4002.

Jossey-Bass also publishes its books in a variety of electronic formats. Some content that appears in
print may not be available in electronic books.

Library of Congress Cataloging-in-Publication Data
Brookfield, Stephen.
  Discussion as a way of teaching : tools and techniques for democratic classrooms / Stephen D.
Brookfield, Stephen Preskill.
      p. cm.
  Includes bibliographical references and index.
  ISBN-10: 0-7879-7808-6 (alk. paper)
  ISBN-13: 978-0-7879-7808-2 (alk. paper)
  1. College teaching. 2. Discussion—Study and teaching. 3. Forums (Discussion and debate) I.
Preskill, Stephen, 1950- II. Title.
  LB2331.B679 2005
  378.1'2—dc22
                                                2005008307

Printed in the United States of America
SECOND EDITION
HB Printing 10 9 8

CONTENTS

The Jossey-Bass Higher and Adult Education Series

PREFACE TO THE
SECOND EDITION

Since the first edition of *Discussion as a Way of Teaching* appeared in 1999 we have received continuous feedback on its benefits and omissions. The benefits seem to be those we had hoped for; readers have told us that the book is a comprehensive "soup to nuts" guide to planning and conducting exercises that is full of helpful exercises and practical suggestions. However, two omissions have been brought to our attention. The first concerns the explosion of online learning that has occurred in the first few years of the twenty-first century. We alluded to this development in the first edition but that analysis was clearly insufficient given developments in this area since 1999. Consequently, Chapters Eleven and Twelve have been added to explore this new phenomenon. Chapter Eleven examines the underlying dynamics of online discussion and concludes that although they are not that startlingly dissimilar to those of face-to-face discussion they do suggest specific practices and approaches uniquely suited to an online environment. Chapter Twelve suggests how the online environment can be adapted to discussion as a way of teaching. We explore how to increase participation, assign students to small groups, link interaction to content modules, and evolve ground rules for discussion. The other omission readers noted was the lack of attention to contemporary theoretical positions such as structuralism and post-structuralism and their relevance for understanding and practicing discussion-based teaching. To remedy this omission we have written Chapters Thirteen and Fourteen. These two chapters explore a number of theoretical concepts—cultural capital, disciplinary power, teachers as judges of normality, repressive tolerance, and the discourse theory of democracy—and describe the discussion practices and exercises that these different ideas call forth.

August, 2005
St. Paul, Minnesota   STEPHEN BROOKFIELD
Albuquerque, New Mexico   STEPHEN PRESKILL

PREFACE TO THE FIRST EDITION

This book is born of friendship, curiosity, anxiety, and service.

The two of us became friends while we were both faculty members at the University of St. Thomas in St. Paul, Minnesota. Our friendship was fostered by a common passion for many things—the films of Woody Allen figured prominently in our early conversations—but what we kept returning to as we talked was the joyful yet contradictory experience of teaching through discussion. In coffee shops, at home, in university corridors, and on the street, we spent hours celebrating the glorious unpredictability of discussion and exploring its purpose and value. Usually our conversations ended with us giving each other advice on the problems we faced as we used the method in our own practice.

During these conversations we often remarked how we'd love to have a book available to us that laid out a rationale for using discussion, guided us through its different configurations, and suggested various resolutions to the problems that arose in its use. What would the authors say about guided discussion (a topic about which we talked heatedly and repeatedly)? How would they conceive of the teacher's role in discussion? What would be their thoughts on using discussion in groups characterized by racial, class, and gender diversity? How would they deal with students who dominated conversation or those who never spoke? As we considered these and other questions, we would often say, "You know, we ought to write a book about this." An idea that was first mentioned lightly and jokingly became a serious possibility when Steve Preskill accepted a position at the University of New Mexico in Albuquerque. We realized that distance threatened our friendship but it stood a better chance of remaining strong if we worked on a common project. The project we chose is the book you now hold in your hands.

What kept us going as we coauthored this book was curiosity about what would end up on its pages. We asked ourselves a series of questions that essentially became the book's chapters. We wanted to know how we would justify the use of discussion to colleagues who saw no connections between how students talked to each other in class and promoting democracy in the wider society. How would we respond to the charge that discussion was a time-wasting distraction from teachers' primary work of transmitting content to students? What advice would we give on how to prepare students to participate in discussion? What were the best ways we knew to get discussion started and keep it going? What were the most creative adaptations we'd seen that kept routine and ennui from creeping into the conversation? How did factors of race, class, and gender play out in discussions? What advice would we give to each other about how to ensure that all students felt their voices were heard and respected? We were intrigued to know what we would say in response to these and other questions. Writing this book became our way of finding out.

Anxiety and service also played their parts. As teachers committed to discussion, we are alarmed that so many of our students and colleagues appear to have lost hope in the moral, political, and pedagogical promises of discussion. To many students, discussion seems like busy work, designed to fill up time or give the teacher a break. Students frequently claim that discussions wander so far off track that what is spoken about bears little relation to the curriculum being studied. Others complain that the experience of discussion is distinctly unpleasant—a time for a few students to dominate or to talk in racist, sexist, or demeaning ways without any control or opposition. We are also concerned that many teachers who continue to use discussion do so in an uncritical, unexamined way that only serves to bring the method further into disrepute. We know, too, that teachers who are committed to using discussion and who use it thoughtfully are constrained by economic forces. Colleges are increasingly held hostage by market forces that force them to run as businesses. Institutional budgets are cut, faculty and staff are reduced, yet student numbers rise. Colleges and universities are forced to demonstrate their profitability and utility by showing how they can serve more and more people. A belief that increased class size equals increased profitability or greater community-mindedness undermines discussion-oriented teaching.

We want to offer this book as a service to educators struggling to preserve their commitment to discussion. We have tried to make the book as practical and helpful as we can. Although we argue strongly for the moral, political, and pedagogical importance of discussion, we are not much concerned with rhetorical exhortation. We want *Discussion as a Way of Teaching* to be a book full of ideas, techniques, and usable suggestions. Our hope is that teachers who feel pressure to abandon discussion in the face of students' complaints or institutional constraints will read our book and find their commitment to discussion renewed. We hope also that they will find many new exercises and approaches to try that will convince students that participating in discussion is worth the effort. And we want teachers to feel that they can experiment with the methods and techniques we suggest without falling behind, sacrificing content, or losing control of the curriculum.

However, we want to stress that we are not out to proselytize. We are not trying to convert skeptics into taking the method seriously. Indeed, our experience has been that this is fruitless. Teachers who resolutely dismiss discussion as time-wasting, touchy-feely, experiential mush only come to take it seriously when they are so dissatisfied with what they're doing that they'll try something new or when they are irresistibly intrigued by the sense of joyful engagement they witness in their own colleagues' experimentations with the method. But we do think there are many college teachers out there who are interested in introducing more discussion activities into their classrooms but who aren't sure how to do this. We also believe that many teachers are trying to use the method but are having difficulties doing so. In some ways we count ourselves among both these groups. So we have written this book for ourselves as well as for them.

ORGANIZATION OF THE BOOK

Before a word of the manuscript was written, we had planned its layout. The opening two chapters make what we hope is a strong and convincing case for using discussion. Chapter One focuses on its moral and political justifications, particularly the experience it provides of democratic process. In that chapter we describe what differentiates discussion from conversation and dialogue, and we blend elements of these ideas into the concept of critical discussion.

The chapter ends with an outline of the dispositions—the attitudes and habits—necessary for democratic discussion. Chapter Two focuses on the benefits of discussion for learning and teaching. We make fifteen claims for the ways in which discussion helps learning and enlivens classrooms (for example, it helps students explore diversity and complexity, it sharpens intellectual agility, and it endorses collaborative ways of working and the collective generation of knowledge). The chapter concludes by summarizing the five most common reasons why teachers lose heart (in our view, prematurely) in their commitment to discussion.

Chapters Three and Four deal with the early stages of discussion. One reason why teachers give up on discussion is that students often seem unprepared to engage in conversation. How to ensure that they come to class able to talk about the discussion topic is the focus of Chapter Three. We show how teachers can use lectures to demonstrate the dispositions of discussion; how to model their own commitment to the method; how to set structured, critical prereading assignments; and how to evolve or clarify ground rules, expectations, and purposes. Getting the discussion started is the theme of Chapter Four. We point out a few of the common mistakes teachers make at the start that can kill discussion. Then we provide some specific exercises that we've found useful in prompting students to talk. We also suggest several ways that students' prior reading or writing can be debriefed.

Chapters Five and Six both deal with how to maintain the momentum of discussion. Chapter Five reviews the different types of questions teachers can ask in discussion and the benefit and purpose of each type. We propose three exercises to improve students' ability to listen carefully and three ways teachers can respond to students' contributions. Chapter Six examines the dynamics of breaking students into small discussion groups. We suggest different ways of bringing small group deliberations back into the larger class and offer some variations on the conduct of small group discussions that we have found useful. The chapter ends with a brief exploration of how e-mail communication can improve classroom discourse.

In Chapters Seven and Eight we move to consider how issues of race, class, and gender affect what happens in discussion. Chapter Seven focuses mostly on race and class. We argue that discussions in culturally diverse groups must begin by honoring and respecting differences. How this could happen is explained through a series of exercises. We offer some diverse formats, such as dramatizing and drawing discussion, and we consider how to introduce verve into conversation. The chapter also proposes ways of monitoring racist speech and of creating outlets for anger and grief. We end with a discussion of middle- and working-class speech codes, and the disproportionate representation they have in discussion. Chapter Eight, written with our friend and colleague Eleni Roulis, looks at how male and female speech patterns manifest themselves in conversation. It begins by offering four vignettes that illustrate the complicated intersections between discussion and gender. The importance of acknowledging relational and rapport talk and the contributions of feminist pedagogy inform the exercises this chapter offers to help clarify the role gender plays in shaping how we talk to each other.

How to keep students' and teachers' voices in some kind of balance and what happens when they are drastically out of balance are the concerns of Chapters Nine and Ten. In Chapter Nine we look at why some students talk too much and others talk too little. We offer suggestions on how to curb those who are overly garrulous and how to bring into speech students who are reluctant to participate. Chapter Ten considers how to keep the discussion leader's voice in balance. We look at the most common reasons why teachers say too much or too little and then offer ways for them to avoid either extreme. The chapter ends with three scenarios that illustrate what happens when the teacher intervenes too much, too little, or just the right amount.

The dynamics and conditions of online discussion are considered in Chapters Eleven and Twelve. In Chapter Eleven we examine the architecture of online courses and lay out the four R's of effective online teaching—research, responsiveness, respect, and relationships. Chapter Twelve reviews how we can create the conditions for effective online discussion—discussion that is participatory, thoughtful, and disciplined. We explore how to increase participation, assign students to small groups, link interaction to content modules, and evolve ground rules for discussion. The next two chapters view discussion through various theoretical perspectives. Chapter Thirteen examines stucturalism, post-structuralism, and repressive tolerance as three perspectives that have considerable implications for how we run discussions. We outline each of these ideas and then consider how they inform the practice of discussion leaders. Chapter Fourteen explores in some detail the work of Jurgen Habermas, the German critical theorist. Habermas believes that a society is more or less democratic according to the discussion processes its members use to come to decisions about matters that affect their lives. We examine his ideas on the way we learn communicative action, practice what he calls the validity claims of discussion, and use standards of discourse to judge whether or not we are behaving democratically.

Chapter Fifteen deals with the thorny question of how to evaluate discussion. We argue against the imposition of a standardized, "objective" evaluative protocol, believing that such an approach ignores the contextuality of most classroom conversations. We favor instead grounding evaluations in the multiple subjectivities of students' perceptions. How these perceptions might be recorded is described through such instruments as discussion audits and logs, course portfolios, and mandatory evaluation forms. The book ends with suggestions on how we might judge the extent to which discussions meet the fifteen claims for discussion advanced in Chapter Two.

COMMON OBJECTIONS TO DISCUSSION

As you read this book, you may find that your interest in experimenting with some of the techniques it contains is contending with some predictable reservations about how realistic this is. We want to acknowledge these reservations and to provide our thoughts on them.

SPENDING TIME IN DISCUSSION WILL ALLOW ME LESS TIME TO COVER NECESSARY CONTENT.

The concern about having insufficient time to cover content is felt by teachers who believe that the material they want students to learn is too important to be left to chance. If they lecture, so their argument goes, at least this ensures that the material is aired in students' presence. We share this same concern. We want our students to engage seriously with ideas and information we think important. In fact, it is precisely for this reason that we think discussion is worth considering. As we argue in Chapter Two, building connections— personal and intellectual—is at the heart of discussion. Ideas that seem disconnected when heard in a lecture come alive when explored in speech. Arguments that seem wholly abstract when read in a homework assignment force themselves on our attention when spoken by a peer. There is no point in covering content for content's sake—the point is to cover content in a way that ensures that students engage with it. It is because we take content so seriously and want students to understand certain key ideas accurately and thoroughly that we feel discussion is indispensable.

A COMMITMENT TO DISCUSSION MEANS THINKING THAT OTHER TEACHING APPROACHES ARE SOMEHOW LESS WORTHY OR IMPORTANT.

Both of us use lectures, simulations, independent study, video, intensive reading, and any other method that works to engage students in learning. We believe that kinesthetic movement needs to be introduced into classrooms to engage the body as well as the mind. For us, anything goes as long as it assists learning. For example, both of us love to lecture and both of us believe that lecturing is often necessary to introduce difficult ideas and to model critical inquiry. But we do believe that discussion can serve many important purposes (which we outline in Chapters One and Two) and that teachers sometimes abandon discussion too early simply for lack of some creative ideas for implementation.

DISCUSSION IS UNREALISTIC TO CONSIDER FOR LARGE UNDERGRADUATE LECTURE COURSES.

We have taught core courses in laboratories or auditoriums with one hundred or more students present. We accept that these are important constraints and that they make experimentation with some of the exercises we suggest virtually impossible. But even under these conditions, we have usually found that it's possible to do some small, though not insignificant, things. For example, as we argue in Chapter Three, a lecture in an auditorium can incorporate two- to three-minute buzz groups or reflection pairs, followed by two minutes of random responses from students. Doing these things stops students from falling into a deep reverie while you're talking and forces them to engage with the ideas you think are important. It also allows you to make reference to students' reflections during the next segment of the lecture, which is one way to keep their attention high.

YOU CAN'T TAKE EXERCISES PROPOSED IN A BOOK
AND SIMPLY PLOP THEM DOWN IN ANOTHER CON-
TEXT WITH THE EXPECTATION THAT THEY'LL WORK.

We couldn't agree more with this point. Both of us now find ourselves working in graduate education, and though our experience
covers high schools, community development, vocational institutes,
community colleges, and adult education centers, our current situations and responsibilities as university professors undoubtedly
shape what we write. So we expect that any ideas that you find
potentially useful here will be adapted, altered, abandoned, or
completely reshaped as you think through how they might work in
your own practice with your own students.

I THINK DISCUSSION IS FINE IN PRINCIPLE,
BUT BECAUSE I'M INEXPERIENCED IN
WORKING THIS WAY, I'M BOUND TO FAIL.

One short response to this, of course, is that the only way to get
experience of leading discussion is to do it! Another is to acknowledge that the two of us fail all the time—things don't work out as
we anticipate, students respond less enthusiastically than we had
hoped, and so on. Indeed, some of the exercises we propose—
particularly those in Chapters Seven and Eight dealing with race,
class, and gender—are quite risky. If you feel so uncomfortable
about an exercise that you're overwhelmed with anxiety, don't
bother with it. Instead, try to find colleagues who are experimenting creatively with discussion and ask if you can sit in on one or two
of their classes, perhaps offering to be a sounding board, resource
person, or cofacilitator. Observing their practice might give you a
better sense of what to expect when you decide to work this way.

DISCUSSION NEEDS AN INVESTMENT OF TIME
I CAN'T MAKE SINCE I ONLY SEE STUDENTS
IN BLOCKS OF THIRTY TO FORTY MINUTES.

There is probably a minimum amount of time needed for a
deep engagement with discussion. Serious consideration of ideas
needs time for these ideas to be stated, heard, restated, questioned,

challenged, refined, and stated again. Listening and responding take up at least as much time as exposition. Also, the time it takes to build the degree of trust among members that is such an important feature of good discussion cannot be rushed. If you take discussion seriously, you could experiment with the timing of classes (for example, canceling class one week and doubling up the next), if that's possible. Or you could try short buzz groups and paired listening exercises. But it may be that you're currently working in a teacher-centered situation where discussion is impossible. That's fine. At the very least, you can try to model through your actions as a teacher some of the dispositions of discussion that we propose in Chapter One.

DISCUSSION DOESN'T HAVE TO BE TIED SO MUCH TO DEMOCRACY—IT'S JUST ONE DIFFERENT TEACHING METHOD AMONG MANY.

We would have to disagree with this contention. For us a commitment to discussion and an honoring of the democratic experience are inseparable. We realize we may have a philosophical difference here with some readers, who see discussion as a method disconnected from any political significance. But for us the respectful engagement with others that lies at the heart of discussion encapsulates a form of living and association that we regard as a model for civil society that has undeniable political implications. Discussion is a way of talking that emphasizes the inclusion of the widest variety of perspectives and a self-critical willingness to change what we believe if convinced by the arguments of others. We believe that most political decisions boil down to choices about who gets what, about how the limited resources available in any social group are used or allocated. The conversations informing such decisions must, in our view, be characterized by the same respectful hearing of the widest possible range of perspectives and the same self-critical openness to changing ideas after encountering these perspectives that undergird discussions held in college classrooms. These classrooms may be one of the few arenas in which students can reasonably experience how democratic conversation feels. Taking discussion seriously moves the center of power away from the teacher and displaces it in continuously shifting ways among group members. It parallels how we think a democratic system should work in the wider society. In this sense, classroom discussions always have a democratic dimension.

DISCUSSION IS FINE FOR "SOFT" SUBJECTS LIKE THE HUMANITIES AND SOCIAL SCIENCES WHERE DISAGREEMENT AND DIVERGENCE ARE POSSIBLE, BUT IT HAS NO PLACE IN "HARD" SUBJECTS LIKE MATHEMATICS, STATISTICS, AND THE NATURAL SCIENCES.

We agree that discussion should be used only when appropriate. In the teaching of unambiguous factual information (for example, the population of Baltimore in 1850, the chemical composition of sodium chloride, or Boyle's law) or inculcation of specific skills (how to load software or how to give an injection), there seems to be little scope for using the method. However, things are not always as simple as they seem. The exact figure given for Baltimore's 1850 population is actually a human construct, dependent on the data-gathering techniques and modes of classification statisticians decide to use, as well as on the learned behaviors of the data gatherers themselves. The hypothetico-deductive method that lies at the heart of intellectual inquiry in the natural sciences is actually a human system of thought, developed at a particular moment and place by a particular person (Francis Bacon) and refined over time by philosophical advances in the logic of the scientific method (for example, Karl Popper's principle of falsifiability). What seem to be standardized, objective, and unambiguous skills of computer usage or nursing care are actually protocols developed by particular groups and individuals. Which program or protocol becomes accepted as professionally dominant, as representing common sense or the norm, depends on which group has the power to promote its way of interpreting good practice over other contenders.

So we would argue that there is no knowledge that is unambiguous or reified (that is, that exists in a dimension beyond human intervention). The seemingly immutable laws of physics are always applied within a certain range, and the boundaries of that range shift according to research and according to who has the power to define standards for acceptable scientific inquiry. It is salutary to reflect on how many intellectual advances have been initiated by thinkers who were ostracized and vilified as dangerous or crazy at the time they were working.

However, we would also acknowledge that there are times when discussion is not the best way to help students learn something. When we attend workshops to learn how to use the World Wide Web, we don't want to spend the first hour problematizing computer technology. Rather than consider how access to this technology is stratified by class, gender, and race and how it reproduces existing inequities, we want to know which search engine to use. Instead of questioning whether or not this technology privatizes people and, by reducing the chance for people to gather physically in public places, thus prevents new social movements that challenge the status quo from forming, we want to know which button to press to display graphics. Of course, we would argue that the best teachers start with learners' needs (such as which search engine to use and which button to press) and then nudge them to question the social organization of the technology they are using.

We would also point to the example of McMaster University in Hamilton, Ontario, where medical students spend three years working in small groups. Ferrier, Marrin, and Seidman (1988) report that according to their supervisors, graduates of the program performed better in their first year of practice than graduates from other universities. When taking the exams of the Royal College of Physicians and Surgeons of Canada, the first-attempt pass rate of McMaster students is higher than the national average. Palmer (1998) describes a large research university he visited where students (under the guidance of a mentor) work in small circles to diagnose and treat real patients. In the words of the dean of the medical school concerned, "Not only did the test scores not decline, but they actually started going up, and during the time we have been teaching this way, they have continued, slowly, to rise. In this approach to medical education, our students not only become more caring but also seem to be getting smarter, faster" (p. 127).

OUR AUDIENCE

The general audience for this book is all teachers and leaders who use discussion to help people learn. Our primary audience is college and university teachers, but we hope that some of the exercises, techniques, and approaches we suggest can be used, or adapted, in secondary schools, adult and continuing education, training and human resource units, community groups, and other areas of learning.

We write out of our experiences working in a variety of settings. Stephen Brookfield has worked with discussion in technical, adult, and higher education, and in community development, in Great Britain, the United States, and Canada. Stephen Preskill has experience using discussion in public schools, colleges, and universities in the United States. Our diverse backgrounds mean that we write about discussion as a method with broad application to any situation in which people gather to learn, whether or not these are officially designated as "education."

We wanted this book to be practical, usable, and accessible. Although our understanding of discussion has been strongly influenced by various traditions and philosophies, we didn't want to add to the already voluminous interpretations of the meanings of discourse and dialogue. Instead, we wanted to write a book we could turn to for help on creating the kinds of conversations we desired. We also wanted the book to be immediately understandable to teachers across disciplines who decide, for whatever reason, to give discussion a try.

So the book is written in a deliberately colloquial tone, one that we believe mirrors the conversational way in which teachers give advice to each other. We took to heart George Orwell's injunction in his essay "Politics and the English Language" (1946) that writers should never use a complicated word where a simple one will do. But this doesn't mean that we've tried to write a gray, utilitarian manual. On the contrary, we've tried to write our own personal experiences as discussion participants directly into the text in the belief that you would appreciate knowing how we try to live the democratic process through group talk. We hope our belief is right.

January 1999
St. Paul, Minnesota   Stephen D. Brookfield
Albuquerque, New Mexico   Stephen Preskill

GRATITUDES

We wish to thank Eleni Roulis for joining us in this project. Her intelligence and spirit were crucial to its completion, and her contributions to Chapter Eight were irreplaceable. We also want to thank the seven reviewers in the United States, Australia, Scotland, and England who read and critiqued the first draft of this manuscript. David Boud of the University of Technology in Sydney, Australia, and Gary Cale of Jackson Community College, Jackson, Michigan, were good enough to identify themselves to us. Gary also gave willingly of his valuable time to help us decide how best to title the book. As always, Gale Erlandson, David Brightman, and John Skelton served as thoughtful, supportive, and constructively critical editors.

Stephen Brookfield wants to thank Stephen Preskill for his friendship and dedicates this book to him. In the preface to his book, *Becoming a Critically Reflective Teacher* (1995), Stephen described Steve as "an inspirational colleague who in his actions embodies much of the critically reflective spirit that this book has tried to convey" (p. xix). Working collaboratively on *Discussion as a Way of Teaching* has only deepened Stephen's admiration for Steve's intelligence and authenticity. It took eight books before Stephen found a coauthor, but the wait was worth it.

Stephen also wants to thank the students and faculty at the School of Education of the University of St. Thomas for many hours of conversation that illuminated the joys and contradictions of discussion. He particularly wants to acknowledge his colleagues in the School of Education—Gene Audette, Bill Carter, Kay Egan, Cathy Guggigsberg, Bruce Kramer, Freddy Kustaa, Don La Magdeleine, and Scott Taylor—who helped him think through the purpose, organization, and format of this book during one of the School's regular "Work in Progress" sessions. He also benefited greatly from the critiques of students and faculty—particularly Tom

Heaney, Scipio Colin III, Craig Mealman, Randee Lawrence, Ian Baptiste, Elizabeth Tisdell, Carol Eckerman, and Martha Casazza— of the National Louis University doctoral program in adult education. Finally, Stephen wants to thank his wife, Kim, and his children, Molly and Colin (The 99ers) for, well, everything.

Stephen Preskill wants to thank Stephen Brookfield for his friendship and generosity. Steve is also grateful to Stephen for lingering in assorted coffee shops for protracted periods whilst painstakingly revising multiple drafts of the new chapters that have been added to this second edition. Steve once again dedicates this volume to Stephen with affection, appreciation, and deep respect.

THE AUTHORS

The father of Molly and Colin, and the husband of Kim, Stephen D. Brookfield is currently Distinguished University Professor at the University of St. Thomas in Minneapolis-St. Paul, Minnesota. He also serves as consultant to the adult education doctoral program at National Louis University in Chicago. Prior to moving to Minnesota, he spent ten years as professor in the Department of Higher and Adult Education at Teachers College, Columbia University, where he is still adjunct professor. He received his B.A. degree (1970) from Coventry University in modern studies, his M.A. degree (1974) from the University of Reading in sociology, and his Ph.D. degree (1980) from the University of Leicester in adult education. He also holds a postgraduate diploma (1971) from the University of London, Chelsea College, in modern social and cultural studies and a postgraduate diploma (1977) from the University of Nottingham in adult education. In 1991 he was awarded an honorary doctor of letters degree from the University System of New Hampshire for his contributions to understanding adult learning. In 2003 he was awarded an honorary doctorate from Concordia University for his contributions to adult education practice.

Brookfield began his teaching career in 1970 and has held appointments at colleges of further, technical, adult, and higher education in the United Kingdom and at universities in Canada (University of British Columbia) and the United States (Columbia University, Teachers College and the University of St. Thomas). In 1989 he was visiting fellow at the Institute for Technical and Adult Teacher Education in what is now the University of Technology, Sydney, Australia. In 2002 he was visiting professor at Harvard University Graduate School of Education. In 2003–2004 he was the Helen Le Baron Hilton Chair at Iowa State University. He has run numerous workshops on teaching, adult learning, and critical thinking around the world and delivered many keynote addresses at regional, national, and international education conferences. In 2001 he received the Leadership Award from the Association for Continuing Higher Education (ACHE) for "extraordinary contributions to the general field of continuing education on a national and international level."

He is a three-time winner of the Cyril O. Houle World Award for Literature in Adult Education: in 1986 for his book *Understanding and Facilitating Adult Learning: A Comprehensive Analysis of Principles and Effective Practices* (1986), in 1989 for *Developing Critical Thinkers: Challenging Adults to Explore Alternative Ways of Thinking and Acting* (1987), and in 1996 for *Becoming a Critically Reflective Teacher* (1995). *Understanding and Facilitating Adult Learning* also won the 1986 Imogene E. Okes Award for Outstanding Research in Adult Education. These awards were all presented by the American Association for Adult and Continuing Education. His other books include *Adult Learners, Adult Education, and the Community* (1984), *Self-Directed Learning: From Theory to Practice* (1985), *Learning Democracy: Eduard Lindeman on Adult Education and Social Change* (1987), *Training Educators of Adults: The Theory and Practice of Graduate Adult Education* (1988), *The Skillful Teacher: On Technique, Trust, and Responsiveness in the Classroom* (1990), and *The Power of Critical Theory: Liberating Adult Learning and Teaching* (2005).

Stephen Preskill is currently Regents Professor of Education in the Department of Educational Leadership and Organizational Learning in the College of Education at the University of New Mexico. For nine years he was an elementary and middle school teacher before earning his doctorate from the University of Illinois at Urbana-Champaign in 1984 in educational policy studies with an emphasis in the history of American education. From 1984 to 1989 he taught at Carleton College in Northfield, Minnesota, and from 1989 to 1994 he was a member of the educational leadership faculty at the University of St. Thomas in St. Paul, Minnesota. He has been teaching at the University of New Mexico since 1994.

He is the coauthor of two previous books. With Stephen Brookfield, he co-wrote the first edition of *Discussion as a Way of Teaching: Tools and Techniques for Democratic Classrooms* (1999). With Robin Smith Jacobvitz, he coauthored *Stories of Teaching: A Foundation for Educational Renewal.* He is currently working on a book for Jossey-Bass in collaboration with Stephen Brookfield tentatively titled *Learning as a Way of Leading: Lessons from the Struggle for Social Justice.*

Preskill's main research activities have focused on the history of American educational reform, leader and teacher narratives, the connections between learning leadership and democracy, and how discussion-based teaching supports democratic processes. He has published more than forty articles in a variety of social science journals.

DISCUSSION AS A WAY OF TEACHING

CHAPTER ONE

DISCUSSION IN A DEMOCRATIC SOCIETY

Recently one of us led a discussion that confirmed for us why we value the discussion method so highly. Steve Preskill was teaching a course on educational ethics and had found a newspaper article describing a local school board's refusal to honor a "do not resuscitate" (DNR) order. A DNR order is issued when a person is gravely ill. It is a legally binding document that is signed by the individual's next of kin and a supervising physician. They declare that the patient's medical condition is so fragile and grave that if the patient goes into cardiac arrest, no effort should be made to resuscitate. The article Steve found involved a schoolchild whose parents had signed a DNR order. The school board took the position that human life is unconditionally sacred. Because preserving life takes precedence over everything else, the board claimed, all efforts must be made to save a child's life, regardless of circumstances or DNR orders.

Steve projected a summary of the article on an overhead screen for the whole class to read. Steve describes the experience in the following vignette.

> I had brought this article into class that day to illustrate what it meant for an organization to take a principled stand on an issue. In previous classes we had been reading articles that took a highly principled view of the value of human life, so I expected that most students would support the school board's position

Note: Parts of this chapter have been incorporated, with permission of the publisher, from Stephen Preskill, "Discussion, Schooling, and the Struggle for Democracy," *Theory and Research in Social Education,* 1997, 25(3).

without much disagreement. I went into class believing that the school board's decision was courageous and morally defensible.

The first students who spoke up after reading the summary supported the school board's decision. As I heard their comments, I smiled and nodded in agreement, all the while quietly celebrating how much my students were learning from my lectures and the readings I had assigned. But as the group probed deeper and as more students spoke, more information as well as opinion emerged. A few students argued that the board showed a marked lack of respect for the parents' carefully reasoned decision. I was taken aback by this dissenting view and was even more surprised by the students' ability to defend it from the same uncompromising position on the sacredness of human life. One student who had had a lot of experience with DNR orders explained that they are written only after agonizing deliberation among parents, health care professionals, attorneys, and educators. They therefore should not be taken lightly. Others pointed out that despite the board's good intentions, the members had acted out of ignorance of the legal, medical, and even ethical issues involved.

By now I was starting to realize that things were not nearly as simple as I'd imagined. What I'd thought would be a straightforward illustration of a principled stand was turning into a deep probing of a situation in which a single, seemingly unassailable principle was being employed to defend diametrically opposing views. This was disconcerting, surprising, and gratifying in equal measure. I felt pleased that things were taking an unexpected turn but uncertain that I could stay on top of the discussion and make some good connections between what students were saying and the concept of taking a principled stand. And at the back of my mind was the contrary thought that it wasn't my duty always to make connections for students.

Despite my uncertainty, I was engaged by this exchange of views and asked someone to explain in what way the school board showed an ignorance of ethical issues. A different student explained that DNR orders are usually inspected by ethicists before they are issued. Another student noted that it wasn't up to any one person or entity to defy such an order, that what to do in such situations was the responsibility of the community as a whole. Furthermore, this student argued, the DNR order was closer to being a reflection of broad community participation than the unilateral fiat of the board was.

This last view showed a sophisticated understanding of communitarianism (a view we hadn't even covered yet!) and led to other students' expressing the opinion that the school board's decision could be defended only if certain conditions were met. The school board members needed to show that they had consulted with as many different people as the authors of the DNR order had, and they also needed to show that they had engaged in the same level of careful forethought as that displayed by the parents and physicians in arriving at their position. I rocked back and forth on the balls of my feet, a bit shaken by this collective display of knowledge and wisdom. My initial conviction that the board was in the right had been thoroughly undermined, causing me to wonder how many more of my beliefs would be thrown into doubt if I exposed them to the consideration of this group. How humbling and disconcerting! And yet how inspiring to take part in a discussion that deepened understanding by allowing many points of view to emerge and to be carefully weighed by all involved.

This vignette demonstrates why we place such store in discussion as a teaching method. As Steve's experience illustrates, discussion is a valuable and inspiring means for revealing the diversity of opinion that lies just below the surface of almost any complex issue. Although there are many ways to learn, discussion is a particularly wonderful way to explore supposedly settled questions and to develop a fuller appreciation for the multiplicity of human experience and knowledge. To see a topic come alive as diverse and complex views multiply is one of the most powerful experiences we can have as learners and teachers. In a discussion where participants feel their views are valued and welcomed, it is impossible to predict how many contrasting perspectives will emerge or how many unexpected opinions will arise.

In revealing and celebrating the multiplicity of perspectives possible, discussion at its best exemplifies the democratic process. All participants in a democratic discussion have the opportunity to voice a strongly felt view and the obligation to devote every ounce of their attention to each speaker's words. In this minidemocracy, all have the right to express themselves as well as the responsibility to create spaces that encourage even the most reluctant speaker to participate.

Discussion and democracy are inseparable because both have the same root purpose—to nurture and promote human growth. By growth we mean roughly the same thing as John Dewey (1916) did: the development of an ever-increasing capacity for learning and an appreciation of and sensitivity to learning undertaken by others. Democracy and discussion imply a process of giving and taking, speaking and listening, describing and witnessing—all of which help expand horizons and foster mutual understanding. Discussion is one of the best ways to nurture growth because it is premised on the idea that only through collaboration and cooperation with others can we be exposed to new points of view. This exposure increases our understanding and renews our motivation to continue learning. In the process, our democratic instincts are confirmed: by giving the floor to as many different participants as possible, a collective wisdom emerges that would have been impossible for any of the participants to achieve on their own.

But we do not prize discussion solely because it helps us attain worthy democratic aims. We practice it eagerly simply because it's so enjoyable and exciting. Unpredictable and risky, it is the pedagogical and educational equivalent of scaling a mountain or shooting dangerous rapids. Never sure what we'll encounter as we push toward the top or as we career around the next bend, our level of alertness and attentiveness remains high. Indeed, there is an exhilaration that we experience in the best of discussions that is not unlike the thrill we enjoy in the most challenging of outdoor activities. This is why we like teaching democratically. In remaining open to the unexpected, we feel engaged and alive. So our commitment to discussion is not just moral and philosophical but also deeply personal and importantly self-gratifying. Even if we lacked a principled rationale for favoring discussion, we would still keep the conversation going because it gives us so much pleasure.

BLENDING DISCUSSION, DIALOGUE, AND CONVERSATION

Certain authors who agree about the potential of group talk have attempted to make distinctions among conversation, discussion, and dialogue. The philosopher Matthew Lipman (1991) argues that conversation seeks equilibrium, with each person in turn taking opportunities to speak and then listen but where little or no movement occurs. Conversation, Lipman claims, is an exchange of thoughts and feelings in which genial cooperation prevails, whereas dialogue aims at disequilibrium in which "each argument evokes a counterargument that pushes itself beyond the other and pushes the other beyond itself" (p. 232). Dialogue for Lipman is an exploration or inquiry in which the participants view themselves as collaborators intent on expeditiously resolving the problem or issue they face. Educational philosopher Nicholas Burbules (1993), while less inclined than Lipman to distinguish sharply between conversation and dialogue, suggests that conversation is more informal and less structured than dialogue and that dialogue focuses more on inquiry and increasing understanding and tends to be more exploratory and questioning than conversation.

David Bridges (1988) claims that discussion is different from conversation and other forms of group talk by its "concern with the development of knowledge, understanding or judgement among those taking par" (p. 17). He believes that discussion is more serious than conversation in that it requires the participants to be both "mutually responsive" to the different views expressed and disposed to be "affected by opinions one way or another in so far as (on some criteria) they merit acceptance or approval" (p. 15). Similarly, James Dillon (1994) argues that whereas conversation is aimless, carefree, and effortless, discussion, in his view, is highly "disciplined and concerted talk" (p. 13) in which people come together to resolve some issue or problem that is important to them.

Other observers prefer the word conversation, meaning something a little less formal and structured than what Lipman, Burbules, Bridges, and Dillon call dialogue or discussion. The neo-pragmatist philosopher Richard Rorty (1979) thinks of philosophy itself as a stimulus to a great and continuing conversation. For Rorty, keeping the conversation going is the most important thing. As long as conversation lasts, he remarks, there is hope "for agreement, or, at least, exciting and fruitful disagreement" (p. 318). Bringing people together in conversation and challenging them to use their imaginations to create new meanings and move toward greater human inclusiveness is, for Rorty (1989), a moral endeavor. To him, conversation extends our sense of "'we' to people whom we have previously thought as 'they'" (p. 192) and provides a forum for acting on our obligation to achieve solidarity with others.

A major influence on Rorty is the English philosopher Michael Oakeshott (1962), who characterizes group talk as an "unrehearsed intellectual adventure" (p. 198) in which as many participants as possible are invited to speak and acknowledge one another. Despite the inevitable and irreconcilable differences between them, the act of conversation allows them to emerge from the experience broadened and enriched. For Oakeshott, participation in conversation is a distinctively human activity. Becoming skillful at this involves us in discerning how each voice reflects a different set of human interests. Through the process of discernment one becomes more sensitized to neglected or discounted voices and to finding room for them to air their views. In Oakeshott's view, conversation is one of the most important ways for human beings to make meaning, to construct a worldview, and to provide a "meetingplace of various modes of imagining" (p. 206). While each person who contributes should have the serious intention of engaging others, the best conversations maintain a tension between seriousness and playfulness. "As with children, who are great conversationalists," Oakeshott offers, "the playfulness is serious and the seriousness in the end is only play" (p. 202).

Although we use the term *discussion* to explore the theory and practice of group talk, we are actually blending or synthesizing the descriptions of discussion, dialogue, and conversation put forward by Lipman, Burbules, Bridges, Dillon, Rorty, and Oakeshott. Our understanding of discussion incorporates reciprocity and movement, exchange and inquiry, cooperation and collaboration, formality and informality. We acknowledge that much can be said for a simple exchange of views that does not oblige the participants to critique one another's opinions. Simply to understand more fully the thoughts and feelings of another increases our capacity to empathize and renews our appreciation for the variety of human experience. We also know that discussion that primarily entertains has merit and is an important part of human experience and education. However, in general we define *discussion* as an alternately serious and playful effort by a group of two or more to share views and engage in mutual and reciprocal critique. The purposes of discussion are fourfold: (1) to help participants reach a more critically informed understanding about the topic or topics under consideration, (2) to enhance participants' self-awareness and their capacity for self-critique, (3) to foster an appreciation among participants for the diversity of opinion that invariably emerges when viewpoints are exchanged openly and honestly, and (4) to act as a catalyst to helping people take informed action in the world.

Discussion is an important way for people to affiliate with one another, to develop the sympathies and skills that make participatory democracy possible. It is, as James Dillon (1994) has said, "a good way for us to be together" (p. 112) so that we can share personal stories of triumph and trouble and stretch our capacity for empathizing with others. In telling our stories, we employ different forms of speech to stimulate and move others, to emote and express strong feelings, and simply to celebrate the joys of coming together.

MAKING DISCUSSION CRITICAL

Whether labeled "discussion," "dialogue," or "conversation," the liveliest interactions are critical. When participants take a critical stance, they are committed to questioning and exploring even the most widely accepted ideas and beliefs. Conversing critically implies an openness to rethinking cherished assumptions and to subjecting those assumptions to a continuous round of questioning, argument, and counterargument. One of the defining characteristics of critical discussion is that participants are willing to enter the conversation with open minds. This requires people to be flexible enough to adjust their views in the light of persuasive, well-supported arguments and confident enough to retain their original opinions when rebuttals fall short. Although agreement may sometimes be desirable, it is by no means a necessity. Indeed, continued disagreement may be a productive outcome of conversation, particularly if some explanation for those differences can be found. An airing of differences can stimulate additional discussion and offer an opportunity to clarify one's own view in relation to another's.

Henry Giroux (1987) offers a view of critical discussion in which teachers become transformative intellectuals who engage and empower their students to probe the contradictions and injustices of the larger society. Building on the tradition of ideology critique in the Frankfurt School of critical social theory, he argues that classrooms are sites where students and teachers converge to make meaning by "interrogating different languages or ideological discourses as they are developed in an assortment of texts" (p. 119). Conceived this way, discussion discloses the ways in which different linguistic, cultural, and philosophical traditions can silence voices. A critical posture leads people to analyze these traditions to understand how they have kept entire groups out of the conversation. Teachers and students probe their own taken-for-granted beliefs and assumptions to uncover the ways these serve dominant interests. This kind of critical discussion helps people see how their choices can either perpetuate injustice and continue silence or contribute to growth and even emancipation.

Autobiographically grounded critical discussion allows discussants to discern the connection between what C. Wright Mills (1959) called private troubles and public issues. By reinterpreting personal difficulties as dimensions of broader social and political trends, we realize that our problems are not always idiosyncratic and due to our personal failings. Also, we are better able to generate strategies for counteracting the most dehumanizing, alienating, and oppressive tendencies of modern society. Discussion, in this sense, not only provides people with opportunities to share their experiences and express concern for one another but can also lead to more effective and more humane action.

PRACTICING THE DISPOSITIONS OF DEMOCRATIC DISCUSSION

If discussion-based classrooms are to be crucibles for democratic processes and mutual growth, students and teachers need to practice certain dispositions. In our own classes, we encourage students to name and learn these dispositions, and we try to model them in our teaching. Our efforts at getting students to approximate these ideals have been mixed at best, but even naming them is useful in helping students become more collaborative and respectful participants in discussion. There are many such dispositions worth considering. Those that are particularly important for us are hospitality, participation, mindfulness, humility, mutuality, deliberation, appreciation, hope, and autonomy.

HOSPITALITY

Parker Palmer writes about hospitality as one of the foundations for good dialogue in his book *To Know as We Are Known* (1993). By hospitality he means an atmosphere in which people feel invited to participate. The conviviality and congeniality that prevail encourage people to take risks and to reveal strongly held opinions. We try to create a hospitable atmosphere in our classes by devoting a good part of the first class or two to giving students opportunities to talk and write autobiographically and by suggesting (while trying hard not to be too intrusive) that they share something important about themselves. It is essential, by the way, that we do everything that we ask the students to do. We therefore spend some class time relating our own personal histories. We also devote one of the initial classes to a presentation of some of our own views on key educational issues and follow this presentation with a critique of these views. We hope to show in this way that every view is subject to criticism but that this can be done with respect and dignity.

Hospitality implies a mutual receptivity to new ideas and perspectives and a willingness to question even the most widely accepted assumptions. There is nothing soft about hospitality. It does not mean that standards are lowered or that heightened concern for one another is taken as an end in itself. Hospitality does not make learning easier or less burdensome, but it does "make the painful things possible, things without which no learning can occur—things like exposing ignorance, testing tentative hypotheses, challenging false or partial information, and mutual criticism of thought" (Palmer, 1993, p. 74). Taking hospitality seriously also means balancing seriousness of purpose with lightness of tone and employing self-deprecating humor, particularly when the tension becomes too great.

PARTICIPATION

In any strong democratic community, everyone is encouraged to participate in significant ways on as wide a range of issues as possible. In other words, democratic discussions work best when a large number of students participate, when they do so on many different occasions and with respect to many different issues, and when what they contribute adds depth and subtlety to the discussion. When a wide variety of learners express themselves, other participants are challenged to consider and digest a diverse range of views. This results in a richer and more memorable learning experience for all.

We don't want to suggest that everyone has to speak during the discussion, though it is desirable if many people do so. What is essential is that everyone finds ways to contribute to others' understanding. Sometimes this happens through speech, sometimes through such alternative media as written assignments and journal entries, informal exchanges during breaks, electronic mail, and even personal communications with the instructor. This places a burden on the instructor, as well as other participants, to seek out the opinions of quiet members and to ensure that these opinions are communicated to the group as a whole in a manner that respects their privacy.

We are quite aware of the students in our classes who are consistently quiet (see Chapter Nine), and often we speak to them privately to find out what we can do to help them participate more actively. Sometimes they say that they prefer to remain silent and that they are otherwise satisfied with the class. Such students, however, often become much more animated when the class breaks up into small groups. Knowing that many students are uncomfortable speaking in a large group has led us to organize small group interactions for our students much more often than in the past. Sometimes another student's dominance is the problem, or our own intellectual zeal prevents some students from joining in. In such cases we must make a greater effort to curb our own eagerness to speak in order to leave room for others to express themselves.

Inseparable from participation is the notion of efficacy—the sense that one's participation matters, that it is having an impact on others. Political philosopher Carol Pateman (1970) has written eloquently about this with respect to industrial democracy, but it is just as important in classrooms. The incentive to participate diminishes when what one says or contributes is ignored or leaves no discernible impact. Everyone in democratic classrooms, but especially the instructor, must work at encouraging widespread participation and finding spaces during class time to receive more than just perfunctory responses from the class. For us this means that we must in some cases ask follow-up questions, at other times rephrase what has been said, and in still other situations show clearly and assertively how one person's contribution is related to other ideas already presented.

MINDFULNESS

In *The Good Society*, Robert Bellah and his colleagues (1991) argue that "democracy means paying attention" (p. 254). Paying close attention to another's words is no small feat. It calls "on all of our resources of intelligence, feeling, and moral sensitivity" (p. 254). As in Hans-Georg Gadamer's notion of dialogue (1989), paying close attention in this manner causes us to lose ourselves, to become completely absorbed in hearing out what someone else has to say. The paying of attention is what we mean by mindfulness. It involves being aware of the whole conversation—of who has spoken and who has not—and of doing what one can to ensure that the discussion doesn't get bogged down in the consideration of issues that are of concern only to a very small minority of participants.

In general, mindfulness is a crucial component of any really good discussion. Without learners who are willing to listen carefully and patiently to what others have to say, discussion cannot proceed beyond the most superficial level. Teachers must model a high level of attentiveness to convey the importance of being mindful. When the two of us lead discussions, we strain to hear and to understand, fully and correctly, what is being said. We often ask follow-up questions to make sure that we understand a comment and to affirm that all our attention and our energy are focused on what each student is expressing.

A component of mindfulness is what political theorist Mark Kingwell (1995) calls *tact*. Kingwell argues that when we share public space, we must curb our compulsion to convey our own moral vision in order to make room for others to receive a full hearing. Tact sometimes involves holding in check our desire to express ourselves fully and vociferously. It doesn't mean compromising our principles or remaining quiet at all times; a tactful person may do a fair amount of talking. But it does oblige us to pay close attention to what others have said and not said and to defer to those who have had few opportunities to speak.

We have found Kingwell's discussion of tact particularly helpful in our own teaching. Teachers, including the two of us, have a tendency to insist on saying all the things they want to say without regard for the group as a whole or the needs of individual participants. This is partly the result of a kind of pedagogical compulsiveness to give the students their money's worth, but it is also a consequence of teachers' viewing their own ideas as superior to and more urgent than the ideas of their students. We have come to realize that group cohesiveness and the give-and-take of a good discussion are usually more important than any particular thing that we feel compelled to contribute.

HUMILITY

Related to mindfulness is humility. Humility is the willingness to admit that one's knowledge and experience are limited and incomplete and to act accordingly. It means acknowledging that others in the group have ideas to express that might teach us something new or change our mind about something significant. It is being willing to see all others in the group as potential teachers. Humility also implies an inclination to admit errors in judgment. Palmer (1993) reminds us that acknowledging our own ignorance is simply the first step in the pursuit of truth. Humility helps us remember that learning is always an uncertain, even uneasy quest. If we admit the limits of our knowledge and opinions, we are more likely to work authentically to create greater understanding among group members.

MUTUALITY

Mutuality means that it is in the interest of all to care as much about each other's self-development as one's own. We demonstrate mutuality when we muster all the resources we can to ensure that all participants benefit from the discussion. When we act with mutuality, we realize that our own flourishing depends in a vital sense on the flourishing of all others. This commitment to others not only generates a spirit of goodwill and generosity but also enhances trust. People become more willing to take risks and speak frankly because these actions are more likely to be seen as mutually beneficial. When we devote ourselves to others' learning as much as our own, the atmosphere of openness that is created encourages engagement with the material to be learned. It instills in students the confidence to be both teacher and student. Instead of being passive recipients of the instructor's wisdom, students alternate between the roles of teacher and learner, sometimes explaining and conveying information and at other times actively absorbing and interpreting what others have to share.

To allow the traditional dividing line between teacher and student to become blurred in this way requires teachers and students to view their enterprise as truly collaborative. In collaborative classrooms, the responsibility for teaching and learning is held in common. Creating such a climate, incidentally, does not absolve teachers of their responsibility to help students learn. Rather, it means that everyone in the group takes that responsibility seriously. When we acknowledge and respect others as teachers and learners, we greatly increase our chances of having those feelings reciprocated. We create a situation in which our efforts to respect and acknowledge our classmates' ideas, opinions, and needs are reflected back to us, thereby spurring our own learning, our identification with the group, and our self-respect.

DELIBERATION

Deliberation refers to the willingness of participants to discuss issues as fully as possible by offering arguments and counterarguments that are supported by evidence, data, and logic and by holding strongly to these unless there are good reasons not to do so. Put another way, democratic classrooms should be highly contentious forums where different points of view are forcibly, though civilly, advanced by as many different participants as possible and abandoned only in response to persuasive arguments or compelling evidence. Deliberative people enter discussions aware that the ensuing exchange of views may modify their original opinions. Political scientist James Fishkin (1995) points out that we often think that when equality and respect prevail, democracy has been attained. He is quick to warn, however, that unless there is a general commitment to deliberative practices that foster reflective and informed judgments, democracy is robbed of its authority and moral meaning. In Fishkin's view, deliberation implies collaboratively addressing a topic or problem as carefully and thoroughly as possible so that the full range of different views in the group is presented and defended.

What Fishkin describes is similar to Jürgen Habermas's ideal speech situation (1984, 1987). In this situation, all discussants are equally able to make and present arguments, all possible arguments are given full and equal airing, and sufficient time is equally given to all participants to question and critique each of the arguments presented so that in the end the issue is resolved in light of the force of the best argument. Michael Collins (1991) summarizes Habermas's ideal speech situation as a

> group learning experience where participants put forward their own views on the problem at hand, listen carefully and respectfully to those of others, and examine seriously all relevantly identified information introduced to the situation. It does not take the form of a debate, or the mere weighing of pros and cons. The process is more rational and democratic—a kind of ongoing, thoughtful conversation. All participants anticipate that their individual contributions will receive serious consideration from others. At the same time, they remain open to changing or to reconstructing their own stance on the problem under consideration in the light of what others have to say and on the weight of all relevantly identified information [p. 12].

Like any ideal, this is an impossible situation to achieve in practice, but it is one standard that we find useful for measuring and critiquing our efforts to conduct democratic discussions. We do not believe, as John Gastil (1993) suggests, that deliberation should result in a "rationally motivated consensus" (p. 25). This may sometimes be a worthy goal, but it may be just as desirable if deliberation results in continuing differences' being better understood and more readily tolerated. Deliberation also frequently involves an evaluation of how effectively the problem has been resolved. It entails a commitment to rethink, reexamine, or reformulate issues or problems in the light of new experiences or new lines of thought.

In our own teaching, we have found the ideal of deliberation to be especially elusive. Our desire to practice the other dispositions mentioned may get in the way of creating a truly deliberative classroom. Specifically, we find that our interest in carving out a safe and hospitable space for people to speak, a place where they can feel affirmed and acknowledged, is itself so difficult that the standard of deliberation must often wait for later. Consequently, the semester is usually more than half over before we think that students in our classes are starting to hold one another account-able for clear and well-substantiated arguments.

Our experience may be unique, but it is fairly consistent. We have been forced to conclude that the kind of teaching we are try-ing to do probably requires an entire academic year of regular meetings, rather than the fairly standard single semester. We con-cede that we must do more to hold our students to a higher delib-erative standard earlier in the semester, but we know that imposing this standard too early is risky. It may prevent the emergence of the kind of trust and mutual respect that form such an important foun-dation for honest and engaged discussion. Margery Osborne (1992) describes this dilemma nicely: "The first few meetings of the class are, for me, filled with tension between creating a place where ideas can be safely aired and questioned and creating a place where we can push, confront, and challenge one another's ideas" (p. 108).

APPRECIATION

Burbules (1993) mentions appreciation briefly as one of a number of important "emotional" factors in dialogue (p. 39). Few of us take enough opportunities in everyday life to express appreciation to one another for a thoughtful comment, a powerful insight, or a wise observation. Because democratic classrooms stress respect, mutuality, and civility, a logical extension of these notions is find-ing space and time to express our appreciation to one another. When a helpful observation clarifies a key point or an intriguing comment excites further curiosity, the disposition of appreciation inclines us to express our gratitude openly and honestly. Like many of the attitudes already mentioned, appreciation brings people closer together and raises the level of trust. But even more impor-tant, openly expressing our appreciation for one another engen-ders a kind of joyous collaboration that is characteristic of the most productive and most democratic of communities.

One of us is especially good at finding ways to express and model appreciation for others. His enthusiasm for the possibilities allowed by dialogue is so great that when it goes well, when people openly exchange their ideas in a respectful, clear, and thoughtful manner, he usually cannot resist the impulse to let people know it. We think this builds trust and community and motivates others to participate in a similar fashion. Of course, such expressions of appreciation can be overdone and seem sentimentalized or inauthentic. When this happens, standards for strong exchanges are lowered, and almost any comment becomes acceptable, leading to the meandering classroom conversation with which many of us are all too familiar. The best way to safeguard against this is to use a classroom evaluation device such as the critical incident questionnaire (CIQ) discussed later in this book.

Hope

Without the hope of reaching new understanding, gaining a helpful perspective, or clarifying the roots of a conflict, there is little reason to go on talking, learning, and teaching. Hope sustains us when we encounter seemingly insurmountable problems or when the amount of time needed to work through a particularly challenging issue grows longer and longer. Hope provides us with a sense that all of the time, effort, and work will benefit us in the long run, even if only in a small way. In one of his last books, Paulo Freire (1994) goes so far as to say that he does "not understand human existence, and the struggle needed to improve it, apart from hope and dream" (p. 8).

Hope also implies what Dewey (1955, 1991) called democratic faith. Faith suggests that people have the capacity to work through their own problems and that each person has something worthwhile and important to contribute to increasing understanding or to resolving conflict. Democratic faith implies that pooling the talents and abilities of individuals increases the likelihood that new light will be cast on old difficulties and everyday common sense will be brought to bear on problems said to require technical expertise.

Hope and faith are cardinal principles underlying and supporting our pedagogy. Despite the recurring and never fully resolved contradictions of building trust and allowing everyone's voice to be heard while maintaining high deliberative standards, we cling to the possibility that together we can make our dialogical encounters incisive, meaningful, and satisfying. Our attempts to do this with our students are always incomplete, always in process; but for the most part the pluses greatly outweigh the minuses, reinforcing our faith that even the most diverse groups of students can have productive dialogues.

AUTONOMY

In a sense this final disposition brings us back full circle. If democratic classrooms seek to promote individual and collective growth, then people who retain the courage, strength, and resolve to hold to an opinion not widely shared by others should be given their due. Autonomy usually denotes a state of being separate and aloof from others and a corresponding dismissal of collaboration, cooperation, and joint deliberation. We want to understand and honor autonomy as a temporary state, a kind of "provisional resting place" (Barber, 1994) where an individual can claim that "this is what I believe in and stand for at this particular point in time." But that same individual should also be willing to subject those convictions to continuous reevaluation and possible revision, on the understanding that these new convictions may, in Barber's words, be "repossessed" again in the future.

Without individuals who are willing to take strong stands and to argue assertively for them, democracy is diminished, and the opportunities for growth and self-development, partly dependent on the clash of contending wills, are greatly weakened. In valuing autonomy, we are reminded of the tension between identifying and collaborating with the group and pursuing our own individual goals. Both are valuable and neither can be neglected, but developing the strong sense of self needed to stand alone occasionally cannot be overestimated (Barber, 1984; Hook, 1946). Our beliefs may be "tentative, fallible, open to further questioning" (Bernstein, 1992, p. 319), but the responsibility to take a stand, however temporary this may be, remains one of the foundations of democratic and moral deliberation.

STRUGGLING FOR DEMOCRACY THROUGH DISCUSSION

One way to sum up much of what has already been said is to consider what Richard Bernstein (1988) has called engaged pluralism. To see why we find this idea helpful for understanding the discussion process, consider the following quote regarding the requirements of an engaged, pluralistic stance: "One accepts the fallibility of all inquiry. One accepts the multiplicity of perspectives and interpretations. One rejects the quest for certainty, the craving for absolutes, and the idea of a totality in which all differences are finally reconciled. But such a pluralism demands an openness to what is different and other, a willingness to risk one's pre-judgments, seeking for common ground without any guarantees that it will be found. It demands—and it is a strenuous demand—that one tries to be responsive to the claims of the other" (p. 271). In this quote Bernstein summarizes many of the fundamental assumptions of democratic discussion. These include the tentativeness of all knowledge, the infinite variety of perspectives and understandings that people bring to discussion, the endless nature of inquiry and the refusal to accept a definitive answer, a genuine receptivity to other views, a striving for agreement that may be impossible to achieve, and the patience to hear out all possible opinions.

What all of this suggests, of course, is that democratic discussion is excruciatingly difficult and that our efforts to realize its promise will always fall short of our hopes. Engaged pluralism calls on us to value and seek out multiplicity—of perspective, interpretation, and background. It spurs us to consider divergent viewpoints and sympathetically to pursue commonalities, with a clear-eyed understanding that agreement and common ground may be illusory. Engaged pluralism puts a claim on us to keep talking with others who have radically different perspectives in a continuing effort to reexamine our own commitments. We do this knowing that we risk eroding our most deeply held beliefs. Implied here is a warning to avoid the trap of complacency. There is always more to be done to make discussion open, fair, diverse, and mutually illuminating.

As Barber (1984) has pointed out, discussion is always at risk as long as hierarchies and power differentials overshadow what transpires. Only when "no voice is privileged, no position advantaged, no authority other than the process itself acknowledged" (p. 183) can a truly rich exchange of ideas occur. Yet as many critical pedagogues have warned, it is impossible to eliminate hierarchy altogether, and it would be naive to think otherwise. The undemocratic traditions and practices of the larger society will always intrude on even the most democratic classroom. Teachers and students who are committed to democratic education must acknowledge this fact and do what they can to combat it.

For social theorist Henry Giroux (1987), the teacher has an especially heavy responsibility in allowing "different student voices to be heard and legitimated" (p. 119). Social relations in the dialogical classroom must be structured to resist the injustices and denial of difference characteristic of the world outside the classroom. Difference and plurality, for critical pedagogues like Giroux, are not merely affirmed and celebrated but are rooted in a "particular form of human community that encourages and dignifies plurality" (p. 119). This process of dignifying plurality and of forming community comes about in part through an assertion of the centrality of difference, as well as through "efforts to identify and recall moments of human suffering and the need to overcome the conditions that perpetuate such suffering" (p. 120). For Giroux (1988), critical discussion depends on giving voice to participants' social, racial, and gender-situated experience and on finding spaces where they can come together freely and openly "to struggle together within social relations that strengthen rather than weaken possibilities for active citizenship" (p. 201).

Still, the problem remains: How can we dialogue with people different from ourselves, genuinely respect those differences, and yet fairly and mutually critique those differences as well? Elizabeth Ellsworth (1989) doubts that this is possible given the oppression and racism that continue to beset society. One of the lessons of Ellsworth's analysis is that educators have not sufficiently confronted the difficulty, the staggering challenge, of teaching democratically in an undemocratic society. Nor have they grappled adequately with the potential for discussion to silence some students and put them at a disadvantage. Indeed, we have too frequently nodded benignly when our classrooms seemed to be alive with the chatter of student voices while allowing to go unheard the voices that were absent or the issues that were ignored.

One of the keys, though, to Ellsworth's argument is not that we should stop talking to one another altogether but rather that we should find alternative ways to talk that force us to deal with the anger and despair that roil beneath the surface of our conventional exchanges of opinion. Even when we do this, however, we must learn to accept that our efforts to open up discussion and counteract injustice will always be partial and incomplete. Nevertheless, the progress that is made and the learning that takes place can still make a real difference in our own and our students' lives.

CONCLUSION

In the end, discussion remains an indispensable part of democratic education. It teaches us dispositions and practices, provides us with the opportunity to serve and connect with others, and tests our ability to confront the most difficult of problems and think them through collaboratively. Perhaps most important of all, it challenges us to consider the different—the other—and to ponder the fragility of our own identities and our ideals. Who we are and what we believe are necessarily imperiled when we continue to encounter others with openness, honesty, respect, and humility.

So the hazards and difficulties of discussion should not be underestimated—but neither should its delights and rewards. At its best, discussion greatly expands our horizons and exposes us to whole new worlds of thought and imagining. It improves our thinking, sharpens our awareness, increases our sensitivity, and heightens our appreciation for ambiguity and complexity. Critical discussion is an ongoing effort to make sense of the chaos of our existence while remaining "true to the natural incoherence of experience" (Elbow, 1986, p. x). Despite the struggle and the prospects of only partial success, it is one of the things that makes life worth living.

The more the two of us study and conduct democratic discussion, the more we realize that this is not a hit-or-miss affair. We want to counter the easy belief that whether or not discussions are good or bad can be put down to the magic of the leader's personal charisma or interpersonal chemistry among group members. Creating the conditions for democratic discussion and realizing them to the extent possible are deliberate, intentional teaching acts. The rest of this book shows how to make them happen.

CHAPTER TWO

HOW DISCUSSION HELPS LEARNING AND ENLIVENS CLASSROOMS

We are unwaveringly committed to teaching through discussion because of the benefits we have consistently enjoyed in its practice. In fact, we have found that at least fifteen arguments can be made regarding the ways in which participating in discussion helps learning.

FIFTEEN BENEFITS OF DISCUSSION

Note that we don't claim that the mere act of engaging students in group talk somehow brings these benefits automatically. The advantages we're claiming for discussion accrue only when students strive to practice the dispositional ideals outlined in Chapter One. If these dispositions are realized, even in part, discussion brings the following benefits:

1. It helps students explore a diversity of perspectives.
2. It increases students' awareness of and tolerance for ambiguity or complexity.
3. It helps students recognize and investigate their assumptions.
4. It encourages attentive, respectful listening.
5. It develops new appreciation for continuing differences.
6. It increases intellectual agility.
7. It helps students become connected to a topic.
8. It shows respect for students' voices and experiences.

9. It helps students learn the processes and habits of democratic discourse.
10. It affirms students as cocreators of knowledge.
11. It develops the capacity for the clear communication of ideas and meaning.
12. It develops habits of collaborative learning.
13. It increases breadth and makes students more empathic.
14. It helps students develop skills of synthesis and integration.
15. It leads to transformation.

Let's examine each of these benefits individually.

DISCUSSION HELPS STUDENTS EXPLORE A DIVERSITY OF PERSPECTIVES

Discussion is one of the most effective ways to make students aware of the range of interpretations that are possible in an area of intellectual inquiry. Teachers can introduce these diverse perspectives themselves through lecturing or prereading, but that is often dismissed as "secondhand" exposure. There is nothing like students' hearing from each other's lips the diversity of interpretations that can be made of the same apparently objective facts or the same apparently obvious meanings. It's much harder for learners to ignore views that are contrary to their own if they're expressed spontaneously by their peers rather than discovered in a text or mediated through a lecturer's words. Physical encounters with equals who hold "inconvenient" opinions are a powerful force. We cannot skip or skim contrary views that are expressed by peers in the same way we can skip a few paragraphs in a book or tune out parts of a lecture.

It helps to increase the chances that discussions will be distinguished by interpretive diversity if participants are drawn from diverse social, ethnic, and gender backgrounds; take a variety of ideological perspectives on common experiences; and express their perceptions in different terms. Discussions that involve students who speak in different voices, express varied viewpoints, and use different expressive forms help students learn about the contested nature of knowledge. Being exposed to different perspectives helps students develop a general tentativeness toward their own (and others') intellectual claims. They come to realize that there is rarely a single, unassailable interpretation of an issue or problem but rather a range of sustainable views, each of which may hold a legitimate claim on at least some participants. This is not to say that all interpretations are equally valid. It is only to aver that coming to hold a relatively secure opinion that may be effectively defended against other views usually results from hearing out and analyzing the diversity of viable perspectives that are available in the whole group.

Groups composed of people who exhibit a diversity of ways of speaking and thinking and who bring many different cultural, class, and gender experiences to the conversation present particular challenges. When people use language differently, there is always the possibility that no one will understand what anyone else is saying. This is the postmodern nightmare—a mutually frustrating Tower of Babel in which no common agreement on the meaning of words is possible. Although some degree of misunderstanding and miscommunication is endemic to discussion, this is more likely to be kept within reasonable limits if people try to observe the disposition of mindfulness discussed in Chapter One. Mindful participants try to understand the meaning of other people's words in the way that they have been framed. We address these challenges fully in Chapters Seven and Eight.

DISCUSSION INCREASES STUDENTS' AWARENESS OF AND TOLERANCE FOR AMBIGUITY OR COMPLEXITY

A good discussion is one that leaves issues open for further inquiry and in which as many questions are raised as are answered. If participants begin a discussion with definitive views, they should conclude it with a sense of tentativeness. They should learn that the topics explored are complex and that our understanding of them is contingent, always requiring further study and reflection. Discussions help students learn to tolerate the ambiguities inherent in so much intellectual inquiry.

Discussion is not suited to teaching that is intended to initiate students into a predefined body of truths, facts, or ideas. Such teaching can be defended as a legitimate and necessary educational process. But we feel strongly that the concept of "guided discussion"—if that phrase is taken to mean that students will be guided during the discussion to learn certain content—is an oxymoron. We have both been participants in—and orchestrators of—discussions where the leader nudges the conversation along to a predetermined conclusion with which the leader agrees. This happens when leaders ignore questions or ideas raised by students that are inconvenient or awkward for the leader's position. It happens when leaders reframe what a student has said in a way that distorts the student's meaning so that it supports the leader's views. Guided discussion is a self-negating concept if it means guiding talk toward a particular position or point of consensus. Whenever this happens, it means that certain perspectives and information have been excluded at the outset. To Paterson (1970), a discussion like this is counterfeit.

At the heart of discussion is the open and unpredictable creation of meanings through collaborative inquiry. For a discussion leader to have decided in advance what these meanings should be is intellectually dishonest. Such a counterfeit pedagogy is manipulative in a way that contradicts the spirit of democratic discourse. Guided discussion makes sense only if what is being guided are the processes by which students are helped to listen respectfully, seek clarification, and create opportunities for all voices to be heard. In discussions we can initiate students into the habits of democratic discourse, but we should never initiate them into predetermined conclusions or preselected meanings.

DISCUSSION HELPS STUDENTS RECOGNIZE AND INVESTIGATE THEIR ASSUMPTIONS

Teachers concerned to develop critical thinking in students know that discussion is an important crucible for this. In conversation we enjoy multiple opportunities for the clarification and scrutiny of each other's assumptions. Sometimes this happens without a teacher's intervention when one participant points out the assumptions underlying another's position. At other times the hunting of assumptions can be an important discussion purpose.

Becoming aware of our assumptions is a puzzling and contradictory task. Few of us can get very far doing this on our own. No matter how much we may think that we know what our assumptions are, we are stymied by the fact that we're using our own interpretive filters to become aware of our own interpretive filters! This cognitive catch-22 is the equivalent of a dog trying to catch its tail or of trying to see the back of your own head while looking directly into a mirror. Becoming critical happens only when we find mirrors that reflect a stark and differently highlighted picture of how and what we think. Our most influential assumptions are too close to us to be seen clearly by an act of self-will.

This is where discussion comes in. In discussions, students can serve as critical mirrors for each other, reflecting the assumptions they see in each other's positions. As students become aware of the diversity of perspectives on an issue that a group represents, they can learn to see the world through multiple lenses. As they question each other about the reasons, evidence, and experiences that lie behind the comments each makes, they start to realize that seemingly random viewpoints are always grounded in assumptive clusters. They learn that what different people consider obvious, factually true, or common sense depends very much on the different assumptions they hold.

Discussion Encourages Attentive, Respectful Listening

In a properly conducted discussion, listening is just as important as speaking. To be heard is to be treated with respect. Conversely, to speak and sense that one is not really being listened to is to feel voiceless, ignored, and demeaned. So a good discussion participant is not necessarily someone who speaks a lot or who voices startlingly original opinions. Participants must learn to listen carefully to what each other is saying; otherwise, there is little chance that the group will be able to do a sustained or probing analysis of a topic, problem, or theme. Such analysis develops organically as various lines of inquiry intersect or double back on themselves. Attentive listening makes it easier to reinterpret earlier comments in the light of later opinions.

Of course, listening attentively is not easy. In fact, it is probably much more tiring than contributing to the discussion. Given the complex multiplicity of expressive styles, the nuances of race, class, and gender, and the variety of idiosyncratic speech forms, it is sometimes amazing to think that anyone ever understands anyone else! Race, class, gender, learning style, personality—all these things complicate our efforts to understand one another in daily conversation without the added difficulties posed by the complexities of intellectual inquiry. Concrete thinkers in a group become frustrated with those who speak only in abstract or holistic terms. Those who express themselves in rambling, disconnected sentence fragments infuriate more task-oriented learners eager to get to the point. What to one person is a permissible question according to standards of critical inquiry can seem rude, bigoted, or hurtful to another.

Grappling with these different patterns of communication is enormously challenging. However, discussion provides the opportunity for students to summarize and reframe each other's comments and to show how their own contributions spring from or build on others' ideas. This ability to summarize other people's views accurately and to see the links between seemingly unconnected ideas is a core process of all intellectual inquiry. Letting another person see that you are striving to understand as closely as possible the exact meaning of what the person is saying is wonderfully respectful and affirming. It is also crucial to the building of democratic trust.

Discussion Develops New Appreciation for Continuing Differences

Sometimes we may expect that discussion will allow participants to resolve their differences. Not only is this an unrealistic expectation, but it may not even be a desirable one. When differences of opinion are strongly felt or when perspectives on an issue are highly divergent for cultural or ethnic reasons, even discussions that take place over a period of years can hardly be expected to overcome such long-standing and deeply rooted differences. Continuing disagreement may be a productive outcome of a conversation, particularly when the participants gain a clearer sense of the basis for that disagreement. In addition, an airing of differences can stimulate more discussion and provide an opportunity to clarify one's views in relation to another's.

Part of the process of confronting differences is to disclose the ways in which dominant groups and prevailing cultural traditions have silenced certain voices and to explore how these traditions have functioned to prevent their contributing to the conversation. Some people would claim that because society is so unequal and racist, discussion is not only unfair but may even exacerbate existing differences and inequalities (Ellsworth, 1989). Although this possibility is always present, the alternative is accepting an inequitable status quo. Therefore, discussion leaders committed to democracy and education for mutual growth must make special efforts to avoid silencing certain students. They can use a variety of methods to make discussion as fair and inclusive as possible and strive to respect and understand enduring differences.

DISCUSSION INCREASES INTELLECTUAL AGILITY

Engaging in discussion requires a certain intellectual agility, an ability to think on our feet and to react to unanticipated comments. Students know this, and that's one of the reasons why some of them fear discussion so much. They realize that they can't anticipate the range of responses that their comments will elicit. Since it's almost impossible to frame a contribution so perfectly that everyone will agree with every aspect of it, students know that what they say will sometimes be challenged, contradicted, even negated. This means they'll have to think quickly to formulate a counterresponse or to mount a defense against arguments that are new to them.

Of course, it's quite permissible in a discussion to ask for time to formulate an informed and useful response. We can say to someone, "I need some time to think about what you've said, so I'd like to deal with your comments later." Students should not feel that they have to have an immediate, intelligent, and articulate reaction to every point that their comments provoke. Discussion is not a performance in which we're all expected to win intellectual Oscars for the brilliance of our speech or the speed of our thought.

But at a minimum we must expect questions about what we say in discussions. People will want to know what's behind our thinking. Sometimes they'll misunderstand what we've said and will ask us to explain our point again, but with different examples. They may want to know what evidence we base our viewpoints on, what assumptions undergird our positions, and the extent to which we're open to critiquing or changing our ideas. So whenever we open our mouths to speak in a discussion, we know that isn't the end of the matter. Every one of our contributions contains an implicit invitation to our listeners to seek clarification.

DISCUSSION HELPS STUDENTS BECOME CONNECTED TO A TOPIC

Building connections, both personal and intellectual, is at the heart of discussion. Ideas that are perceived as distanced or irrelevant when presented through a lecture come alive when we have to explore them through speech. Arguments that were abstract when read in a text grab our attention when spoken by a peer. Interpretations that might be skipped over when encountered outside the classroom cannot be dismissed when proposed by a colleague.

When we're introducing students to a new topic, it's usually safe to assume that no inherent point of connection exists between students' experiences and the topic of discussion. In these situations, we can help create this connection by asking students to play certain predefined roles in a discussion. Some can be provocateurs, arguing a certain line of analysis in the strongest and most controversial terms. Others can be devil's advocates, with a charge to counter every element in a particular line of argument. Still others can be intellectual detectives concerned to point out biases that keep recurring in the discussion or to bring the group's attention to areas of inquiry it keeps approaching and then steering away from. As students begin to adopt these roles, there is often a sense of playfulness, a feeling that this is just a game of artful pretense (which, of course, it is). However, after a while this sense of artificiality starts to diminish, and students find that they actually care about what others think and say about the topic being discussed. A commitment develops to understanding the topic fully and to seeing its exploration through to whatever the end might be.

The insights gained through discussions sometimes connect directly to action in the world outside. When students analyze their experiences in discussion, they often start to make connections between this analysis and their lives. How do the insights they are developing affect how they live as parents, friends, lovers? What do these new understandings mean for their political commitments and involvements? In what ways does a point raised in discussion cause them to rethink what it means to work responsibly and ethically? Some discussions veer back and forth between the analysis of a problem and considerations of how participants might act in response to it. In this way discussions become crucibles for the kind of praxis—the continuous spiral of action, reflection on action, further action, further reflection on action, and so on—envisaged by Freire (1993). Some of the best discussions we have participated in have caused us to locate our private troubles in the context of wider public issues (Mills, 1959). When this happens, the next step is usually to think about how we might join with others similarly affected to take collective action to change our individual histories.

Discussion Shows Respect for Students' Voices and Experiences

The two of us espouse democratic ideals in our teaching. We want to turn the hierarchical experience of higher education into a collaborative and respectful adult educational process. We believe that college students should be treated as adults, irrespective of their chronological age. They should not be talked down to, infantilized, or demeaned. Their experiences must be recognized and valued. Teachers who believe in inclusivity and who value students' voices and experiences can't avoid using discussion. And in discussions, students will sooner or later invoke their experiences as evidence to justify the truth of their assertions.

At the forefront of discussion is the analysis of experience, in particular the attempt to understand how individual experience is socially formed. In discussion, we value formal knowledge and theoretical understanding, but we also dignify (in a critical way) participants' experiences. Discussion participants often dismiss their own experiences as anecdotal and idiosyncratic. They denigrate their personal experiences in deference to "book knowledge," which seems codified, legitimated, somehow "more true" than individual stories. Good discussions affirm that personal experience is an important object of study, but they take the analysis of experience beyond individual storytelling to an analysis of the generic, recognizable elements that are embedded in particular tales. In discussion, we apply formal theory to review individual experience and to point to its social formation. This helps us realize that our individual stories are held in common and that they are shaped by the same economic and political forces that exist in the larger capitalist society.

A good discussion leader will try to encourage students to talk about the experiences that have shaped how they think and act. As the adult educator Myles Horton observed, "You can't say you respect people and not respect their experiences" (Horton and Freire, 1990, p. 178). In a very real sense, we are our experiences. But dignifying and valuing people's experiences doesn't mean treating them reverentially or uncritically. As Horton said to Paulo Freire, "Often when I say you start with people's experience, people get the point that you start and stop with that experience. There's a time when people's experience runs out" (p. 128). He argued that "people know the basic answers to their problems, but they need to go further than that, and you can, by asking questions and getting them stimulated, coax them to move, in discussion, beyond their experience" (p. 136).

So while we believe that recognizing, honoring, and celebrating experiences in discussion is important, we don't believe this is all that should happen. Experience is problematic. It is constructed by us as much as it happens to us. Our experiences can be understood in multiple ways, depending on the culture, gender, class, and history of the person interpreting them. Experiences can also be distorting. Understood in a certain way, they can teach us habits of bigotry, paranoia, and exclusion. The fact that a theoretical idea contradicts a student's experience doesn't mean that the student should ignore the theory. For a discussion to be considered educational, students should be encouraged to subject their experiences to critical analysis. Good discussion leaders ask provocative questions about experience. They supply alternative interpretations of students' experiences and new perspectives on those experiences. But they do this in a respectful way. They acknowledge that ultimately the experience is the students' own, and they never insist that students must agree with teachers'—or anyone else's—interpretations of experience.

DISCUSSION HELPS STUDENTS LEARN THE PROCESSES AND HABITS OF DEMOCRATIC DISCOURSE

Learning democratic discourse is difficult. In the immediate aftermath of World War II, the adult educator Eduard Lindeman (1947) proposed eight democratic disciplines that, taken together, formed "the natural code of behavior for a citizen living under democratic conditions" (p. 113). These disciplines included learning to live with diversity, learning to accept the partial functioning of democratic ideals, learning to avoid false antitheses, learning to ensure that means and ends are as congruent as possible, learning to value humor, and learning to live with contrary decisions and perspectives.

If discussions are introduced and conducted with careful attention to these disciplines, we believe they can become laboratories in which students learn democratic habits. A discussion group can constitute a safe space in which the democratic experiment can be tried, adapted, and reframed with a minimum of serious consequences for participants. Discussion in which participants are given opportunities to voice concerns, work collaboratively, formulate ideas, express disagreement, and solve problems collectively is both a foundation for democracy and a sign that democracy is taking hold. Without this kind of constant experience of the democratic process, it is hard to see how people can become citizens in any but the most nominal sense. But with the opportunity to learn and practice democratic disciplines and dispositions, the possibilities are limitless.

Discussion Affirms Students as Cocreators of Knowledge

In discussion, students have the same right to be heard as teachers. Because the flow of conversation and the development of contrasting lines of inquiry can't be predicted, students and teachers share responsibility for the evolution of the group's knowledge. Creating insights, validating or refuting claims, and exposing group members to alternative perspectives are all shared responsibilities.

When teachers declare passionately that they view their students as cocreators of knowledge, students who have been burned by experiences of false and spurious democracy in the past may react with skepticism, hostility, or cynicism. Given the usually submerged power dynamics of higher education classrooms, it would be surprising if this were not their reaction. But if these espousals of the democratic creation of knowledge come over time to be seen as sincere and acted on, the effect is remarkable. When students feel respected and treated as coequal creators of knowledge, they are much more likely to take the discussion process seriously.

Having one's views attended to carefully and granted public credibility is a powerful experience for students who have learned to think of themselves as failures or imposters. In the best discussions, students should feel that their contributions are indispensable. The feeling should prevail that to lose anyone's participation would be a loss to the group as a whole.

DISCUSSION DEVELOPS THE CAPACITY FOR THE CLEAR COMMUNICATION OF IDEAS AND MEANING

Postmodern theorists challenge the idea that the unambiguous communication of transparent meanings between individuals, let alone among groups, is possible. Yet the human impulse to create shared meanings and understandings shows no sign of abating. In fact, the era of increased electronic communication is usually celebrated for the way in which it has increased the possibility for all kinds of new information exchanges. Through electronic networks, we can communicate immediately and relatively cheaply with people all over the world. Yet in societies that are increasingly fragmented along lines of race, gender, class, and ideology and in which ever more specialized communities of interest speak their own private languages, the possibility of dialogue across differences begins to seem increasingly remote.

Through discussion, we can help students grapple with the difficulties of trying to communicate ideas and meanings not immediately clear to others. Discussions can be a training ground in which people learn the importance of giving examples to illustrate complex propositions. Through conversation, students can learn to think and speak metaphorically and to use analogical reasoning. They can become more adept at entering into other participants' frames of reference and seeing the world through the multiple lenses these represent. They can learn to vary the pace at which they disclose new ideas according to the complexity of the ideas and the relative sophistication of other learners. They can get better at knowing when using specialized terminology is justified and when it is just intellectual posturing. As they respond to questions asked by their peers, they can learn to recognize what aspects of their own communication styles are creating difficulties for others.

The object of discussion is to create a climate in which all participants are supported in articulating clear and convincing arguments while remaining open to different or newly emerging perspectives. Finding one's voice, expressing views that are true to oneself, and articulating claims forcibly should not interfere with the imperative to communicate clearly and to be open to the wide diversity of opinion found in any group.

DISCUSSION DEVELOPS HABITS OF COLLABORATIVE LEARNING

The importance of learning to work collaboratively with peers and colleagues is, like motherhood and democracy, difficult to criticize. Not surprisingly, the rhetoric of collaborative learning has swept through the educational world in the past three decades (Bruffee, 1993). Yet true collaboration—people combining their efforts to help each other learn and to create something that is greater than the sum of their individual energies—is rare. The pressure of time and the lack of collectively developed ground rules often conspire to turn collaborative efforts into a series of individual projects spuriously linked together. It probably doesn't help that most collaborative work takes place within a system of competitive grading.

But if the conditions for democratic, critical discussion are carefully created and respected, students can end up learning collaborative habits. They learn to listen respectfully and attentively to each person's contributions to the group. Through valuing devil's advocacy and critical analysis, they learn to reduce the tendency toward groupthink whereby certain ideas come to be regarded as off limits, sacred, unchallengeable. They learn to create spaces in which everyone's efforts are recognized. They learn that being a productive group member is not the same as directing everybody else or speaking all the time. They learn to value silence and reflective speculation. Learning to do these things is crucial if students are to work well in collaboration.

Collaboration is addictive. The more successful people are at collaborating with others, the more they seek out the chance to do it. Unfortunately, opportunities for collaboration are all too infrequent. Discussion can give us the sense that by collaborating with others, we can solve problems and realize purposes that would be out of reach on our own. It provides an important outlet for the kind of communal sharing that many people crave.

Sometimes discussion groups decide to try to reach some kind of consensus. This does not and should not come easily. Consensus doesn't come about merely by accepting the group's collective judgment. It emerges out of much sharing, haggling, and compromise by everyone involved. A consensus viewpoint transcends the views of any one member yet incorporates, to some degree, the views of all. In striving for consensus, we often increase our identification with the group by hearing out everyone's individual views. Reaching consensus is a collaborative process that can promote mutual respect and help people place concern for the common good above immediate self-interest. It also teaches vocal members of the group to adopt a somewhat more self-effacing attitude.

DISCUSSION INCREASES BREADTH AND MAKES STUDENTS MORE EMPATHIC

One of the irreplaceable benefits of discussion is the opportunity it affords people to expand their horizons, develop new interests, and appreciate new perspectives. Discussion can take us out of ourselves and open us to new realms of experience. In especially intense and engrossing discussions, we actually surrender a part of our identity for the sake of the group. This may not entail the wholesale adoption of the interests and opinions of one's classmates, but it often means gaining a different perspective on these interests that puts them in a new and more understandable light.

Through discussion, we can increase our capacity to empathize with others, to walk in their shoes, and in the process to gain new sensitivity about what they have experienced and the burdens they must continue to shoulder. Individual problems shrink in magnitude just a bit, and the challenges of tackling problems that affect the entire group take on a new intensity. The more we learn about the people in a group, the more chance we have of probing sensitive and challenging issues. Giving class members license to speak freely about their experiences, ideas, and feelings invariably increases the level of trust. Although we believe that discussion should eventually move beyond uncritical personal disclosure, we know that such disclosure is an important starting point in opening people to a broad range of experience.

Discussion Helps Students Develop Skills of Synthesis and Integration

Students with good discussion habits know that some of the most important ways they can contribute to a discussion are by linking apparently unconnected insights, by drawing the group's attention to emerging themes, and by pointing out similarities of reasoning or evidence embedded in multiple arguments. Students who are skilled in discussion will work dialectically (Basseches, 1984). On the one hand, they encourage an exploration of the widest range of interpretive perspectives possible. On the other hand, they strive to discover commonalities and previously unnoticed connections. Over time, they learn to keep in mind several apparently disparate strands of analysis. Occasionally, this leads to a creative and exciting synthesis. More usually, it helps students become comfortable with ambiguity. They accept the fact that discussions are open and not always supposed to lead to some form of conclusion.

Discussion Leads to Transformation

Although discussion is intrinsically satisfying when it fosters mutual enlightenment and strengthens social bonds, it can also be the catalyst for social change. At the most basic and local level, discussion can promote understanding, explain ongoing differences, encourage reciprocal respect, and generally make human interactions more productive and enjoyable. But sometimes it also sets the stage for probing the roots of enduring conflicts and for beginning to implement plans for transformation. In Paulo Freire's terms (1993), discussion represents the reflective phase in the cycle of praxis out of which comes critically informed social action. To Myles Horton (1990), discussion is a way to get a taste of democracy on a small scale that must then be extended to a wider world. The same practices and principles that underlie good discussion also underlie the decent society. To participate in conversations that model these practices and principles is a first step toward the reconstruction of a more humane and just society.

The Limitations of Discussion

Of all the pedagogies college teachers talk about, it is discussion that inspires them to the loftiest flights of rhetoric—the chapter so far demonstrates this very point! In expressing the high hopes the two of us have for discussion, we have fallen into the semireverent and uncritical tone we often employ in characterizing its virtues. Sadly, discussion is not a panacea for all educational ills. Viewing it as the only method of any consequence in higher education is as pedagogically myopic as refusing to do anything other than lecture because "the material has to be covered in a set time." Having a commitment to discussion does not automatically turn you into the embodiment of an empathic, respectful, student-centered teacher. Putting students into circles and telling them to speak to each other rather than to you does not alter the fundamental power dynamics in the classroom. Announcing to students that you've decided to use discussion will not in and of itself unleash a hunger for learning and communication. In fact, one of the most common mistakes made by teachers experimenting with discussion is to assume that if it doesn't immediately transform their classrooms, it should be abandoned.

In our experience, generating the conditions for critical and democratic conversation takes considerable time. It requires a serious modeling of the dispositions outlined in Chapter One and the setting of ground rules that prevent the power dynamics of the wider society from reproducing themselves inside the classroom. Unless we understand the complexities of this method, it's easy to conclude prematurely that it isn't working and that we should give up hope of ever galvanizing a class through its use.

Why Teachers Lose Heart for Discussion

Teachers new to discussion methods can easily lose heart at their first experiments with the method. Given the complexity of the process, this is hardly surprising. It would be almost miraculous if one's early attempts at teaching through discussion were not accompanied by moments of failure and the accompanying temptation to return to tried and trusted methods. In this section, we will examine the most common reasons why teachers jump to the mistaken conclusion that their experiments with discussion are doomed to fail:

1. They have unrealistic expectations about the method.
2. They have not prepared students for the experience.
3. They have not paid sufficient attention to evolving ground rules for the discussion.
4. They have not created an explicit connection between the activity of discussion and the reward system for the class.
5. They have not modeled participation in discussion before asking students to engage in this process—or if they have, it's in a form of discussion that privileges loquacity and high-status discourse.

Let's examine each of these errors in turn.

Teachers' Unrealistic Expectations

One reason teachers feel their discussion sessions are not working is because they have hopelessly inflated images of what a "successful" discussion looks like. In these visions of "good" discussion, silence never fills the room. The conversation focuses only on relevant issues, at a suitably sophisticated level of discourse. Talk flows scintillatingly and seamlessly from topic to topic. Wildean epigrams dart impishly across the room, interspersed with haikus of great profundity. Everyone listens attentively and respectfully to everyone else's contributions. People make their comments in a way that is informed, thoughtful, insightful, and unfailingly courteous. The Algonquin round table or a Bloomsbury dinner party pales in comparison to our febrile imaginings.

The reality is that discussions like this rarely, if ever, happen. Learning to participate in discussion is a lifelong learning project, and most of us go to our graves feeling we still have a lot to learn. Compounding the problem is the fact that two of the most common models of public discourse we have available to us—political debate and television or radio talk shows—foster an image of conversation as loud, dichotomous, oppositional, and inflammatory. Students who see themselves as members of minority groups and whose past experiences have produced legitimate fears about how they will be treated in an academic culture may reject these models and elect for silence. Students who are introverts or who need time for reflective analysis may find the pace of conversation intimidating. If students have suffered public humiliation in previous discussions or if teachers mandate participation without demonstrating why students should take the process seriously, discussion will not work. If students don't know what the teacher's image of a good discussion looks like or if teachers haven't first modeled their participation in critical, respectful discussion in front of students, teachers can't blame students for not acting appropriately.

STUDENT UNPREPAREDNESS

At the beginning of a course, teachers often issue declarations that "in this class, we're going to use discussion" as a learning tool, confident that students will sigh in appreciative relief that they have finally met a teacher who believes in active learning and the democratic process.

In reality, many students are suspicious—and rightly so—of such pedagogical fiats. Sometimes they sense that the teacher has a hidden agenda for the discussion, which the students are supposed to guess. Sometimes students think they don't know enough about things to be able to discuss them intelligently and thus fear looking stupid in front of their peers. Often they have no idea what kinds of contributions the teacher values. When discussions become games in which students try to guess what kinds of comments will earn the teacher's approval, the conversation is stilted and hesitant. What looks on the surface like a participatory democratic experience only serves to reinforce the existing power dynamic.

LACK OF GROUND RULES

Students learn quickly how to gain the teacher's attention in a discussion. Get in quickly and say something—anything—so that your participation is noted and logged. In students' minds, participation becomes equated with speaking, and not saying anything becomes an indication of mental inertia or stupidity. Students' perceptions in this regard are often pretty accurate. Many teachers have an implicit sense that the "best" kind of discussions are those in which everyone speaks for roughly the same amount of time, with no awkward silences. For students, the pressure they feel to participate, to say something intelligent, forces them to devote a great deal of energy to thinking of a point, silently rehearsing what they will say and how they will say it, and then interjecting it when they've got their contribution word-perfect. The purpose of this careful rehearsal is to make them look smart. Of course, in a perverse, catch-22 manner, by the time they intervene with their perfectly rehearsed contribution, the discussion will probably have moved on, so they end up feeling ridiculous anyway.

Students know too that discussion groups can quickly become emotional battlegrounds, arenas in which only the strongest egos survive relatively intact. We've all been in discussion groups where a small minority of participants accounted for the greater part of the conversation. We've all seen one forceful individual's personality shut down any meaningful discourse. We've all seen people disagree with another's point in a way that seems personally abusive. And we've all watched while factors of race, gender, and class played themselves out in our discussion groups, reproducing the unequal patterns of communication found in the wider society.

Without clearly defined ground rules that try to ensure an equal chance for everyone to participate, there is little to prevent the dominant few from setting the agenda and claiming the air space. Without ground rules that work to help people understand how disagreement can be respectfully expressed, attempts at critical discussion soon descend into abuse or disengagement. Without ground rules that stress that periods of silence are as integral to conversational rhythms as is the most garrulous speech, students think that good discussion participation involves making as many comments as they can fit into the time available.

Poorly Integrated Reward Systems

Asking students to invest time and energy in discussion and then grading them on how well they do on midterms and finals is akin to telling faculty that teaching is important and then giving tenure only to those with good publishing records. In both situations, people know what the real rules of the game are and what behaviors get rewarded. If students know that their final grade depends on the quality of their written work in term papers or examinations, that is where they're going to direct their efforts.

If you're going to ask students to take discussion activities seriously, you need to underscore your intentions by adjusting the reward system for the course. Indispensable are clear statements at the outset of the course—both verbally and in the syllabus—of the ways in which serious discussion participation will be expected, recognized, and affirmed. The establishment of unequivocal criteria for participation is of the utmost importance. Bland, generalized declarations that students will be graded in part on their "participation" ignores the subtleties and complications of race, class, gender, and personality and serves chiefly to induce panic and suspicion in anyone who feels less than comfortable in the culture of academe. Unfortunately, the situation described by Bean and Peterson (1998) is typical. In studying core curriculum syllabi at their university, they note that "93 percent of courses included class participation as a component of course grades. Our informal discussions with professors, however, suggest that most professors determine participation grades impressionistically, using class participation largely as a fudge factor in computing final course grades" (p. 33). Chapter Eleven contains suggestions on establishing clear criteria for assessing participation in discussion.

FAILURE TO MODEL PARTICIPATION

One of the mistakes we have both made many times is to walk into a classroom on the first day of a new course, announce to students that we believe in discussion, and tell them why the experience will be good for them. Then we assign topics to students and put them into small discussion groups. The trouble with this scenario is that it omits a crucial element: we have neglected to model for students how to engage in the activity we are urging on them, participating in group discussion with peers. As teachers, we have to earn the right to ask students to engage seriously in discussion by first modeling our own serious commitment to it. If we want students to believe us when we say discussion is good for them, we have to show them that it's good for us too. So in any course in which discussion methods will be used, it's a good idea to invite a group of colleagues into the classroom at an early stage in the course. We can then hold a discussion about some aspect of the course's content in which we try to show the kinds of behaviors we'd like students to exhibit in their own subsequent discussions. More details of this are given in Chapter Three.

CONCLUSION

Throughout this chapter we have tried to maintain a balance between describing the virtues and benefits of discussion and acknowledging that group talk always falls short of our ideals. One of the things we've had to learn as discussion leaders is the importance of living with what Lindeman (1951) called the discipline of the partial functioning of ideals. We are constantly frustrated by our own inability to ensure that the conditions for good discussion are created at every moment in our teaching. We are constantly researching our classrooms to find out new procedures that will lead to democratic talk. And we never feel that we get it completely right.

However, never being able to get it completely right doesn't mean that we can't get better at creating the conditions under which good discussion is more likely to occur. Our chances of being successful with discussion depend on planning carefully, having realistic expectations about its benefits, and being willing to monitor closely its value for students. We hope you can see that we are enthusiastic supporters of discussion; it does boost learning and enliven classrooms. But we remain, as well, painfully aware of its pitfalls and limitations. In the chapter that follows we explore ways to prepare for discussion that may help you avert some common problems and get discussion going in fruitful directions.

CHAPTER THREE

PREPARING FOR DISCUSSION

Teachers cannot expect students to share a common understanding of the term discussion. Nor can they assume that students have any positive disposition toward the method. In fact, many students will actively resist discussion and do their best to undermine it with sarcasm, silence, or acting out for the benefit of peers. They may have learned from past experience that supposedly democratic discussions are often a thin veneer for maintaining traditional teacher power through apparently nontraditional means. They may also have seen discussions reproduce the differences of race, class, and gender that exist in the wider society. So teachers cannot expect that students are ready and willing to engage in discussion, much less able to do so. Teachers must earn the right to ask students to take the process seriously by showing them what democratic discussion looks like and convincing them that participating in discussion is worth their time and energy.

Learning the dispositions and practices of democratic talk takes time and effort. Given that engaging in critical discussion is difficult, how can we help people learn to do this sooner rather than later? One of the keys to good discussion is preparing students and teachers adequately for what lies ahead. In this chapter we offer a number of suggestions on what might be done before the discussion begins to prepare people for democratic talk.

ENSURE EARLY AND EQUAL ACCESS TO RELEVANT MATERIALS

One prerequisite for good discussion is that participants be as fully informed as possible about the topic under consideration. Of course, being fully informed is an ideal. Few people could be said to be completely informed about all aspects and dimensions of a phenomenon at any one time. As an ideal, however, striving to ensure that participants have access to full information is of enormous political significance. Educators concerned to help learners gain access to all relevant information about an issue fight to ensure that all relevant perspectives, no matter how politically contentious, are available. This gives them a clear mandate to engage in political action when it is obvious that certain interests wish to keep information (about, for example, conditions of economic inequity or moral injustice) in the hands of the few and out of the minds of the many.

How can we ensure that all students have equal access to as full a range of relevant materials as possible? One way is to place these materials in an accessible location well before a course starts. This might be a physical location, as in the case of a university library that has the course's required materials on reserve or a bookstore that sells copies of them. Or it might be an electronic location, as in the case of an electronic bulletin board or listserv that either provides the resources or explains how they can be accessed via electronic means. But all these approaches depend on students' being relatively privileged. They must be fortunate enough to own a car so that they can drive to the library, and they must have enough discretionary time to be able to consult library materials beforehand. If they are purchasing required texts, they need money over and above what they're paying for tuition, traveling expenses, and child care. And they may have to find this money out of a budget that's further reduced by the students' not being paid while they are away from work. To access electronic information, they must have access to computer technology and have enough discretionary time to learn how to manipulate computer software. If they are enormously privileged, of course, they can pay someone to drive to the library or bookstore or to retrieve the materials electronically on their behalf.

A simple way to equalize access to resources is to make sure that a package of materials is sent to all students well before the course begins. This means planning the opening sessions of a course several months beforehand so that you have time to track down, duplicate, and distribute these materials. If all students in a course are lucky enough to have access to computers, you can send disks containing prereading material to them through the mail.

You could also post the materials on your Web site several weeks before the course begins and have students download them at their leisure. It is important that when students receive these materials, they know what to do with them. We like to ask students to do the prereading before class begins and to bring to the first class meeting photocopies of a short paper they have written in response to the prereading. These photocopies are distributed to other class members, who read them and use them to frame the opening discussions.

USE LECTURES TO MODEL DEMOCRATIC TALK

One of the traps that advocates of discussion methods often fall into is setting up a false dichotomy between lecturing and discussion. They give the impression that anyone who lectures combines the moral sensitivity of Caligula with the democratic impulses of Stalin. If you lecture, so their argument goes, you only serve to confirm your authoritarian, demagogic tendencies. This is a disservice to well-intentioned colleagues and a gross misunderstanding of pedagogical dynamics. Exhorting colleagues to stop lecturing altogether and use only discussion forces teachers to make a choice between what seem to be two mutually exclusive options.

We believe that this pedagogical bifurcation is wrong. Lectures are not, in and of themselves, oppressive and authoritarian, and lecturers are not, by definition, demagogues. Similarly, discussions are not, in and of themselves, liberating and spontaneous, and discussion leaders are not, by definition, democratic. We have both been participants in discussion sessions where leaders manipulate the group to reach certain predefined conclusions. Through their power to control the flow of talk, to summarize and reframe students' comments, and to respond favorably to some contributions and unfavorably to others, discussion leaders can act in extremely authoritarian ways.

Instead of reducing questions of pedagogical method to a simplistic dichotomy—discussion good, lecture bad—we see these two methods as complementary. We agree with Paulo Freire's observation that "a liberating teacher will illuminate reality even if he or she lectures" (Shor and Freire, 1987, p. 40). So we want to argue that lectures can provide a wonderful opportunity for teachers to model the forms of democratic dispositions they wish to encourage in discussion. Here are some ideas on how this might happen.

- *Begin every lecture with one or more questions that you're trying to answer.* Posing these questions at the outset of your talk means you frame the lecture as part of your continuous effort to make sense of a subject. This suggests that you see education as a never-ending process of inquiry in which you're constantly trying to come to a point of greater understanding, all the while acknowledging that whatever truths you claim are provisional and temporary. If students are used to you opening all your lectures by raising a series of framing questions, they'll be more accepting when you frame discussions around a question or questions to be explored.

- *End every lecture with a series of questions that your lecture has raised or left unanswered.* Lecturers are often told that the golden rule of effective lecturing is to "tell 'em what you're going to tell 'em, tell 'em, and then tell 'em what you've told 'em." The problem with this rule is that it presents the lecture as a statement of indisputable truth. Doing this is inimical to intellectual inquiry. In particular, ending with a summary of what's already been said establishes a sense of definitive closure—the last word on the subject has been spoken. We believe that good lecturers should end their presentations by pointing out all the new questions that have been raised by the content of the lecture and also by pointing out which of the questions posed at the start of the lecture have been left unanswered or been reframed in a more provocative or contentious way. This prepares students for the practice we advocate of ending discussion sessions by asking students to volunteer the questions the discussion has raised for them (rather than by giving a summary of "what we've learned today in our discussion").

If possible, lecturers should spend the last ten minutes of a lecture asking students to write down the questions the lecture has raised for them and then find a way to make some of these public. Students can be asked to announce their questions to the whole class, to share them with each other in groups of two or three, or to write them down, pass them to the lecturer, and have the lecturer read out a random selection.

- *Deliberately introduce periods of silence. One barrier to good discussion is people's belief that conversation means continuous talk.* We believe that periods of reflective silence are as integral to good discussion as the most animated speech. Participants in discussion must feel comfortable saying, "I need to think about that a minute or two before I respond," and then be ready to take that time to think before speaking. Others in the group should not feel they have to fill this "vacuum" of silence with speech. They need to learn that silence does not represent a vacuum in discussion. Rather, it signifies a different but equally significant and intense engagement with the subject of discussion.

Lecturers can prepare students for periods of reflective silence in discussions by introducing such silences into their lectures. They can tell students they need a minute to think about what they want to say next and then take that full minute. After every twenty minutes or so of uninterrupted lecture, they can call for three to five minutes of silent reflective speculation. During this time students can think about the preceding twenty minutes and write down the most important point they felt was made, the most puzzling assertion, or the question they most would like to ask. At the end of these few minutes of silent reflection, students can spend a couple of minutes sharing their ideas in pairs or triads, volunteer to announce their ideas to the whole class, or write them down and pass them to the lecturer, who will read out a random selection.

• *Deliberately introduce alternative perspectives.* Participating in discussion involves exposing oneself to a variety of alternative ideas and perspectives. We can use lectures to model this willingness to consider different viewpoints seriously and nondefensively. One way to do this is to present as part of our lecture any arguments that counter our own assertions. A dramatic and theatrical approach is to state your opening position while you stand in one part of the room and then to move to another part of the room, look back at where you were standing, and direct a second set of comments at that spot. This second set of comments should be counterarguments or rebuttals. When you do this, you address your imaginary other selves by name, saying things like "Stephen, what you're omitting to mention is" or "Of course, Stephen, you could pursue a very different line of reasoning if you argue that. . . ."

Another approach is to bring one or more colleagues into your lecture who disagree with your presentation and give them some time to speak their views. By listening respectfully and then following their presentations with a brief period of discussion in which you acknowledge and explore your differences, you model the kind of respectful attention to diverse perspectives that you hope will be paralleled in students' discussions.

• *Introduce periods of assumption hunting.* One of the purposes of discussion is to encourage critical thinking, which involves students in identifying and scrutinizing the assumptions that inform their ideas and actions. We can show students what this looks like by first introducing periods of "assumption hunting" into our lectures. These are moments when we stop professing what we believe and spend a few minutes in a "time-out" compiling the assumptions on which our beliefs rest and musing on how we might investigate them. We do this musing aloud in front of our students. When students see us identifying our assumptions and subjecting them to critical scrutiny, it gets them used to the idea that doing this is a regular part of discussion.

• *Introduce buzz groups into lectures.* Students can begin to acquire the habit of discussion by participating in brief buzz group sessions during lectures. Buzz groups are usually made up of three or four students who are given a few minutes once or twice during a lecture to discuss a question or an issue that arises. The best kind of questions ask students to make some judgments regarding the relative merits, relevance, or usefulness of the constituent elements of the lecture. Here are some examples of such questions:

What's the most contentious statement you've heard so far in the lecture today?

What's the most important point that's been made in the lecture so far?

What question would you most like to have answered regarding the topic of the lecture today?

What's the most unsupported assertion you've heard in the lecture so far?

Of all the ideas and points you've heard so far today, which is most obscure or ambiguous to you?

In their buzz groups, students are asked to take turns giving a brief response to the question asked and to note if one response draws particular agreement or produces significant conflict. When the three-minute buzz group period is up, the lecturer asks for random responses to the questions asked or for comments about the discussions that occurred. Buzz groups are useful minidiscussions that get students used to talking to each other while completing a task at hand. If you split students into triads during a lecture and ask them to "discuss the significance of what they've heard so far," that task can seem so momentous or impenetrable that it precludes productive conversation. But a focused buzz group gets students involved in discussion almost without their realizing this is happening. We will have more to say about buzz groups in Chapter Six.

USE CRITICAL INCIDENT QUESTIONNAIRES

One of our strongest convictions about discussion is that students learn to speak in critical and democratic ways by watching people in positions of power and authority model these processes in their own lives. As teachers committed to modeling critical thinking in our own practice, we have found the critical incident questionnaire (CIQ) to be very useful in this process.

The CIQ is a simple classroom evaluation tool that we use to find out what and how students are learning. It consists of a single sheet of paper (with attached carbon) containing five questions, all of which focus on critical moments or actions in a program or class, as judged by the learners. Beneath each question, space is provided for learners to write down whatever they wish. The CIQ is handed out to learners about ten minutes before the end of the last class of the week. The five questions are always the same:

1. At what moment in class this week were you most engaged as a learner?
2. At what moment in class this week were you most distanced as a learner?
3. What action that anyone in the room took this week did you find most affirming or helpful?

4. What action that anyone in the room took this week did you find most puzzling or confusing?

5. What surprised you most about the class this week?

As learners write their responses to these questions, the carbon provides a copy that they can keep for themselves. This allows them to review their responses over the length of the course and to notice habitual preferences, dispositions, and points of avoidance in their learning.

As learners exit the room, they leave the top copies of their CIQ facedown on a table by the door, or they give their sheets to a peer who then hands the whole bundle to the teacher. The CIQ sheets are never signed, so teachers have no idea who wrote what. This anonymity is crucial. It means that participants can be as brutally honest and critically frank as they like, with no possibility of recrimination. If some learners put their names on the forms in the early stages of a course, we ask them to stop doing this. We explain that we're looking for honest, accurate commentary on the class, and we know they will feel constrained about what they write if they have to put their names to their comments. We address the power differential in college classrooms head on and stress that the reason CIQ responses are anonymous is so that no one will feel that writing negative comments will adversely affect his or her grade. We also say that we know the students won't believe that we welcome their criticism, since they've probably seen too many professors espouse that belief and then punish students who challenge professorial competence and authority.

After everyone has left the room, we start to read the responses. For a typical class of about thirty students, it will take us fifteen to twenty minutes to get a sense of the clusters of ideas and main themes on the forms. We jot down notes on the chief clusters and themes and sometimes verbatim comments that encapsulate several people's reactions. Sometimes we type this information up on a sheet of paper and make photocopies for everyone in the class. Sometimes we simply use the notes as the basis of a verbal report.

At the first class each week, we report the results of the previous week's CIQ responses. We invite students' reactions, comments, questions, and elaborations concerning these responses; then we spend some time discussing what we need to do about what they've said or written. Sometimes all that the CIQs reveal is that things are fine and no change or renegotiation is necessary. Sometimes it becomes clear that there are problems we need to talk about. Perhaps the pace of the class is wrong for a substantial number of participants. Perhaps there's confusion concerning the required assignments. Maybe expectations that we thought we had explained thoroughly didn't really sink in. Maybe criteria aren't clear. Or maybe an activity that we thought was going well is actually confusing for some participants. We then spend some time clarifying and negotiating these matters.

Each week students see us trying to understand how our actions as teachers look to them. As we report their CIQ responses to them, we thank them for clarifying and challenging our assumptions. Students' written responses help illuminate power dynamics in the classroom that we may have thought were absent or unimportant. They point out to us ways in which our affirmations of the democratic process are contradicted by our instinctive, automatic moves to control what happens. When comments critical of our actions turn up on the form, we try to highlight these in our report to the students. Week in, week out, students see us react to their criticisms of us as nondefensively as we can. We try to celebrate their criticisms and point out how much we are learning from them and how this learning is invigorating our practice.

Sometimes it's very hard to do this. We take their criticisms personally, and we're devastated by suggestions that we're acting in anything other than good faith or from the best of intentions. We let them know how hard it is for us to make these criticisms public but how important it is for us to do this if we're going to ask students to apply the same process of critical analysis to their own ideas in discussion. We explain that we're trying to earn the right to ask students to think and speak critically by first modeling this in front of them. The overall effect is often very powerful, particularly when students see us putting ourselves in the uncomfortable position of highlighting comments that show us in a bad light. Over time, using the CIQ in this way earns us the right to turn to students and ask that they take the same risk of inviting critical scrutiny of their ideas and actions in discussion.

HAVE FACULTY DEMONSTRATE THEIR OWN PARTICIPATION IN AND COMMITMENT TO DISCUSSION

Before you can get skeptical students to take discussion seriously, you need to demonstrate your own readiness to engage in this activity. African American educator bell hooks (1994, p. 21) writes forcefully about this: "In my classrooms, I do not expect students to take any risks that I would not take, to share in any way that I would not share. It is often productive if professors take the first risk, linking confessional narratives to academic discussions so as to show how experience can illuminate and enhance our understanding of academic material." One way to demonstrate one's commitment to the method is to spend some time during the first couple of weeks of a course holding a discussion with colleagues in full view of the group. You can invite to your class several colleagues who are experienced discussion participants or discussion leaders and ask them to engage with you in an unrehearsed discussion of some contentious issue in front of the students. As you do this, you should listen attentively to each other's comments, reframe and rephrase what you've heard, and check with colleagues to make sure you've caught their meaning accurately. Try to show how it's possible for you to disagree respectfully with each other, focusing your critical comments on each other's ideas rather than being personally derogatory.

Introduce new perspectives by showing how they have been prompted by or are intended to illuminate earlier contributions from others. If possible, clarify in the midst of the discussion how others' comments are helpful in getting you to recognize and examine critically some familiar assumptions you hold. Thank colleagues for suggesting radically new interpretations or perspectives you had not previously considered. But also allow yourself to reject these and to show that you don't feel obliged to change your views because of colleagues' comments. You want to show students that it is quite permissible to be the only one holding a dissenting view in a discussion and that groups should avoid trying to convert holdouts to the majority opinion. And make very sure that you don't finish by giving a set of conclusions. Instead, finish by listing all the unresolved issues and areas for future inquiry that the discussion has prompted.

You can also use this modeling to show students that silence is a necessary and desirable part of conversation. If one colleague asks another a question that the other has no ready response for, the person asked should feel comfortable saying, "I'm not sure; I'll need a minute or two to think about that," and then take that time before responding. During this period, everyone else waits silently. It's been interesting for us to observe how shocked and uncomfortable students are when they see their teachers just sitting quietly as a group while one of us thinks about what to say next.

Finally, try to avoid talking in a rarefied, overly academic manner. Use specialized terminology when you feel it's warranted, but try to mix in plenty of colloquial speech and familiar metaphors. Don't worry about hesitating in midsentence, stumbling to find the right words to express your meaning, starting over, pausing to regroup your thoughts, or letting your words trail off. Better to do this than to strive to make ringing, grammatically impeccable, eloquent, and unequivocal declarations of truth. Our concern is that faculty avoid putting on a beautifully articulated, seamless, exemplary display of dazzlingly erudite, high-status, academic discourse. We want students to see that hesitations, pauses, and colloquial language are a normal part of discussion. If we model discussion participation for students, the last thing we want to do is act as if we are characters in a play by Noel Coward or Tom Stoppard.

Although we advocate modeling the discussion process with colleagues, we admit that we have done so far less than we would like. Time is one factor. We often worry that we've sacrificed too much time working on process that should be spent studying content. To add a role-played discussion to a course already full of participatory learning activities can seem like overkill. But mostly our problem is that it's difficult to convince colleagues that it's worth their while to spend time modeling the discussion process with us. At the very least, we can offer to return the favor by helping out our colleagues in whatever way they think is useful.

Evolve Ground Rules for Conducting Discussions

Rules of conduct and codes of behavior are crucial in determining whether or not students take discussion seriously. Although we've emphasized that discussions should be completely open regarding the possible directions the conversation could take, and though we've condemned the concept of guided discussion, this doesn't mean we're opposed to structuring the process of democratic conversation. There is no contradiction in guiding the ways in which people talk to each other while refusing to guide what they talk about. Our experience is that when students know that there are fair and democratic ground rules that frame how people speak, there is a much better chance of getting them involved.

We advocate spending some time at the start of a discussion-based course talking with participants about the ground rules for conversation they'd like to see in operation. How would they like to be spoken to by their peers? What are their feelings about good manners, respect, or courtesy in discussion, and what do these things look like? Do they want discussions to be nothing but talk, or would they like some periods of silence? How do they want to indicate that they're ready to speak? Should we call on people by a show of hands, deciding on the order of contributions by the order in which people volunteer? Or should we allow the same few people to have two or three contributions in short order if this leads to a deeper analysis of a particular theme or idea? Perhaps before bringing new people into a discussion the leader should check whether their comment applies to the current theme or takes the discussion on a new tack. Is it OK for the leader to call directly on individuals known to possess particular knowledge or experience that's relevant to the theme being discussed, even if they have not indicated that they wish to speak?

One way to generate ground rules is to work from students' most vivid recollections of their experiences as discussion participants. Here are the instructions we give to groups to do this.

Generating Ground Rules for Discussion

As a first step in organizing this discussion group, I suggest that we set some ground rules for our participation. Ground rules are the rules we follow to ensure that the discussion is a useful, respectful, and worthwhile experience for all participants. To help us decide on some rules, I would like each of you to do the following:

1. Think of the best group discussions you've ever been involved in. What things happened that made these conversations so satisfying? Make a few notes on this by yourself.

2. Think of the worst group discussions you've ever been involved in. What things happened that made these conversations so unsatisfactory? Make a few notes on this by yourself.

3. Now form a group with three other people. Take turns talking about what made discussion groups work well for you. Listen for common themes, shared experiences, and features of conversation that a majority of you would like to see present in this course.

4. Take turns talking about what made discussion group work awful for you. Listen for common themes, shared experiences, and features of group conversation that a majority of you would like to see avoided in this course.

5. For each of the characteristics of good discussion you agree on, try to suggest three things a group might do to ensure that these characteristics are present. Be as specific and concrete as you can. For example, if you feel that good conversation is developmental, with later themes building on and referring back to earlier ones, you could propose a rule that every new comment made by a participant be prefaced by an explanation as to how it relates to an earlier comment.

6. For each of the characteristics of bad discussion you agree on, try to suggest three things a group might do to ensure that these characteristics are avoided. Be as specific and concrete as you can. For example, if you feel that bad conversation happens when one person's voice dominates, you could propose a rule that someone who has spoken may not make a second comment until at least three other people have been heard (unless asked a direct question by another group member).

7. Try to finish this exercise by drafting a charter for discussion that comprises the specific ground rules you agree on. We will make each group's rules public and use them to develop a charter for discussion to guide the entire class in the coming weeks.

Our role as teachers in this exercise is not to suggest images of how we think good discussants behave. That's the business of group members. However, when it comes to translating these images into specific rules of conduct, we have found that students do need some help. If the class agrees that good discussions involve lots of people talking, we'll suggest ways to make this more likely to happen, such as putting a time limit on individual contributions or regularly calling for a circle of voices where each person in turn is given the floor.

Another approach to evolving ground rules is to ask participants to focus on the "golden rule": ask them how they would like to be spoken to in a discussion, and use their responses to frame a code of conduct for speaking to others. Again, our role would be to help students move from general declarations such as "I want people to listen carefully to what I'm saying" to specific behaviors (such as suggesting a weekly circular response discussion period in which students take turns to listen carefully, paraphrase, and then respond to each other's contributions).

In their work on cooperative learning, Johnson, Johnson, and Smith (1991a, 1991b) emphasize that we cannot assume that students possess the social and communicative skills necessary for collaboration; these need to be taught. They propose a technique, the "T-Chart," that can be adapted to help students develop ground rules for discussion. The characteristic of discussion that students desire is written at the top of a large piece of newsprint. Assume that students say they want their discussions to be respectful. Under the heading "Respectful," the teacher divides the sheet in two, labeling one side "Sounds Like" and the other side "Looks Like." Students and teachers then suggest behaviors and procedures that would fall in each column; after a few minutes, a picture emerges of how students think respectful discussions should look and sound.

Finally, you can use videos of discussion vignettes—filmed excerpts of powerfully inspiring or troublingly contentious episodes of actual discussions—as a useful way to focus students' attention on how they want their own discussions to look. Here are the instructions for such an exercise that you might give to students.

Videotaped Discussion Vignettes

You are going to see two five-minute excerpts of different discussions. Please watch for the kinds of comments, contributions, and actions that you think are good or bad discussion behaviors. Note these down by yourself. Don't discuss your reactions with others at this stage. You might find it helpful to watch the videos with the following questions in mind:

1. In your view, which participants made the best, most helpful, or most useful contributions to the discussion? Why were these contributions so worthwhile?

2. In your view, which participants made the worst, least helpful, or least useful contributions to the discussion? Why were these contributions so irrelevant or unproductive?

3. What changes would you introduce to improve either of these discussions?

Afterward, compare your responses with the reactions of others in your group. Look particularly for areas of agreement. Based on these, could you suggest any guidelines that would ensure that helpful discussion behaviors are encouraged?

When we reconvene, we will see if your notes can help us decide on the discussion guidelines we want to follow in this course.

HAVE STUDENTS DO STRUCTURED, CRITICAL PREREADING

Having participants do a serious, critical prereading of materials to prepare themselves for a discussion increases enormously the chance that you will have good conversation. However, asking students to do this purely to improve the quality of subsequent talk won't have much effect. Students' lives are simply too full for such a request to rise to the top of their priorities. Even those who want to do the reading will often be forced to give time to other, more pressing tasks. They'll rely on their peers to have done the reading for them and will gamble on being able to improvise a comment or two that will make them look properly prepared.

So if you want participants to prepare for a discussion, you have to show them that it's in their own best interests to do so. From their point of view, there has to be some incentive for them to spend time in this effort. Our approach is to ask students to write brief papers based on the prereading as part of a homework assignment. They bring multiple copies of these papers to class for sharing with peers.

Prereading works best when it is structured around a series of critical questions that preclude any clear resolution or answer. In a graduate adult education class one of us teaches, for example, the following protocol of questions has proved useful for showing students what it means to read an adult education text critically.

A Protocol for Critical Reading

Critical reading happens when readers (1) make explicit the assumptions authors hold about what constitutes legitimate knowledge and how such knowledge comes to be known, (2) take alternative perspectives on the knowledge being offered so that this knowledge comes to be seen as culturally constructed, (3) undertake positive and negative appraisals of the grounds for and expression of this knowledge, and (4) analyze commonly held ideas for the extent to which they support or oppose various political ideologies. It's often useful to structure a critical reading of texts around four general categories of questions: epistemological, experiential, communicative, and political. Asking questions like the examples shown here provides a template for the critical analysis of a text that makes this activity seem less daunting.

Epistemological Questions

These are questions that probe how an author comes to know that something is true. Here are some examples:

- *To what extent does the writing seem culturally biased?* For example, does the author make universal claims about adult learners or learning that are based on studies of learners drawn from a small number of cultures at one period in history?

- *To what extent are description and prescription confused in an irresponsible and inaccurate way?* For example, does the author write as if the philosophical ideals she or he holds about self-directed learning, critical thinking, or the democratic process are empirically accurate summaries of reality?

- *To what extent are the central insights grounded in documented empirical evidence?* (Remember, empirical evidence includes personal experience.)

- *To what extent are the ideas presented an uncritical extension of the paradigm within which the author works?* For example, does the author's view of the purpose of adult education as liberating empowerment or as preparing a skilled workforce skew his or her treatment of various theories of learning?

Experiential Questions

These are questions that help you review the text through the lens of your own relevant experiences with the issues covered in the text. Here are some examples:

- *How do the metaphors used in the text compare to the metaphors you use to describe your own similar experiences?* For example, if the text describes teachers as coaches or midwives, do these metaphors have meaning for you? Do they capture accurately your sense of your own practice and philosophy? If not, what metaphors work better for you?

- *What experiences are omitted from the text that strike you as important?*

- *If the text addresses experiences with which you are familiar, to what extent are these congruent with or contradicted by your own experiences?* For example, does the way the author describes ethical dilemmas faced by adult educators echo ethical dilemmas you have faced?

Communicative Questions

These are questions having to do with how authors convey meaning and whether or not the forms they choose tend to clarify or confuse. Here are some examples:

- *To what extent does the text use a form of specialized language that is unjustifiably distant from colloquial language?*

- *To what extent is the text connected to practice?* For example, does the text analyze problems of practice you face in a helpful way, and does it suggest useful responses to these problems?

- *Whose voices are heard in the text?* For example, are the most important voices those of the learners studied, the author, or major gatekeepers and theoreticians in the field?

Political Questions

These are questions that alert us to the ways in which published works serve to represent certain interests and challenge others. Here are some examples:

- *Whose interests are served by the publication of this text?* For example, is this book written primarily to advance the author's career, to help practicing adult educators, or to enhance the reputation of the foundation that sponsored the research?

- *What contribution does the text make to the understanding and realization of democratic forms and processes?* For example, does reading this book help us create more opportunities for self-evaluation, classroom discussion, collective educational action, or a negotiated curriculum?

- *To what extent does this text challenge or confirm existing ideologies, values and structures?* For example, does it routinely use capitalistic metaphors for learning and education, such as "buying into" ideas, "owning" ideas, treating students as "customers" and teachers as "instructional managers," and setting up curricula to "produce outcomes" (educational "goods")?

Clarify Expectations and Purposes

As teachers, we need to justify to students why we believe so strongly in using discussion. Many students will likely have experienced classes where teachers manipulated the discussion's outcome and even humiliated their students. Being clear about what we hope to achieve through discussion helps combat students' cynicism and raises our chances of drawing them into conversation.

Truth in Advertising Statements

We can clarify our expectations and purposes in a number of ways. For example, a strong statement as to why discussion will be used so much in class can be inserted into the syllabus. One of us includes in his course syllabus a section titled "What You Need to Know About This Course." This section is a kind of "truth in advertising" statement that sets forth the nonnegotiable elements of the course.

What You Need to Know About This Course

As a student, I very much appreciate the chance to make informed decisions about the courses I take. I want to know who the educator is, what his or her assumptions are, and what he or she stands for before I make a commitment to spend my time, money, and energy attending the class. So let me tell you some things about me and how I work as an educator that will allow you to make an informed decision as to whether or not you wish to be involved in this course.

I have framed this course on the following assumptions:

1. That participating in discussion brings with it the following benefits:

   - It helps students explore a diversity of perspectives.
   - It increases students' awareness of and tolerance for ambiguity or complexity.

- It helps students recognize and investigate their assumptions.
- It encourages attentive, respectful listening.
- It develops new appreciation for continuing differences.
- It increases intellectual agility.
- It helps students become connected to a topic.
- It shows respect for students' voices and experiences.
- It helps students learn the processes and habits of democratic discourse.
- It affirms students as cocreators of knowledge.
- It develops the capacity for the clear communication of ideas and meaning.
- It develops habits of collaborative learning.
- It increases breadth and makes students more empathic.
- It helps students develop skills of synthesis and integration.
- It leads to transformation.

2. That students attending will have experiences that they can reflect on and analyze in discussion.

3. That the course will focus on the analysis of students' experiences and ideas as much as on the analysis of academic theories.

4. That the chief regular class activity will be a small group discussion of experiences and ideas.

5. That I as teacher have a dual role as a catalyst for your critical conversation and as a model of democratic talk.

So please take note of the following "product warnings"!

If you don't feel comfortable talking with others about yourself and your experiences in small groups, *you should probably drop this course.*

If you don't feel comfortable with small group discussion and think it's a touchy-feely waste of valuable time, *you should probably drop this course.*

If you are not prepared to analyze your own and other people's experiences, *you should probably drop this course.*

You can also involve former students in communicating your expectations and purposes to new students. We like to use panels

of former students as contributors to the first or second class. These former students come to class and talk about their experiences of the course a year or so previously. They are asked to pass on to new students whatever advice they have on how to survive and flourish in the class. Frequently, they end up making the case for discussion that you would have made and elaborating on the benefits that you would have stressed, but their testimony is far more powerful. Former students talking about the value of discussion have far more credibility in the eyes of new students than anything that you as the teacher could say or do.

LETTERS TO SUCCESSORS

A variant on this approach is the "letter to successors" technique. An interesting way to discover what students feel are the most crucial elements in your teaching is to ask them to identify what they regard as the essential things new students need to know and do to survive in your classroom. One of us likes to assign the writing of such a letter as an exercise at the end of a course. Current students are asked to compose a letter that will be sent to new students entering the same course the next time it is offered. The letter encapsulates departing students' insights about the experience.

After these letters have been written, students form small discussion groups to read each other's letters. Group members look for common themes, which are then reported in a whole-class plenary session. Because responses are given by a group reporter, anonymity is preserved, and no one is required to say anything about a particular concern unless he or she wishes to do so.

These are the instructions given for this exercise.

Writing a Letter to Successors

In this exercise, I want you to write a letter to be sent to new students who will be in this course next year. I want you to tell them—in as helpful and specific a way as possible—what you think they should know about how to survive and flourish in this class. Some themes you might consider writing about are "what I know now about this course that I wish I'd known right at the start," "the most important things you should do to keep your sanity in this class," "the most common and avoidable mistakes that I and others made in this class," and "the words that should hang on a sign above your desk concerning how to make it through this class." Feel free to ignore these themes and just write about whatever comes into your head around the theme of survival.

After you have finished your letter, make three photocopies. Bring these to class so that you can give them to colleagues. In class, you will be forming a group with three other people to read what each of you has written. As you do this, you will be looking for common themes and recurring pieces of advice. I will be asking you to appoint someone to report to the whole class the main suggestions and advice that were given.

If one or more of these letters contain passages that urge skeptical students to prepare for discussions and to take them seriously, we try to obtain permission from the students concerned to let us reproduce these comments in the syllabus for the next version of the course.

CONCLUSION

We've argued in this chapter that even before a word is spoken in discussion, there's an enormous amount that can be done to prepare students for democratic talk. Good discussions don't just happen. They are partly the result of thoughtful planning, consistent modeling by the teacher, and respectful consideration of the experiences of students. In the next chapter we consider how such talk might be initiated once students are gathered together.

CHAPTER FOUR

GETTING DISCUSSION STARTED

The first few minutes of any new discussion are often somewhat uncomfortable, particularly if the group members don't know each other very well or if there has been a contentious atmosphere in the previous session. In this chapter we want to focus on ways of opening up conversation that concentrate participants' attention on the theme at hand and that model democratic process at the outset. We do want to stress, however, the importance of the preparatory steps outlined in the preceding chapter. If teachers and students lead into discussions by doing the kinds of things that Chapter Three describes, there's a much better chance that the conversation will flow relatively easily.

But what do you do if you've modeled democratic talk in your lectures, held unscripted discussions with colleagues in front of students, helped students draft their own guidelines for conversation, organized provocative preparatory reading, and clarified your expectations—and still silence descends on the group in the first few minutes?

MISTAKES TO AVOID AT THE START OF A DISCUSSION

We have noticed, in ourselves and others, five things that teachers sometimes do at the start of discussion sessions that we feel kill the spirit of democratic talk. So here are our five "don'ts" to discussion leaders regarding the opening moments of the class.

DON'T LECTURE

Don't start the discussion by giving a minilecture in which you summarize salient points, outline different perspectives, and introduce your own concerns. You have already shown students what you think is important through your introductory lectures, your choice of preparatory reading material, and your previous assignments. Even the most judiciously evenhanded prologue conveys subtle messages about what you want or expect students to say once the discussion starts.

DON'T BE VAGUE

Don't always open the discussion by posing vague, general questions like "What do you think?" or "Would anyone like to react?" or "Who wants to start us off?" This opening works only when two conditions are in place: when participants know and trust each other and are used to talking easily and democratically and when they are so immersed in and provoked by the topic or preparatory reading that they are bursting to speak.

DON'T PLAY FAVORITES

Don't allow a pecking order of opening contributors to develop. Every teacher knows the one or two students who are so committed to learning (or to impressing the teacher) that they can be relied on to speak up and get the discussion going. Since the two of us are introverts, we have often been grateful for the presence of extroverted, garrulous students in our classes and have sighed with relief when they've saved us from embarrassment by responding to our opening questions. This is misplaced gratitude. After watching this happen two or three times at the start of the discussion, the others in the group lose their desire to participate because they can predict that the usual suspects will speak up. The majority of students can then mentally doze off.

DON'T FEAR SILENCE

Don't panic at silence. At the start of a discussion, there may be long periods of silence as people settle into the new intellectual project that the conversation represents. Something we both struggle with is letting silence exist without panicking. Like many teachers we know, we tend to assume that silence means things aren't going well. This is an erroneous inference. As Palmer (1993) points out, "We need to abandon the notion that 'nothing is happening' when it is silent, to see how much new clarity a silence often brings" (p. 80). A typical conversational dynamic in discussion is for teachers to start the session by asking a provocative question designed to spark some fruitful responses. Sometimes, though, students choose not to say anything, and in panic, teachers start to answer their own question. Do this even once and you let students know they can rely on you to answer the question and do their thinking for them.

Don't Misinterpret Silence

Don't mistake students' silence for mental inertia or disengagement. Conversation is halting, tentative, and circuitous, filled with hesitations and awkward attempts at reformulating thoughts even as we speak them. In a culture in which talk shows advance the idea that talk consists of a string of inoffensive, humorous, and seamless anecdotes or vicious and theatrical attacks on other people's beliefs or integrity, it is sometimes hard to insist on the value of reflective silence. Silence is the condition the media dread above all else—they even call it "dead air"—but real-life discussion is not a talk show! Effective discussion leaders take steps to ensure that periods of reflective silence became accepted as a normal and necessary element of people's deliberations.

Now that we've covered what not to do at the start of a discussion, let's look at some of the things you *should* do.

Declaring a Classroom Speech Policy

We have noted that students will often look to you to start off a discussion session rather than take the responsibility for doing this themselves. They will assume that their silence will impel you into speech. If this is the case, a good way to get things going is to make an opening statement regarding the value of silence. It may seem strange to suggest that you launch a discussion by advocating silence, but our experience has been that this puts diffident or introverted students at their ease.

Many students from working-class backgrounds, female students, or students from underrepresented ethnic groups will approach discussion sessions with a justifiable sense of distrust. They will feel, sometimes accurately, that success in academe is often correlated with a glib facility to spring confidently into speech at the earliest possible opportunity, thus impressing the teacher. You can do a great deal to destroy this perception at the outset if you acknowledge the power of silence and students' right not to speak. What follows is an example of a declaration to students that not only expresses the teacher's tolerance of silence but also informs students that participation in class discussion is entirely voluntary and should never be used to curry favor with the instructor:

> I know that speaking in discussions is a nerve-racking thing and that your fear of making public fools of yourselves can inhibit you to the point of nonparticipation. I, myself, feel very nervous as a discussion participant and waste a lot of my time carefully rehearsing my contributions so as not to look foolish when I finally speak. So please don't feel that you have to speak in order to gain my approval or to show me that you're a diligent student. It's quite acceptable to say nothing in the session, and there'll be no presumption of failure on your part. I don't equate silence with mental inertia. Obviously, I hope you will want to say something and speak up, but I don't want you to do this just for the sake of appearances. So let's be comfortable with a prolonged period of silence that might or might not be broken. When anyone feels like saying something, just speak up.

We believe in the power of this kind of early declaration because we've seen how well it works. Students will often come up to us afterward and say that by granting them public permission not to say anything, we actually emboldened them to speak. By deliberately destroying the link between student speech and teacher approval, we reduce the pressure on students to "look smart" in front of us.

DEBRIEFING PREPARATORY WORK

In Chapter Three we argued that discussion works best when participants can start off by expressing reactions to preparatory reading, writing, or reflection. Here we want to give some more specific examples of how this might happen.

FRAME THE DISCUSSION AROUND STUDENT QUESTIONS

We believe that it's best for students when discussion topics are framed as questions. There are two ways such questions can be generated. First, teachers can assign questions themselves and then structure students' prereading around them. The subsequent discussion would then be an analysis of students' responses to the questions. This is the approach taken in the prereading assignment described in Chapter Three. Another approach is to ask students to generate the questions themselves. The first approach is probably more appropriate at the beginning of students' acquaintance with a subject, the second one when students have some familiarity.

With this second approach, we like to assign the task of generating questions as homework. One way to do this is to say to students, "Imagine that the author of the chapter, article, or book you've been assigned to read as preparation for the discussion next week will be visiting the class. What are the top three questions you'd like to ask the author about the work?" Another is to provide some guidelines regarding the kinds of questions they might ask that are less detailed than the questions outlined in the protocol for critical reading presented in Chapter Three. For example, students could be asked to look for questions prompted by omissions, contradictions, ambiguities, unsupported assumptions, or unacknowledged ethical dilemmas they discover in the text.

Whichever of these options they choose, students bring their questions to class, share them in small groups, prioritize them in these groups, and post their favorites on large sheets of newsprint. These questions can also be posted on an electronic bulletin board or listserv before the class meets. We then ask students to wander around the real or virtual classroom looking for common categories of questions they have posted. We also ask them to look for striking differences. Our intention is to ground the discussion in the exploration of these questions so that students feel the conversation originates in their own efforts and interests. Usually three or four clusters of questions emerge that provide provocative starting points for the discussion.

A more intensive approach is to ask students to suggest the most pressing questions that need to be explored regarding a particular idea, area of knowledge, or piece of work. Here students are given no guidance as to what these questions might be. Their task is to come to class with one or more questions that they feel need to be asked in the course. By prioritizing these questions in small groups or by posting them on newsprint around the room, the individual concerns students have about the course become a public agenda around which discussion can be framed. Sometimes these questions are posed within the boundaries of already established discourse—for example, why a particular view prevails, why certain skills are deemed so crucial, or why a particular author's ideas are so influential. Occasionally, however, students pose questions that challenge the power and authority of teachers and curricular decision makers. They will ask, "Why do we need to study this?" and "Why is it necessary to know or do this before we're licensed to practice in this field?"

E-mail lends itself particularly well to these activities, provided that all class members have an e-mail address. You can then create a class listserv, bulletin board, or chat room that allows students to come to class already having had a chance to look for clusters in the questions posed electronically and to think about their responses. In effect, e-mail allows you to do electronically what was previously accomplished by posting questions on newsprint in class.

Ask Students to Choose a Concrete Image

For students who are visual rather than auditory learners, Frederick (1986) and Van Ments (1990) suggest asking students to choose a specific image that is actually contained in the text or suggested by something they have read. Frederick puts it like this: "Go around the table and ask each student to state one concrete image/scene/event/ moment from the text that stands out. No analysis is necessary—just recollections and brief description. As each student reports, the collective images are listed on the board, thus providing a visual record of selected content from the text as a backdrop to the discussion. Usually the recall of concrete scenes prompts further recollections, and a flood of images flows from the students" (p. 142).

Debrief the Last Week's CIQs

Another approach is to ground the discussion in a debriefing of the critical incident questionnaire responses to the last session. As described in Chapter Three, the CIQ requires that teachers begin the first class each week by summarizing students' anonymous responses to the previous week's class. If you've given a lecture on a topic the week before it's going to be discussed, many of the CIQ responses will refer to the content of the lecture. It's particularly useful to read the responses to the second, fourth, and fifth questions (on most distancing moments, most puzzling actions, and most surprising aspects, respectively). Responses to the "most distancing moment" question tend to identify elements in the topic that are particularly problematic. Responses to the "most puzzling action" question often describe comments that a student or teacher made that another student found contentious. Responses to the "what surprised you most" question tend to bring to the surface ideas and perspectives that students had not considered before. All these responses tend to be somewhat open-ended, and this openness can be used to generate some good conversation.

START WITH A SENTENCE COMPLETION EXERCISE

Another way to focus students on the topic at hand and to ensure that what gets talked about is in some way connected to their own concerns is to start the discussion session with a sentence completion exercise. We have found that the brief time we spend on this exercise is very worthwhile in terms of generating some enthusiasm and drawing participants into speech. Here's how it works.

Students are asked to complete whichever of the following sentences seems appropriate:

What most struck me about the text we read to prepare for the discussion today is . . .

The question that I'd most like to ask the author of the text is . . .

The idea I most take issue with in the text is . . .

The most crucial point in last week's lecture was . . .

The part of the lecture (or text) that I felt made the most sense to me was . . .

The part of the lecture (or text) that I felt was the most confusing was . . .

After students have written down their responses, they share them with one another. If the class is large, we put students into groups of four or five and have them read their sentences to one another. If the class is fairly small, this can be done in a whole-class group. As students hear one another's responses, they jot down the ones they would most like to hear more about. After all responses have been read, students begin the discussion by asking other students about the responses they wanted to hear more about.

STATE AND RESPOND TO CONTENTIOUS OPENING STATEMENTS

Sometimes a strongly worded statement—spoken or written—is a good way to get a conversation going. It can be taken from the public domain or created by the teacher or a student. The statement should be provocative, even inflammatory. It should challenge assumptions that students take for granted or cling to fiercely. It's important to tell the class not to assume that the person introducing the opinion agrees with its sentiments. The statement is being made only to generate conversation.

We have found that this technique works especially well with statements uttered by authority figures. The credibility students tend to invest in authority figures ensures that the statement cannot be dismissed out of hand as the ravings of a crank. Also, students can often more easily criticize a controversial statement made by an authority than they can one made by a peer. Some students will be reluctant to state a contentious view, no matter how much they are assured that no one assumes they agree with that view. Other students will be unwilling to criticize the words uttered by a peer in front of a teacher, no matter how much that teacher strives to create a safe atmosphere.

Here are a couple of contentious opening statements that one of us has used to stimulate discussion in courses on adult education:

"To talk about a theory of adult learning is empirical and conceptual nonsense. Children learn in ways that are very similar to adults. The only reason a field of study called adult learning exists is because professors of adult education need to justify their own existence."

"Paulo Freire's ideas are nothing more than Marxist agitation dressed up as educational philosophy. Moreover, their context-specific genesis in Latin America means they have absolutely no relevance for Western Europe or North America."

After the statement has been made, the conversation opens with group members trying to understand the reasoning and circumstances that frame the statement. Why would someone hold these views? What in the author's experience led to such ideas? What possible grounds could we advance to support the making of such an argument? For a while students are asked to be devil's advocates, coming up with evidence and rationales that are completely outside their usual frames of reference. This kind of perspective taking is a cognitive warm-up. It serves the same function in discussion as stretching does at the start of an aerobic workout. By examining the grounds for a view that is contrary to their own, students engage in a form of intellectual muscle flexing. Moreover, being forced to take seriously opinions that one strongly disagrees with guarantees that students are drawn into the discussion at an emotional level.

GENERATE TRUTH STATEMENTS

One task that Frederick and Van Ments suggest for the start of a discussion is to ask students to generate what they call "truth statements" (Frederick, 1986, p. 144) or "statements worth making" (Van Ments, 1990, p. 38) based on their preparatory reading. Students are split into small groups, and each group is asked to generate three or four statements that group members believe to be true on the basis of their reading. Frederick observes that "I have found this strategy useful in introducing a new topic—slavery, for example—where students may think they already know a great deal but the veracity of their assumptions demands examination. The complexity and ambiguity of knowledge is clearly revealed as students present their truth statements and other students raise questions about or refute them" (p. 144). The point of this exercise is not so much to produce undeniable facts or theories but to generate, and then prioritize, questions and issues around which further discussion and research are undertaken. The exercise helps participants develop an agenda of items for discussion and suggests directions for future research they need to conduct if they are to be informed discussants.

Find Illustrative Quotes

Frederick (1986) and Van Ments (1990) also advocate asking students to find relevant quotes from a preparatory text as a way of focusing their attention on the topic at hand and of generating conversation. For example, students can be asked to spend the first ten minutes or so reading through the articles or chapters assigned as prereading to find one or two brief quotes that they especially liked or disliked. These might be quotes they found that best illustrate the major thesis of the text or that are the most difficult to understand. Students then read out their chosen quotes as all class members follow the specific page and passage with them.

In addition to generating good conversation, this exercise has the virtue of respecting the text. One of the most frequent complaints from discussion participants regarding prereading is that the subsequent conversation does not draw explicitly enough on the text they have been asked to spend time reading. Asking students to find illustrative quotes underscores your own commitment to a careful reading of the text. Frederick (1986) observes of this exercise, "Lively and illuminating discussion is guaranteed because not all students will find the same quotations to illustrate various instructions, nor, probably, will they all interpret the same passages the same way. It is during this exercise that I have had the most new insights into texts I have read many times previously. And there may be no more exciting (or modeling) experience than for students to witness their teacher discovering a new insight and going through the process of refining a previously held interpretation" (p. 143).

Use Quotes to Affirm and Challenge

A variant on the illustrative quotes exercise that we have used is asking students to choose quotes from a text that they wish to affirm and quotes that they wish to challenge. Students form small groups, and each member takes a turn to propose a quote to affirm and the reasons for wanting to do so. The quote does not have to be defended as empirically true. Sometimes a participant will propose a quote because it confirms a cherished point of view. Sometimes the person feels that the quote states the most important point in the text. At other times the quote is affirmed because it is rhetorically rousing or expressed so lyrically. When everyone in the small group has proposed a quote to affirm, the group then chooses one to be presented to the entire class.

The choice of which quote to present to the whole class can be done randomly or through deliberation. Using the random approach, the small group members each type out their quote beforehand. At the end of the small group conversation, group members hand all the pieces of paper to one person, who then randomly selects a quote. This quote is read out to the whole class with everyone (not just the student who originally chose the quote) trying to explain what it was about the quote that was so compelling. In contrast to this random approach, the small group can simply report the quote that drew the greatest support.

The "quote to challenge" activity follows the same procedure, only this time students choose a quote that they disagree with, find contradictory, believe to be inaccurate, or consider reprehensible or immoral. Each person proposes a quote to the small group, and group members choose one to present to the class. One thing that has surprised us in this full-class phase is the unexpected advantage of randomly choosing a small group quote. Because group members don't know which quote will be drawn out of the hat, they have to stay alert to hearing comments on all the quotes proposed. When a quote is chosen by consensus in the small group, groups often pick one quote early on and then spend their time rehearsing a presentation on all the reasons why it's terrific or appalling. This ensures an impressive small group report, but it also means that the opportunity for fruitful discussion of the merits of diverse and even contradictory quotes is lost.

RECALLING A MEMORABLE EXPERIENCE

One of the chief reasons people don't speak up in groups is their sense that the topic of the discussion is removed from their experience, that it has no meaning or relevance to their lives. Their prereading may convince them that the topic is one about which only experts have knowledge and opinions. Or they may feel that they are being asked to talk about a theory or concept that exists only as an abstraction. A useful way to combat this sense of distance is to start a discussion by getting students to talk about a memorable experience in their lives that somehow connects to the topic. Because most students think they are experts on their own experience, starting out with personal stories is often much less intimidating for them than launching straight into a discussion of the strength and weaknesses of a theory.

Starting with students' memorable experiences is much easier to do when the topic deals with familiar issues. Discussions on racism, for example, often begin with personal stories from participants of their experiences of this. If students seem to have no obvious personal connection to the topic (for example, a discussion of international economics), it is often possible to ground the conversation in people's reactions to a story told by a third party in writing or on video (for example, a worker's account of how she lost her job when her employer moved a factory to a country with cheap labor and no unions).

For discussions on topics that seem to have no personal dimensions whatever, people can still be drawn into the conversation by focusing on critical moments in their attempts to understand the topic. They can talk about the moment of greatest frustration or confusion they experienced during their preparatory reading. They can pick out the moment when they felt most connected to the content of a preparatory lecture or the moment when they felt completely and utterly distanced from the material.

If you choose to use this latter approach, it is often a good idea to start the ball rolling by speaking about your own struggles with the topic. When we have opened a session by talking about our difficulties in understanding the same reading we've asked students to grapple with, the effect is often very dramatic. Students are first puzzled and then enormously reassured that their teacher, too, can feel inadequate when reading difficult texts. In their learning journals or critical incident questionnaires, the most engaging moment is often reported to be the time when the teacher admitted to struggling with the same material that the students find difficult.

Because of the ascribed authority associated with titles such as "professor," "lecturer," or "college teacher," students sometimes assume that we have read everything and know everything. By talking about our struggles as learners, we make it possible for students to admit to the same confusions. Getting group members to identify the aspects of a discussion topic that produce the greatest confusion is a good way to get conversation going. If clear clusters of opinion emerge about the most obscure or inaccessible parts of the preassigned reading, the discussion can start with everyone giving personal reactions to the various ideas and passages concerned.

We don't want to leave this section without giving a warning. One of the dangers of getting students to talk about memorable experiences in their lives that connect to the topic is that of spending the whole class time in a storytelling mode. Both of us believe strongly in the power of narrative and use it in our own teaching, but both of us try also to critique the content of our narrative and the narrative method itself. The purpose of a discussion is not to celebrate personal experience in an uncritical way. A discussion that only affirms the experience of each participant is not a critical conversation.

In the early stages of a group's life, a great deal of time can be spent on hearing people's stories and letting them stand on their own with no critical commentary. Out of such storytelling often comes trust. But sooner or later, good teachers will start to encourage students to look at their stories from different perspectives. They will ask other members of the class to give their interpretations of the story or try to get the storyteller to scrutinize the assumptions underlying the framing of the story and the teller's own actions in it.

Events happen to us, but experiences we construct. How we live through events, how we interpret them, how we feel as they are happening to us, and the meanings we ascribe to them are human creations. In telling our stories, it's easy to distort our place in the narrative by presenting ourselves as heroes and by omitting or overlooking significant details. It's tempting to describe our experiences in ways that are self-serving and that reconfirm the accuracy of our prejudices. A critical discussion will open people to the possibility of seeing their stories from different perspectives and understanding their experiences in new ways.

TELLING TALES FROM THE TRENCHES

One useful way to encourage students in professional courses to reflect critically on their field is to use the "tales from the trenches" exercise. It works well in courses with students who work full time or are involved in some kind of internship or clinical practice. At the start of class, students describe their most vivid recent experiences as neophyte practitioners. There is no order for speaking and no guidance other than the announcement that "now's the time when anyone who wants to can talk about something especially memorable that happened at work since our class last week." Sometimes people talk about strongly felt emotional peaks when a technique "finally came together" or "everything fell into place" and they were able to perform a procedure as they thought it ought to be performed. At other times they speak of the blissful joy they experience as they finally get to work in the roles they've been preparing for over such a long period.

We've found, however, that the more usual tale from the trenches is one of frustration as students recount their dismay at the gap between theory and practice, between the training laboratory and real life. Students describe situations in which the skills learned in the classroom don't seem to fit the context for which they are intended or in which the supposed benefits or results of applying a certain skill just don't occur. Usually these stories are told as if they are idiosyncratic, unique to the particular student and situation involved. Invariably, however, other students jump into the conversation with tales of similar problems. The discussion then evolves into a troubleshooting session with each of the participants submitting interpretations and experiences and describing personal attempts at resolution. Sometimes the discussion of just one tale from the trenches can occupy the greater part of a class. We're pleased when this happens, provided that the tale told is analyzed critically from different perspectives and that the time taken doesn't violate earlier promises made about the use of class time.

One of the best ways to provoke some good student tales from the trenches is for teachers themselves to open the class with a brief tale of their own. We recommend that these generally be tales of frustration and failure. Telling tales of one's triumphs and pleasures as a teacher or practitioner tends to widen the expert-neophyte divide that already exists. But giving a five-minute description of something you did during the previous few days that caused you to feel stupid or inadequate usually engages people's attention in a dramatic way. Just as it reassures students to hear that you have difficulty with the same ideas or theories they've been struggling with in their prereading, it often exhilarates them to learn that you, too, still make elementary mistakes.

For example, one of us regularly reads out in class some of the bad evaluative comments he's received from participants at courses or workshops he's given. The effect on students is immediate and profound. They say they can't believe that he gets such comments, and they love the fact that he lets them know he's as demoralized as they are when he receives less than perfect reviews of his practice. Some of the best "tales from the trenches" sessions have happened after he's read out to students comments such as these:

"Really there was little that I could appreciate. The speaker's ego and overall approach were so off-putting that any viable content was obviated."

"There should be far less personal illustrations and cutesy anecdotes. The first hour was remarkably dull."

"His personal asides were totally overdone. His attitude was so egotistical. His approach, . . . [his introduction, was] 55 minutes of clever autobiographical prattle that made me question his competence and wonder how he lasted in academia as long as he has."

After students get over their astonishment at our being willing to make such comments public, there is usually a flood of conversation around situations in which students themselves received similar appraisals, the perceived reasons for these, and the demoralization they felt as a result.

DISCUSSION IN THE ROUND: HEARING ALL VOICES

A common room arrangement for discussion groups is the circle. Many discussion leaders place chairs in a circle as a way of showing students that no one individual is in a favored spot for catching the teacher's eye. The circle is regarded as a physical manifestation of democracy, a group of peers facing one another as respectful equals. Everyone has the same chance of being seen and heard, and everyone can see everyone else. That the teacher is not placed apart from the rest of the participants sends a clear message regarding the value of students' opinions and experiences. Their voices are front and center, and there is an obvious expectation that they will be active contributors to the session.

Both of us regularly use circles for the reasons just stated. However, we know that things are not quite as simple as we have made them seem. For confident, loquacious students, the circle is liberating. But many others, especially those who have suffered from sexism, racism, or class bias, find the circle an ambiguous and even humiliating experience. The circle strips students of the right to privacy. It denies them the chance to check from a distance before deciding whether or not the teacher is to be trusted. These students interpret the teacher's implicit invitation to speak as pressure to say something, anything, just to be noticed and to gain favor. As Gore (1993) and Usher and Edwards (1994) have pointed out, you don't remove power dynamics from the room merely by changing the seating arrangements, nor do you automatically cause students to relax and trust you. In fact, the circle can be experienced as a mechanism for forced disclosure as much as a chance for people to speak in an authentic voice.

So when we use the circle to kick off a discussion, we like to introduce some procedures to ensure that this arrangement has the effect we want. To help people feel that all voices are valued equally, we use two techniques: the circle of voices and the circular response method.

THE CIRCLE OF VOICES

The circle of voices is an activity revered in Native American, First Nation, and Aboriginal cultures. It describes the very simple procedure of giving each person an equal chance to contribute to the discussion. As we note in Chapter Five, the circle of voices can be introduced in the middle of discussion to allow those who haven't yet spoken some time designated for their voices alone. When we use it to open a discussion, we do it in the following way.

Four or five students form a circle. They are allowed up to three minutes of silent time to organize their thoughts. During this time, they think about what they want to say on the topic once the circle of voices begins. Then the discussion opens, with each student having up to three minutes of uninterrupted time. During the three minutes each person is speaking, no one else is allowed to say anything.

Students can take their turns to speak by going around the circle in order or volunteering at random. Although the latter arrangement sounds relaxed and informal, we have found that the opposite is often the case. Moving sequentially around the circle removes the stress of having to decide whether or not to try to jump in after another student has finished speaking. An important benefit of using the circle of voices at the start of a discussion is that it prevents the development early on of a pecking order of contributors. Introverted or shy students, those whose experience has taught them to mistrust academe, or those who view discussion as another thinly veiled opportunity for teachers to oppress or offend will often stay silent at the beginning of a course. The longer this silence endures, the harder it is for these individuals to speak up. By contrast, in the circle of voices, everyone's voice is heard at least once at the start of the session.

After the circle of voices has been completed and everyone has had the chance to speak, the discussion opens out into a more free-flowing format. As this happens, a second ground rule comes into effect. Participants are allowed to talk only about other people's ideas that were expressed in the circle of voices. A student cannot jump into the conversation to expand on his own ideas; he can only talk about his reactions to what someone else has said. The only exception to this rule is if someone else asks him directly to expand on his ideas. We like this simple ground rule because it short-circuits the tendency toward "grandstanding" that sometimes afflicts a few articulate, confident individuals.

CIRCULAR RESPONSE DISCUSSIONS

As we point out in the next chapter, one of the habits students find most difficult to acquire is the habit of attentive listening. The circular response exercise is a way to democratize participation, promote continuity, and give people some experience of the effort required in respectful listening. We learned of this technique from David Stewart (1987), who in turn learned of it from Eduard

Lindeman (1987). In this process, students sit in a circle so that everyone can see everyone else, and each person in turn takes no more than three minutes to talk about an issue or a question that the group has agreed to discuss.

Speakers are not free, however, to say anything they want. They must make a brief summary of the preceding speaker's message and then use this as a springboard for their own comments. In other words, what each speaker articulates depends on listening well to the preceding speaker as much as on generating new or unspoken ideas. We often tell students they must respect the following six ground rules:

1. No one may be interrupted while speaking.
2. No one may speak out of turn in the circle.
3. Each person is allowed only three minutes to speak.
4. Each person must begin by paraphrasing the comments of the previous discussant.
5. Each person, in all comments, must strive to show how his or her remarks relate to the comments of the previous discussant.
6. After each discussant has had a turn to speak, the floor is opened for general reactions, and the previous ground rules are no longer in force.

Through this exercise, all participants must demonstrate that they heard and understood what the preceding speaker said and that their own ideas are at least partly prompted by someone else's. In circular response, no one can prepare remarks ahead of time because what each person says depends on paying careful attention to the words of the preceding speaker. Everyone is under the same expectation to speak clearly and listen attentively. This activity gives students practice participating in discussions where collective and cumulative understanding is more important than the contribution of any one individual. The downside is that under the ground rules of circular response, there is really no obligation to absorb and review critically what anyone except the previous speaker has said or to keep track of the general direction of the discussion. So although this exercise is a valuable way to enhance listening skills, it has only limited value in fostering conversational continuity.

Circular response can be altered, however, to give at least a few students experience in tracking and summarizing the discussion and in identifying recurring themes. The adaptation is simple. The ground rules remain the same except that two or three students are designated as summarizers before the exercise begins. Their job is to listen carefully to all participant contributions, taking notes where necessary, and to end the exercise with a synthesis of the discussion's highlights. They recount key points and recurring themes, giving everyone involved some sense of the whole.

Ensuring Participation Through the Hatful of Quotes

One question that invariably arises regarding exercises such as the circle of voices and circular response is whether or not teachers should require all students to participate. Mandating speech seems like an exercise of teacher power that violates the spirit of democratic conversation. However, we believe that there are occasions when it is justifiable to exercise power in this way. In Teaching to Transgress, bell hooks (1994) describes how she requires students to read out paragraphs from their journals in class so that no one feels invisible or silenced. To her, this is a responsible exercise of teacher power. We agree. Always allowing students the option to pass in discussion circles means that those who are shy and introverted, or uncomfortable because they perceive themselves as members of a minority race, gender, or class, end up not contributing. The longer this pattern of nonparticipation persists, the harder it is to break. So what seems like an empathic, benign action by the leader—allowing students the right to silence—serves to reinforce existing differences in status and power. Those who are used to holding forth will move automatically to speak, while those whose voices are rarely heard will be silenced.

One way through this dilemma is to make the required act of contributing as stress-free as possible. Such is the purpose of the "hatful of quotes" exercise. Three doctoral students at National Louis University—Connie Huber, Kenneth Smith, and Jane Walsh—demonstrated this idea for us. Prior to a discussion of a text, the leader types out sentences or passages from the text onto separate slips of paper. In class, she puts these into a hat and asks students to draw one of the slips out of the hat. Students are given a few minutes to think about their quote and then asked to read it out and comment on it. The order of contribution is up to the students. Those who feel more fearful about speaking go last and take more time to think about what they want to say. Because the same five or six quotes are used, students who go later will have heard their quote read out and commented on by those who spoke earlier. So even if they have little to say about their own interpretation of the quote, they can affirm, build on, or contradict a comment a peer has already made on that quote. This exercise is a good way to create a safe opportunity for everyone to speak. Those who are diffident get to say something, thus building confidence for subsequent contributions. They avoid the feelings of shame and anger that come from feeling excluded from the discussion while lacking the confidence to break the prevailing pattern and project their voice into the mix.

CONCLUSION

The ideas we've presented in this chapter and in Chapter Three should decrease the likelihood that your attempts to start a discussion will be met with silence. But no matter how carefully you plan against this eventuality, it will happen. Remember, silence is not always indicative of hostility, confusion, or apathy. It could just as easily signal students' need to collect their thoughts on a complicated topic before they venture into speech. If, however, conversation refuses to catch fire and is desultory or nonexistent, a wider structural problem is probably manifesting itself. Perhaps the institutional culture and reward systems are working against your commitment to discussion. Perhaps differences of race, class, and gender between yourself and the group or between various group members are generating a silence born of mutual suspicion. Perhaps students' past experiences have taught them that participating in discussion is a waste of time, a chance for a teacher or peer to catch them out, trip them up, and put them down. In such situations, the best course of action is to place the problem before the group and seek reactions and advice, to rethink the dynamics of your pedagogy and how you use discussion, and to ask your colleagues (perhaps by getting them to sit in on a session) for their perceptions of the situation and recommendations on how to remedy it.

CHAPTER FIVE

KEEPING DISCUSSION GOING THROUGH QUESTIONING, LISTENING, AND RESPONDING

We emphasize throughout this book that democratic discussion is open and fluid, building on the diverse experiences and interpretations of its participants. Although teachers have some responsibility for guiding the discussion, no one person controls its direction entirely. Consequently, good discussions are unpredictable and surprising. They reveal things about the discussants and the topics under examination that are illuminating and eye-opening. At the same time, however, because democratic discussions have a life of their own, they can falter and even expire quite unexpectedly.

Even when discussion gets off to a good start and seems to have momentum, a variety of circumstances can intervene to bring group talk to a grinding halt. Sometimes the teacher or one or two students assume too dominant a role. Sometimes the question or issue to be discussed just isn't controversial enough. Often the pace seems too slow, or the process for exploring the question lacks variety. In other cases, the students may not be ready to explore a topic in a large group setting or for some reason have lost their enthusiasm for the subject. Although it is frequently difficult to pinpoint the reasons why attention is wandering or commitment to the subject is waning, action needs to be taken to reinvigorate the conversation when these things happen. Part of the secret of dealing with these situations lies in refusing to panic or to berate oneself for allowing things to get off track. Fortunately, it is often possible to revive discussion and regain the sense of "controlled spontaneity" (Welty, 1989, p. 47) characteristic of good conversation.

This is not to say, however, that we regard discussion as a panacea for turning bored, disinterested, or hostile students into enthusiastic advocates for learning. Neither do we believe that simply talking about problems leads inevitably to students' deciding to take action to address pressing social concerns. As we argued in Chapters One and Two, discussions, in general, tend to increase motivation, promote engagement with difficult material, and give people appreciation for what they can learn from one another and for what can be accomplished as a group. But we want to acknowledge that we have both been responsible for classes where discussion failed miserably, inducing boredom, resentment, and confusion. We have no magic formula to guarantee success, just some ideas that have proved useful to rejuvenate conversations that seem to be stuck.

Sometimes a discussion can be considered successful even if the original intentions of the leader go unrealized. When participants learn that a problem is more complex than they had thought or when their appreciation for existing differences is deepened, these can be counted as significant accomplishments, even though they might be different from the teacher's anticipated outcomes. We can say unequivocally, however, that discussion fails when participants avoid similar dialogical encounters in the future or when they lose interest in the topics under consideration. If part of the point is to keep conversation going, to stimulate people to keep talking in the future, then discussions that inhibit this desire must be regarded as counterproductive and miseducational.

The question remains, what conditions inhibit dialogue and what measures can be taken to overcome them? This chapter and the next will focus on a variety of procedures to keep discussion moving and propose ways to make discussion a process of continuous discovery and mutual enlightenment. Getting students to view problems from a variety of perspectives and helping them frame these problems more critically and creatively helps keep discussion fresh. How teachers maintain the pace of the discussion, how they use questioning and listening to engage students in probing subject matter, and how they group students for instruction all affect how the discussion proceeds and how motivated the students are to participate in similar discussions in the future.

QUESTIONING

To reiterate, an important focus of democratic discussion should be on getting as many people as possible deeply engaged in the conversation. Whatever the teacher says and does should facilitate and promote this level of engagement. As a number of commentators have pointed out, at the heart of sustaining an engaging discussion are the skills of questioning, listening, and responding (Christensen, 1991a, 1991b; Jacobson, 1984; Welty, 1989). Of the three, learning to question takes the most practice and skill (Freire, 1993; Bateman, 1990). Although it is certainly true that the kinds of questions one asks to begin a discussion set an important tone, it is equally true that subsequent questions asked by both the teacher and the students can provide a powerful impetus for sustaining discussion. Indeed, as Palmer (1998) has noted, how we ask questions can make the difference between a discussion that goes nowhere and one that turns into a "complex communal dialogue that bounces all around the room" (p. 134).

TYPES OF QUESTIONS

Once the discussion is moving along, several kinds of questions are particularly helpful in maintaining momentum.

Questions That Ask for More Evidence

These questions are asked when participants state an opinion that seems unconnected to what's already been said or that someone else in the group thinks is erroneous, unsupported, or unjustified. The question should be asked as a simple request for more information, not as a challenge to the speaker's intelligence. Here are some examples:

How do you know that?

What data is that claim based on?

What does the author say that supports your argument?

Where did you find that view expressed in the text?

What evidence would you give to someone who doubted your interpretation?

Questions That Ask for Clarification

Clarifying questions give speakers the chance to expand on their ideas so that they are understood by others in the group. They should be an invitation to convey one's meaning in the most complete sense possible. Here are some examples:

Can you put that another way?

What's a good example of what you are talking about?

What do you mean by that?

Can you explain the term you just used?

Could you give a different illustration of your point?

Open Questions

Questions that are open-ended, particularly those beginning with how and why, are more likely to provoke the students' thinking and problem-solving abilities and make the fullest use of discussion's potential for expanding intellectual and emotional horizons. Of course, using open questions obliges the teacher to take such responses seriously and to keep the discussion genuinely unrestricted. It is neither fair nor appropriate to ask an open-ended question and then to hold students accountable for failing to furnish one's preferred response. As Van Ments (1990) says, "The experienced teacher will accept the answer given to an open question and build on it" (p. 78). That is, as we all know, easier said than done.

Here are some examples of open questions:

Sauvage says that when facing moral crises, people who agonize don't act, and people who act don't agonize. What does he mean by this? (Follow-up question: Can you think of an example that is consistent with Sauvage's maxim and another that conflicts with it?)

Racism pervaded American society throughout the twentieth century. What are some signs that things are as bad as ever? What are other signs that racism has abated significantly?

Why do you think many people devote their lives to education despite the often low pay and poor working conditions?

Linking or Extension Questions

An effective discussion leader tries to create a dialogical community in which new insights emerge from prior contributions of group members. Linking or extension questions actively engage students in building on one another's responses to questions. Here are some examples of such questions:

Is there any connection between what you've just said and what Rajiv was saying a moment ago?

How does your comment fit in with Neng's earlier comment?

How does your observation relate to what the group decided last week?

Does your idea challenge or support what we seem to be saying?

How does that contribution add to what has already been said?

These kinds of questions tend to prompt student-to-student conversation and help students see that discussion is a collaborative enterprise in which the wisdom and experience of each participant contributes something important to the whole. Too often discussion degenerates into a gathering of isolated heads, each saying things that bear no relationship to other comments. The circular response exercise (see Chapter Four), which requires students to ground their comments in the words of the previous speaker, gives students practice in creating discussions that are developmental and cooperative. Skillfully employing linking questions can also help participants practice discussion as "a connected series of spoken ideas" (Leonard, 1991, p. 145).

Hypothetical Questions

Hypothetical questions ask students to consider how changing the circumstances of a case might alter the outcome. They require students to draw on their knowledge and experience to come up with plausible scenarios. Because such questions encourage highly creative responses, they can sometimes cause learners to veer off into unfamiliar and seemingly tangential realms. But with a group that is reluctant to take risks or that typically answers in a perfunctory, routinized manner, the hypothetical question can provoke flights of fancy that can take a group to a new level of engagement and understanding.

Here are some examples of hypothetical questions:

How might World War II have turned out if Hitler had not decided to attack the Soviet Union in 1941?

What might have happened to the career of Orson Welles if RKO Studios had not tampered with his second film, *The Magnificent Ambersons?*

In the video we just saw, how might the discussion have been different if the leader had refrained from lecturing the group?

If Shakespeare had intended Iago to be a tragic or more sympathetic figure, how might he have changed the narrative of Othello?

Cause-and-Effect Questions

Questions that provoke students to explore cause-and-effect linkages are fundamental to developing critical thought. Questions that ask students to consider the relationship between class size and academic achievement or to consider why downtown parking fees double on days when there's a game at the stadium encourage them to investigate conventional wisdom. Asking the class-size question might prompt other questions concerning the discussion method itself, for example:

What is likely to be the effect of raising the average class size from twenty to thirty on the ability of learners to conduct interesting and engaging discussions?

How might halving our class size affect our discussion?

Summary and Synthesis Questions

Finally, one of the most valuable types of questions that teachers can ask invites students to summarize or synthesize what has been thought and said. These questions call on participants to identify important ideas and think about them in ways that will aid recall. For instance, the following questions are usually appropriate and illuminating:

What are the one or two most important ideas that emerged from this discussion?

What remains unresolved or contentious about this topic?

What do you understand better as a result of today's discussion?

Based on our discussion today, what do we need to talk about next time if we're to understand this issue better?

What key word or concept best captures our discussion today?

By skillfully mixing all the different kinds of questions outlined in this chapter, teachers can alter the pace and direction of conversation, keeping students alert and engaged. Although good teachers prepare questions beforehand to ensure variety and movement, they also readily change their plans as the actual discussion proceeds, abandoning prepared questions and formulating new ones on the spot.

The Case Against Teacher Questions

James Dillon (1994) begins his discussion about teacher questions with the following unambiguous injunction: "Do not put questions to students during a discussion" (p. 78). He claims that when teachers start asking questions, discussion turns into recitation, which inhibits student deliberation and exchange. Instead, he says, teachers should find other means to stimulate participation and thought. Dillon allows only two exceptions to this: (1) the initiating question posed at the beginning of a discussion to orient the participants and set the boundaries for the conversation and (2) the "self-perplexing question" that the teacher may raise once or twice during the course of a discussion out of "genuine wonderment" (p. 79). As an alternative to asking questions, Dillon urges teachers to develop a broad repertoire of responses to student comments and questions. This repertoire includes statements, silences, and nonverbal signals of encouragement, all of which are designed to keep students talking to each other. (More information about some of these alternatives to teacher questions will be covered later in this chapter in the section headed "Responding.")

Having referred to Dillon's concerns about teacher questions, which we think have some merit, we hope it is also clear that we think this is an extreme position. There are many occasions—some of which we have already identified—when a question is an appropriate and effective way to keep the conversation going. Furthermore, teachers are curious people; their natural inclination to express puzzlement or to seek clarification or further information should not, in our view, be artificially suppressed.

Listening

It is a platitude (but nonetheless true) that listening continues to be the most undervalued and least understood aspect of discussion. Good teachers are artful listeners who don't just remain quiet when their students are talking. Instead, they strain to hear both the explicit and the underlying meanings of their students' contributions. This involves teachers in trying to understand the speaker's point of view in the terms in which it is expressed and in judging how authoritatively or tentatively that view is being expressed. It also means judging when and how the speaker is willing to entertain challenges to the view advanced. Discussion leaders who listen carefully can weigh how well the students understand the subject and the degree to which their comments relate to and advance the ongoing discussion. Listening well also helps us know when it's important to encourage contributions that neither advance understanding nor enhance continuity but nevertheless add something valuable.

Still, one of the most valuable benefits of good listening is that it increases continuity. When a comment seems unrelated to what has preceded it, the discussion leader will frequently ask for evidence of a connection or help the student clarify the link. But this is not a hard-and-fast rule. Even when a student takes the discussion off on what appears to be a tangent, the departure can become a productive move if it is a logical extension of the preceding exchanges. So discussion leaders need to use their listening and questioning skills to hold students accountable for making connections between their contributions and earlier points and helping the entire group see new links as the discussion grows increasingly complex.

Listening is useless without retention. Although all participants in a discussion have the responsibility to listen and remember at least some of the contributions, teachers have a special responsibility to try to retain virtually everything said. They must develop the ability to recall at appropriate times, and on behalf of the group, earlier comments that illuminate points made later in the discussion, thus ensuring a sense of continuity. If the conversation is experienced as evolving developmentally, this helps forge a more closely knit dialogic community. Listening in this way also obliges teachers to be self-effacing enough to allow their students to be at the center of classroom conversation. Palmer (1998) has written eloquently about this: "Attentive listening is never an easy task—it consumes psychic energy at a rate that tires and surprises me. But it is made easier when I am holding back my own authoritative impulses. When I suspend, for just a while, my inner chatter about what I am going to say next, I open room within myself to receive the external conversation" (p. 135).

Listening takes great effort, but as with many difficult skills, practice helps. Periodically, it makes sense to ask students to do some exercises that sharpen their listening skills and that add variety and a change of pace to democratic discussions. Three exercises we have found useful are described here.

PAIRED LISTENING

In this exercise, students work in pairs and practice listening to each other with great intensity. Each person takes a turn as speaker and as listener. The speaker takes no more than five minutes to share something personal, but it's the listener who has by far the more difficult role. This person must strain to hear everything the speaker says while actively demonstrating listening and understanding. Body language, head nodding, verbal interjections like "yes" and "uh-huh," paraphrases of the speaker's statements, and even repetitions of the speaker's actual words all show the listener's active involvement. Here are the instructions we give to students for this exercise:

> Because listening is such an important part of successful discussion, you are going to engage in an active listening exercise to gain practice in attending closely to another person's message. You will be paired with another person for

about ten minutes. One of you will assume the role of the speaker, and the other will serve as the listener. The speaker will have no more than five minutes to talk about something personal; then we will reverse roles for another five minutes. Although the speaker's words are important, the burden is on the listener to make this exercise successful. The listener doesn't just passively receive the words of the speaker; she must attend carefully to their meaning. This means she uses every resource at her disposal to show that her first priority is witnessing and understanding the speaker's words. Body language, eye contact, head nodding, paraphrasing of the speaker's meaning, and echoing the actual words are all part of the active listening process.

If you are the listener, you may ask questions to get clarification on key points, but please ask them sparingly. This activity can feel a little awkward, especially when you're just parroting another person's words. Echoing is OK, but don't take it to an extreme; try to keep your responses varied. Take this activity seriously, but try to enjoy it as well. Most of all, when it's your turn to be the listener, devote every ounce of your attention to the speaker's message. To listen this closely can be exhilarating and illuminating.

This exercise not only enhances communicative accuracy but also gives students valuable practice in empathizing with others and in simply accepting what is heard without imposing interpretations or making premature judgments. It follows closely the protocol for active listening developed by Gordon (1977) and others. As Palmer (1998) notes, it is sometimes tiring to listen to another person this attentively, but making the effort helps us catch the cues, shades of meaning, and emotions that we miss when not attending so carefully. This exercise is also a simple way to affirm others, to show them that what they say and think matters a great deal. Of course, paired listening is very different from discussion in large groups, where participants must attend to many diverse voices, but it is a useful first step in practicing the kind of respectful listening that supports all good discussion.

HEARING THE SUBJECT

Palmer (1993, p. 98) reminds us of something that is easy to forget when the focus turns to the value of listening well. "There are really three parties to the conversation," he says, "the teacher, the students, and the subject itself." Of these three parties, the subject is the most frequently neglected, but it too has a voice that "we must strain to hear . . . beyond all our interpretations." Although interpretive filtering is inevitable, Palmer advises that a text, a lecture, a film, or even a picture needs to be understood, at least initially, on its own terms. The tendency to jump to conclusions that fit personal experience or that address a currently pressing problem should be resisted to allow the relatively unfiltered message of the subject to come through.

One way to learn to listen to the subject is through an exercise similar to paired listening that puts the focus on the subject instead of another person. In this exercise, students "listen" to a text, film, or picture and try to paraphrase and echo as much of what they witness as possible. They try to "hear" the subject even if what they encounter at first seems quite incomprehensible. Here are the instructions:

> You have done some active listening exercises that were intended to give you practice in comprehending what others are saying. Now I want you to try an exercise called "hearing the subject." We sometimes read a text or view a film that is quickly dismissed because at first glance it doesn't make much sense. But by giving that text or film another chance, by "listening" more closely to its meanings and forms of expression, we discover surprising and revealing dimensions to it.
>
> Take about thirty minutes to witness one of the following: (1) a short scene from a twentieth-century existentialist play, Pirandello's *Six Characters in Search of an Author;* (2) a twentieth-century abstract painting, Picasso's *Girl Before the Mirror;* or (3) a brief surrealist film, Buñuel and Dalí's *Un chien andalou.* Don't be overwhelmed by the difficulties of making meaning out of the work you are perceiving; just listen to it as closely as you can. You might want to jot down some parts verbatim, paraphrase others, or recount images, shapes, colors, and textures. Please restrain the impulse to express emotion about the work being examined or to generate your own interpretation. Experience the work in as unmediated a fashion as possible—don't try to make meaning out of it.
>
> When the thirty minutes are up, join two other people who have been experiencing the same work. Share your perspectives on the experience of the work, but do this without any interpretational filters. What are the actual words, images, shapes, textures, and colors that were employed? Generate as

full an account as you can. We will end by asking everyone to return to the
large group and converse about this experience of listening to the subject with
a high degree of intensity. How did it enhance or detract from your enjoyment?
Did it help you make meaning of what you perceived?

The point here is simply to get students to experience texts and
other media as directly as possible so that they take the time to listen deeply to what these materials are conveying, just as it has been
suggested that students and teachers do with one another. This
kind of exercise can teach students to attend sympathetically to
even the most confusing or off-putting voices and to derive a certain level of understanding and meaning from them instead of dis-
missing them out of hand. There is no guarantee, however, that
this activity will result in increased understanding. It may instead
produce frustration and an increased intolerance for certain kinds
of unorthodox or obscure messages. But the result could be an
increased appreciation for the amount of effort and attention that
must sometimes be devoted to making sense of experiences and
ideas that are complex and multifaceted.

Designated Listener

As useful as the foregoing exercises are, the most valuable listening
practice occurs in discussion itself. We recommend that individual
students occasionally be designated official listeners in discussion
with the expectation that eventually all students will have the
chance to assume this role at least once. As designated listeners, students do not contribute any ideas of their own. But in listening
intently, they may ask occasional questions, check for understanding or clarification, or acknowledge comments with a brief word or
a simple gesture. Their focus is entirely on the words and body language of the other participants. At the end of the conversation, they
are expected to summarize the main ideas expressed and to comment on the participation levels of the various group members.

When assigning designated listeners, we ask students to do the
following:

- Listen to understand the words spoken rather than thinking
  about what to say next.

- Strive to understand the point before either approving or criticizing.
- Take note of points of agreement as well as disagreement within the group.
- Raise questions with participants that help clarify and explain key points.
- Raise questions with participants that extend and deepen the conversation.
- Forget about what others in the group are feeling about the speaker's comments.
- Try to be aware of the speaker's level of confidence and be ready to support him or her.

RESPONDING

The first and perhaps most important thing to be said about responding to a comment in discussion is that this is never the sole responsibility of the instructor. One of the best ways for teachers to respond to others' comments or questions is by remaining silent, thereby giving students the opportunity and space to respond to what their peers have to say. Nevertheless, how to respond to what individual students say so as to sustain discussion over the long haul is one of the most elusive and context-dependent skills discussion leaders can learn. By responding with silence, teachers can create an opportunity for collective reflection and give other students a chance to speak. Or they might respond with a question directed at the previous speaker or at the class as a whole. They can paraphrase what has just been said or request further information. They might offer a few words of praise for a brilliant insight. Or perhaps a few gentle words of criticism or clarification are called for because the last comment seemed to show little understanding of the issue at hand. Choosing the most appropriate response to a student's comment depends on a variety of factors, including what you know about the student, your goals for the class, how deeply the group has so far probed the subject matter, what has been said by others, and the pace you want to maintain in the discussion.

Christensen (1991a, 1991b) offers excellent advice about the options available to teachers in responding to student comments.

He suggests that there are two major courses of action: continuing teacher-to-student interaction by taking it upon oneself to query the student further or extending student-to-student interaction by leaving it to the other students to respond to the most recent set of remarks. Our preference is to focus on ways to extend student-to-student interaction, so we will not pursue the options available to the discussion leader who wants to prolong an interchange with a student. However, these options tend to complement what we have already said about teacher questions.

If you make the decision to extend student-to-student interaction, there are a variety of options available. One is to remain silent and to await responses from the other students. Another is to invite a student who you know has a contrasting view to present his or her ideas as a way of stimulating the whole group to confront conflicting perspectives. You might lead into this by saying, "I was talking to Karen during the break, and she had a very different view of how class size affects achievement because her definition of achievement is so different from Leroy's. Karen, would you kindly talk about how your view differs from Leroy's?"

A third option is to ask a question or raise an issue that is directly related to what was just said by a student. For example, if the student has made a claim about the effects of class size on academic achievement, you might ask the whole group, "What assumptions about achievement does this claim make? What if we defined achievement as one's ability to participate in a discussion group? How might class size affect achievement then?"

RESPONDING WITHOUT QUESTIONS

Dillon (1994) suggests that leaders can respond to comments in ways that do not involve questioning. One choice is simply to make declarative statements that reflect one's honest opinion. These statements may contrast with what students have said, or they may complement student comments. Discussion leaders can also restate concisely what they have heard for the benefit of the group. On other occasions they may want to ask for clarification about what has been said or to point out how a recent contribution has cleared up some earlier difficulties. Still another response is to restate what two or more students have said to get these students to examine their disagreements more closely.

Dillon also emphasizes that teachers should create conditions that encourage student questions. Leaders can ask questions that reveal the complexity of issues and praise students when they pose similar questions. They can comment specifically on how particular questions help the group probe the topic more deeply. Another approach is simply to invite all of the students to ask at the end of the session at least one question that the discussion has suggested to them. Still another option is to call on students to identify one question that remains unanswered about a topic to which the group has devoted a fair amount of study time. However this is done, discussion leaders should give a high priority to student questions.

AFFIRMATION

Whatever course of action you take, it is a good idea to be as encouraging as possible when responding to student comments. Students take risks when they ask a question, volunteer an answer, introduce an argument, or venture a criticism, particularly if they don't know what to expect of teachers or when they have limited experience as discussants. When teachers find ways to be hospitable and inviting, they lay the groundwork for good discussion later on. How much affirmation teachers should give students is an open question, one that continues to be sharply disputed. One extreme insists on "lavish affirmation" (Vella, 1995) as a response to all comments, regardless of their quality. The other, advocated by the Great Books Foundation (1991), advises discussion leaders to refrain from praise of any kind. Advocates of this view believe that the practice of affirming students leads to dependence on the instructor. In general, we lean toward affirmation, though to affirm every comment, regardless of its content or connection to the rest of the discussion, seems excessive. One way through this contradiction is to thank students routinely for the act of making a contribution but to differentiate those expressions from appreciative comments you make on the quality of a contribution.

Praise should be specific and concrete. Look at some examples of the kinds of affirmative responses we have found ourselves using in discussion. These responses tend not only to be concrete but also to foster continuity and momentum.

Your comment has made clear for me the dangers of overgeneralizing in this case.

Your contribution strikes me as a synthesis of the points made by Angel and Jade yesterday. It moves us to the next level of analysis.

I was trying to paraphrase what Trang said earlier, but you have helped me see that I omitted his most important point. Thanks for listening so closely.

"Methodological belief" is a good name for what we all have been talking about. I'm glad you found a label that works so well.

RESPONDING WITH SILENCE

Another mode of responding is through silence. The tendency to answer students without hesitation is a hard one to unlearn. Silence is frequently viewed as a sign of resistance, poor pacing, or lack of interest. As we asserted in Chapter Four, however, silence can also be a constructive, positive aspect of discussion. Research indicates that students learn more in discussion when the teacher takes five to ten seconds before responding to what students say (Dillon, 1994, p. 90).

We believe that even more time, up to a full minute, can occasionally be used to model unhurried deliberation and to emphasize the importance of reflection. Structuring silence can give participants a chance to take the time needed to think through a new idea, make sense of it, and fit it into an existing mental schema. When teachers at least occasionally resist the frenetic give-and-take that passes for stimulating discussion and slow the pace to allow time for taking stock, they remind their students that group thinking and problem solving should be punctuated by moments of silence as much as by energetic outbursts.

Silence can also be a way of responding that shows respect. Sometimes words cannot express the depth of feeling we experience or the level of appreciation we want to communicate. One of the authors has for years regularly shown a very moving film called Weapons of the Spirit, about the residents of a small French village who risked their own lives by hiding thousands of Jews from the Nazis during World War II. He has learned that when the film ends, silence must be observed as a kind of wordless witnessing of their remarkably selfless actions. The two of us saw the film *Schindler's List* together and could not speak for many minutes after the credits had finished rolling. Sometimes an exchange of ideas is so powerful or poignant that a silent expression of appreciation and respect is the only appropriate response.

CONVERSATIONAL MOVES

Throughout this chapter we have emphasized the teacher's responsibility to develop skills of questioning, listening, and responding. But students must become proficient in them too. Even if the teacher consistently displays these skills, there is no guarantee (though it is probably more likely) that students will ask questions of each other or try to build on others' contributions. This exercise asks students to practice these skills in very specific ways. Here's how it works.

Prepare one three-by-five-inch card for each member of the class. On each card, write a "conversational move" from the following list, and distribute the cards randomly among participants before a discussion session. Ask students to practice the move indicated on their card during the ensuing discussion. When the discussion is over, distribute the entire list of moves so that people can see the wide variety of ways in which questioning, listening, and responding can be practiced. Point out to students that virtually all of the moves listed are designed to strengthen connections among group members and to reinforce the notion that discussion is a collaborative process. Note as well that these are just a few suggestions from the wide range of moves that are possible in lively conversation. If there is time, ask participants to recap how they tried to make the conversational moves they were allocated.

Ask a question or make a comment that shows you are interested in what another person has said.

Ask a question or make a comment that encourages someone else to elaborate on something that person has said.

Make a comment that underscores the link between two people's contributions. Make this link explicit in your comment.

Use body language (in a slightly exaggerated way) to show interest in what different speakers are saying.

Make a comment indicating that you found another person's ideas interesting or useful. Be specific as to why this was the case.

Contribute something that builds on or springs from what someone else has said. Be explicit about the way you are building on the other person's thoughts.

Make a comment that at least partly paraphrases a point someone has already made.

Make a summary observation that takes into account several people's contributions and that touches on a recurring theme in the discussion.

Ask a cause-and-effect question—for example, "Can you explain why you think it's true that if these things are in place, such and such a thing will occur?"

At an appropriate moment, ask the group for a minute's silence to slow the pace of conversation and give you and others time to think.

Find a way to express appreciation for the enlightenment you have gained from the discussion. Try to be specific about what it was that helped you understand something better.

Disagree with someone in a respectful and constructive way.

Conclusion

Keeping a discussion going is a complex challenge. It entails leaving plenty of space for students to speak, giving them an opportunity to learn from others, and showing them that what they say has an impact on how their peers think. It involves asking questions that stimulate and provoke students to examine their own and others' experiences and that establish an atmosphere for critical inquiry. Listening to students in an active and affirming manner is another crucial ingredient in sustaining discussion. Teachers who take time to listen carefully to students are more likely to keep discussions going in directions that are satisfying and fruitful for everyone. Furthermore, when teachers respond thoughtfully to students, they create a kind of conversational momentum and continuity that may lend new meaning and purpose to discussion.

CHAPTER SIX

KEEPING DISCUSSION GOING THROUGH CREATIVE GROUPING

It should be clear by now that we think teachers can do a lot to keep discussion going. Pacing the discussion to keep it from lagging and varying the format so that it doesn't become stale or perfunctory are two of the most important responsibilities teachers can assume. Changing pace and format helps accommodate the different learning styles of students and allows for the pursuit of a broader range of goals and objectives. Variety also imparts the sense that discussion should be experimental, a never-ending search for different ways to frame issues or analyze difficult problems.

In this chapter we describe a variety of simple strategies that teachers can employ to keep up the pace of discussions, maintain interest in the subject matter, and help participants view the subject and each other from diverse angles and perspectives.

VARYING GROUP SIZE

Many of the options available to teachers for introducing variety relate to creative grouping. Some teachers prefer to keep discussions chiefly in a whole-class setting, usually with all the students gathered together in a circle or a U shape. There is nothing inherently wrong with whole-group discussions. They can be stimulating and productive, and they bear the distinct advantage of allowing the teacher to monitor the understanding and participation of all learners simultaneously. There are also many times when it is helpful for students to hear the wide range of voices that only the entire group can provide.

However, the large scale of whole-group discussions can inhibit the participation of some individuals, allowing the most socially confident or aggressive to dominate. Whole-class discussions are also more likely to perpetuate the inequalities of class, race, and gender that exist in the larger society. Furthermore, whole-group exchanges can be unwieldy, difficult to manage, and occasionally chaotic. Even when the large group is well organized, whole-class discussions can be overdone, leading to tedium and a reluctance to speak up about issues that may involve self-disclosure. So even if discussion gets off to a good start in the large group, it makes sense eventually to divide students into different small group configurations.

RELAXED BUZZ GROUPS

In relaxed buzz groups, students gather in groups of four or five to discuss issues from a reading assignment. There are no prepared questions to answer, and there is no obligation to return to the large group with a report of any kind. The only requirement is that group members keep their talk focused on issues that emerge from the reading. They may raise questions with each other, highlight difficult or interesting passages, try to draw out the text's thesis, or simply note serious flaws. It is up to the group to decide how to handle the conversation and to do it in a way that is most comfortable for its members. At the end of the group discussion, or "buzz" (we usually allow ten to fifteen minutes for this activity), group members may want to share recurring themes or try to summarize what was said, but there is no expectation that this will happen.

Relaxed buzz groups are good icebreakers. They get people acquainted and build enthusiasm for future conversation. Because there is no need to come up with findings or conclusions, they are relatively unpressured. Consequently, inexperienced discussants find them especially congenial. But even for old hands, relaxed buzz groups can provide a welcome change of pace. By avoiding the pressure induced by having to come up with a probing question or a brilliant insight, we limit the competition that sometimes results when experienced groups try to best one another. Relaxed buzz also implicitly promotes the idea that discussion can stand on its own, that it doesn't always have to lead to some tangible outcome. The problem with this exercise is related to its strengths. Its looseness can cause discussion to degenerate into chitchat, so that the reading and topic are ignored altogether. Or the lack of structure may lead to aimlessness and a sense that discussion isn't helpful in clarifying issues.

STRUCTURED BUZZ GROUPS

In structured buzz, students have twenty minutes to answer a few questions about the reading prepared by the instructor. Although they don't have to cover all the questions, they try to finish as many as they can and to record their answers in writing. The group's answers are either submitted to the teacher or reported in some summary form to the reconvened large group.

The advantage of structuring buzz is that it gives the small groups an agenda to cover. They are obliged to focus on the questions and, assuming these are skillfully written, to examine some fairly important issues. A drawback to this activity is that it takes a lot of initiative out of the hands of the students. If the small group feels strongly about something in the reading that isn't covered in the questions, the issue may go unexplored because there isn't the flexibility to pursue unanticipated directions.

One way to deal with this dilemma and also to accommodate different learning styles is to supply groups with prepared questions but give them the option of holding to these fairly closely or ignoring them entirely and exploring a theme of mutual interest to the group. Of course, the problem here is that groups are rarely of one mind. Those who prefer the structure of prepared questions will fight those who abhor any kind of constraint on their freedom and creativity.

SOME GENERAL GUIDELINES FOR ORGANIZING SMALL GROUPS

You may have noted that we recommend that buzz groups be limited to about five people. This is not an arbitrary number. In his summary of research on group size, Bruffee (1993) advises five as the ideal number for small group discussion. Anything larger gets increasingly unwieldy; anything smaller results in an unproductive level of subgroup contentiousness.

Determining the size of small groups is easy, however, compared to the question of how to organize them. Those of us who use small groups frequently wonder whether we should assign students to groups or just let them choose with whom they wish to converse. We're not sure what the most common practice is, but we do know that there are advantages and disadvantages to both approaches.

When students select their own groups, they are likely to choose peers with whom they feel comfortable. These will be people they know and trust and with whom they are likely to speak openly and honestly. These are real advantages, especially when exploring highly sensitive or personal issues. In self-selected groups, students don't need to get to know one another and can begin conversing about the topic immediately. Conversely, when students form their own groups, they often choose to be with people who hold similar opinions. This reduces the likelihood that they will have to grapple with differences of ideology and perspective that are such a challenging and important part of good discussion.

When teachers take the opposite approach and assign students to groups, they can bring together people with different views and experiences. They can ensure that groups are mixed by gender, race, and class and that both talkative and quiet students are represented. They can also include students with different learning styles in each group. Of course, teachers can easily make the mistake of bringing together people who don't get along, thereby forestalling the chances for good discussion. Teachers may also be so intent on forming small groups that display diversity that they lose sight of the advantages of occasionally creating groups distinguished by gender, race, native language, or learning style. Bruffee (1993) cites research showing that heterogeneous groups sometimes foster discussion that is more challenging and critical, though he, too, notes that too much heterogeneity can be self-defeating.

In general, we recommend that teachers let their students form their own groups at least some of the time, depending on the topic or the purpose of the activity, and that just as frequently the teacher take the initiative in assigning group membership. Over the course of a semester, it is good practice to maintain a fairly equal balance between teacher-selected and student-selected groups. In this way students can benefit from the advantages of both while avoiding the disadvantages of relying too heavily on either.

Irrespective of how groups are composed, we cannot emphasize enough the importance of keeping their assignments short and manageable. Bruffee's guidelines (1993) are useful in this regard. He suggests that if there is text to be analyzed, you should limit it to a few pages or even just one paragraph. If you want students to answer questions, don't assign them more than one or two. How the questions are posed is especially important. They should be written in clear, straightforward prose with as little jargon as possible. Use concrete particulars, and try to avoid grandiose abstractions. Students have a difficult enough task responding to the questions; they should not have to wrestle with the meaning of your words. Also, write questions about which you are genuinely puzzled and for which there is no ready-made answer. As we have noted, discussion works best when the questions that are asked provoke many legitimate responses. Finally, show students that you expect them to back up their responses to the questions by referring to concrete examples from the text or their experience. The more specific and precise they can be in their use of these examples, the better.

STRATEGIES FOR REPORTING TO THE LARGE GROUP

It is standard procedure to have small groups report the substance of their conversations to the large group. How this is done can make the difference between students' feeling that they are just going through their paces and the sense that they are engaged in a powerful exchange of ideas. Typically, teachers approach the task of reporting to the whole class in a number of ways. The most straightforward is to invite each group to summarize the themes explored in response to the question assigned. Although admirably thorough, this can also be drawn out and repetitive. A variation is to call on each small group to share the one or two insights group members found most surprising or illuminating. A different version of this procedure is to ask each small group to address to the whole class a particularly challenging question that emerged from group discussion. On other occasions, small groups can offer the key themes or concepts that seemed to recur throughout their conversation. These can spark strong reactions from others, stimulating new lines of inquiry.

Newsprint Dialogue

One way to avoid the more ponderous aspects of reporting is to suggest that small groups summarize their conversations on large sheets of newsprint or the chalkboard. Individual members of the class are then free to wander about the room reading all the responses and comparing them to those of their own groups. Here are the instructions we give to our students:

> In this activity, you will be working in small groups most of the time. I have prepared some questions for you to consider in these groups, but don't follow them too slavishly. Use them as a jumping-off point for ideas you find especially worth exploring. You will have thirty minutes to discuss these questions in your groups and to write your answers to these on the newsprint provided. You should appoint someone to be recorder, but don't start writing immediately. Take some time to let your responses emerge from the discussion. Covering all the questions is not important, but you should begin to jot some ideas down on the newsprint within fifteen or twenty minutes of starting. When the thirty minutes are up, post your newsprint sheets around the classroom and tour the answers recorded by other groups. Look especially for common themes that stand out on the sheets and for possible contradictions that arise within or between groups' responses. If possible, write your responses to others' comments on the same sheet of newsprint containing the point you're addressing. Finally, note any questions that were raised for you during the discussion on the separate sheets of newsprint specially provided for this. We will bring the activity to a close with a short debriefing in the large group.

Attractions of this activity are that it provides a different approach to reporting by taking people out of groups for a while and letting them act as relatively autonomous free agents. It also reminds people that dialogue can work as a written as well as spoken exchange. On the downside, written exchanges lack the spontaneity and excitement of group talk. And in the limited space and time allotted, it is frequently difficult for students to provide full explanations of the words and phrases on the newsprint. Still, this is an interesting alternative way to keep the conversation going.

ROTATING SMALL GROUP STATIONS

Another way to avoid the usual format of reporting through a series of summaries is to place each small group at a station where members have ten minutes to discuss a provocative issue and record their ideas on newsprint or a chalkboard. When time is up, the groups move to new positions in the classroom, where they continue their discussions, treating the comments written on the newsprint or chalkboard by the preceding group at the station as a new voice in the mix. Rotations continue every ten minutes until each group has been at all of the positions and has had a chance to consider all of the other groups' comments. Here are the instructions we give to students for this exercise:

> We're going to do another small group activity, but this time you won't be staying in one place for long. Each of you should join a group of about five participants at one of the stations that has been established around the classroom. Together you will have the responsibility of answering some questions by making comments on the newsprint directly in front of your group. You will have ten minutes to do this. When the time is up, move with your group to the next station, where you will continue your conversation by responding to the comments left behind by the group that has just vacated that station. You have ten minutes to record the main points of your discussion at this station. When that time is up, move on to the next station, where you will now have the comments of two other groups to consider.

> Again take ten minutes to respond, and move on when the time is up. When every group has occupied each station, leaving remarks behind at all of them, break out of your groups and read all of the newsprint comments. Add questions, comments, or criticisms to these sheets whenever you are inspired to do so. Remember that each station will include comments from all groups, making orderliness a challenge. Write as small and as legibly as you can, please!

In addition to fostering healthy confusion, rotating stations encourages students to examine critically ideas that originate outside their group. The safety and intimacy of small groups is retained while incorporating the diversity of viewpoints experienced in whole-class discussion. Momentum and excitement tend to grow as groups rotate from one station to another, and participants enjoy a sense of exhilaration and connectedness unusual in small group activities. People feel they have heard and responded to many voices in the classroom in a way that is less threatening than in large group exchanges. On the debit side, the ten-minute period for each rotation is not particularly conducive to deep discussion. But longer periods of fifty to sixty minutes, we have found, are impractical. Using fewer groups with a greater number of members is one option for getting around this, but the larger group size makes it harder for shy, diffident, or introverted members to contribute.

SNOWBALLING

One way to make a discussion developmental and increasingly inclusive is to use a process called "snowballing" or "pyramiding" (Jacques, 1992). Students begin this activity by responding to questions or issues as individuals. They then create progressively larger conversation groups by doubling the size of these groups every few minutes until the large group has been re-formed. Here are the instructions students follow:

> We are going to try something a little different today. It's called "snowballing," and it gives you a chance to think and talk about issues in a variety of configurations. Notice that there are some questions at the bottom of this sheet. Begin this activity by gathering your thoughts on these questions in private reflection. Jot down some of these reflections if you wish. After five minutes of solitary thought, you will begin a dialogue on the questions with one other person. After another five minutes, you and your partner should join another pair to form a group of four. You will continue the discussion for ten minutes and then merge with another foursome to create a group of eight. The discussion proceeds for twenty minutes this time, after which two groups merge again, and the process continues in twenty-minute intervals until the whole class has been brought together at the end of the session. The discussion can end when the class is reunited, or continue for a final twenty minutes (or however much time is available).

On the one hand, this exercise gets a lot of people talking to each other while retaining much of the value of small groups. It also contributes a festive quality to the class. People mill about excitedly and greet each other warmly as they meet in new configurations. On the other hand, snowballing can sometimes have a frenetic, disjointed feel. But sometimes the regular change of group membership is just the thing needed to shake students up a little.

COCKTAIL PARTY

A variation on snowballing is the cocktail party. In this exercise, the teacher brings in and serves hors d'oeuvres and nonalcoholic drinks. The ground rules couldn't be simpler. To create the right mood, the teacher serves students from a tray carried around the room, frequently replenishing it with more food and drink. Just as at a party, students munch and drink as they mingle with as many of their peers as they can. The only expectation is that in chatting with different people, students find interesting and engaging ways to explore an issue. Like snowballing, this exercise encourages a festive atmosphere while offering a relaxed setting for conversation. Strange and sometimes wonderful things happen in unique settings such as these. Although we don't promise miracles, we do recommend an occasional activity such as this to cultivate the unexpected and the spontaneous.

JIGSAW

Still another way to retain the advantages of small groups but to infuse them with more diverse perspectives is to use the cooperative grouping technique called "jigsaw" (Aronson, 1978; Slavin, 1990). Teachers and students begin by generating a short list of topics they would like to study. Each student becomes an "expert" on one of those topics, first individually and then in discussion with other experts. Later these student experts become responsible again, through dialogue, for helping nonexperts to become as knowledgeable as they are. The sequence of steps that one would use in implementing this process is as follows:

1. A class of twenty-five students chooses five topics they would like to know more about (the number of topics chosen should be roughly equal to the square root of the number of students in

the class—four in a class of sixteen, five in a class of twenty-five, six in a class of thirty-six).

2. Each student selects one topic in which to become an expert (with the teacher checking that the topics are reasonably distributed among the students) and studies that topic to develop the required level of expertise before the class meets.

3. In class, students who have selected the same topic gather in a small group to raise questions, explore understandings and misunderstandings, and discuss what they have learned.

4. When students have finished pooling the insights they gained in the course of becoming experts, new small groups are formed that include at least one expert representative for each of the original topics.

5. Each student expert takes a turn leading the groups in a discussion of his or her particular area of expertise.

6. These small groups end when all members of the group express satisfaction with their knowledge and understanding of all of the topics covered. The exercise may end there or be extended to having the whole class sum up the discussions on all the topics.

The following is an example of the jigsaw technique as applied to a graduate-level course one of us taught called "Leadership and Biography":

> For today's class I am going to hand out six biographies for you to read. Since there are thirty-six students in the class, each bio will be read by six students. You should read your chosen biography carefully so that you are knowledgeable enough about this person's life to be designated an "expert" on this person for the purposes of our discussion. When we return to class, you will meet in a small group with the other people who have chosen the same biography—thus everyone reading about Susan B. Anthony will meet together, everyone reading about Frederick Douglass will form a group, and so on. In these groups you will touch on as many different aspects of the person's life as possible, focusing on key accomplishments, missed opportunities, character flaws, personal history, and unanswered questions.

> Once all the members of each group have mastered their chosen subject, we will form a second set of small groups, containing one representative from each of the expert groups. Thus each group will include one person who read about Anthony, one who read about Douglass, and so on. These second discussions

allow each expert to share perspectives from the expert group and to lead the rest of the new group in a discussion of the chosen person's life. These discussions should not come to a conclusion until each expert has had a chance to lead the group in discussion and everyone is reasonably familiar with each life discussed. The activity will end with debriefing as a class.

In this activity, students benefit from having extended discussion with twice the usual number of students. The jigsaw gives even the most reticent students reason to speak up, thereby bolstering their confidence. Both sets of discussion are rich, but in different ways. In the initial expert conversations, everyone is on roughly equal ground. They have a common focus and a lot to share with one another. In the second round of discussions, everyone has a basis for contributing substantively, and everyone is obligated to participate. Each person has a chance to be in the spotlight for part of the discussion. The chief drawback to the jigsaw is that the amount of information to absorb in the second round of discussion can be overwhelming.

SUSTAINING DISCUSSION BY ASSUMING DIFFERENT ROLES

Sometimes students renew their enthusiasm for discussion when they are invited to assume a variety of roles. Experimenting with different ways of participating broadens their perspectives and stimulates them to engage one another in novel ways. Doing this may put learners in uncomfortable situations. Sometimes they have to deal with their classmates in a more confrontational manner than they would wish. This can be productive, but it can also be unsettling. So it's important that the guidelines for assuming different discussant roles be clear without being constraining and that the activity be justified because of its effectiveness in casting new light on difficult or troubling issues.

CRITICAL DEBATE

In critical debate, learners are asked to explore an idea or to take a position that they find unfamiliar, unsympathetic, even objectionable. They do this as members of a debate team, rather than in a full role play. This makes the exercise more palatable to those who, for whatever reason, are so opposed to the view they are being asked to explore that it is difficult for them to participate. Here's how critical debate works:

1. Find a contentious issue on which opinion is divided among participants. Frame the issue as a debate motion.
2. Propose the motion to participants. Ask people to volunteer by a show of hands to work on a team that is preparing arguments to support the motion or one that is preparing arguments to oppose it.
3. Announce that everyone will be assigned to the team opposite the one volunteered for.
4. Conduct the debate. Each team chooses one person to present its arguments. After initial presentations, the teams reconvene to draft rebuttal arguments. A different person presents these.
5. Debrief the debate. Discuss with participants their experience of this exercise. Focus on how it felt to argue against positions you were committed to. What new ways of thinking about the issue were opened up? Did participants come to new understandings? Did they change their positions on this issue at all?
6. Ask participants to write a follow-up reflection paper on the debate. Students should address the following questions:
   What assumptions about the issue were clarified or con-firmed for you by the debate?
   Which of these assumptions surprised you during the debate? Were you made aware of assumptions that you didn't know you held?
   How could you check out these new assumptions?
   What sources of evidence would you consult?
   What new perspectives on the issue suggested themselves to you?
   In what ways, if any, were your existing assumptions chal-lenged or changed by the debate?

Critical debate asks students to make the strongest possible case for a position that is diametrically opposed to their own. It's the kind of exercise that may help them strengthen their own argu-ment by anticipating the claims of opponents, or it may cause them to look at the issue in a new light, bringing about a shift in their point of view. Most important, it is a highly structured and provocative process for reinvigorating discussions that may have lost some of their verve. The biggest disadvantage is that it's not always possible to identify an issue over which there is sufficient contention to split the class roughly in half. Also, this is the kind of exercise that cannot be used unless the trust level is high. Therefore, it should not be tried until the students know each other fairly well and trust the teacher to deal with them fairly. Under the right conditions, though, taking a position that is at least somewhat at odds with one's actual view builds tolerance of other views and gives everyone practice in concisely articulating an argument.

SPECIFIC TYPES OF CONVERSATIONAL ROLES

As we have noted, a few individuals sometimes dominate discussion, leaving other students bored and disinclined to talk. One way to deal with this problem, and to introduce some variety to the class, is to assign specific conversational roles. These may help certain students speak more often and get other participants to hone their listening skills and restrict their opportunities to talk.

Practice in playing different conversational roles helps students see that expressing a point of view is only one way to contribute to a discussion. It also helps create opportunities for the more tentative students to speak, thereby building their confidence. Because it's unfair always to give talkative students roles that require them to say little, any roles assigned must be alternated so that everyone gets a chance to play most of them. We have found the following designations to be particularly helpful:

Problem, dilemma, or theme poser: This participant has the task of introducing the topic of conversation, drawing on personal ideas and experiences as a way of helping others into conversation about the theme.

Reflective analyst: This member keeps a record of the conversation's development, giving every twenty minutes or so a summary that focuses on shared concerns, issues the group is skirting, and emerging common themes.

Scrounger: The scrounger listens for helpful resources, suggestions, and tips that participants have voiced as they discuss how to work through a problem or situation and keeps a record of these ideas that is read out before the session ends.

Devil's advocate: This person listens carefully for any emerging consensus and then formulates and expresses a contrary view. This keeps groupthink in check and helps participants explore a range of alternative interpretations.

Detective: The detective listens attentively for unacknowledged, unchecked, and unchallenged biases related to culture, race, class, or gender that emerge in the conversation and brings them to the group's attention.

Theme spotter: This participant identifies themes that arise during the discussion that are left unexplored and that might form a focus for the next session.

Umpire: This person listens for judgmental comments that may be offensive, insulting, and demeaning and that contradict ground rules for respectful conversation generated by group members.

We maintain that an important benefit of assigning roles for participants is their realizing how varied participation in a discussion can be. Although some students at one time or another may have assumed the roles of theme poser or devil's advocate in a discussion, most of these roles are probably quite unfamiliar to them. Playing them reveals surprising perspectives on the different ways people contribute to group talk.

The greatest challenge in an activity like this is for everyone to stay alert. To perform these roles, students need to pay attention to everything that is said, which, of course, is excellent practice for subsequently participating in lively and productive exchanges. It is also difficult to observe the constraints imposed by many of these roles. But doing this helps students live and learn the dispositions of mindfulness and humility.

CRITICAL CONVERSATION PROTOCOL

We have argued that good discussion must contain a critical element. Students must be willing to question assumptions, to subject their views to a continuing round of analysis and critique, to insist on strong evidence to support claims, and to be as clear as possible. But engaging in critical discussion involves risks. Criticisms intended to be helpful can be perceived as sharp-edged, hostile, and demeaning. When this happens, conversation falters, and quick action is needed to get people talking to each other again.

One way to do this is to provide a structure for critical conversation in which students have the safety of playing one of three clearly defined roles. These roles are (1) the storyteller, the person who becomes the focus of critical conversation by presenting an incident from personal experience or a perspective on an important issue or idea; (2) the detectives, the people who critique that presentation by hunting for unacknowledged or unquestioned assumptions; and (3) the umpire, the person who monitors the conversation to make sure that participants talk to each other in a respectful and nonjudgmental manner. Here is the sequence of steps to follow when using this three-role structure:

1. The storyteller begins by relating her interpretation of an experience or developing an argument that reflects her position on an important issue or idea. She speaks without interruptions of any kind.

2. While the storyteller speaks, the detectives listen very attentively. Their task is to identify the assumptions underlying the storyteller's remarks. What do the storyteller's biases appear to be? What assumptions seem to be conscious and acknowledged? What assumptions seem to be implicit? The detectives also consider alternative interpretations that could be given for the same facts and circumstances.

3. When the storyteller is finished speaking, the detectives may ask descriptive, nonjudgmental questions to get additional information about the storyteller's ideas. This helps them propose alternative interpretations to the storyteller and uncover her unquestioned assumptions. The storyteller gives all the information detectives ask for, provided that it is requested in a nonjudgmental way. The storyteller may also ask detectives why they are asking particular questions. No more than one question at a time may be asked of the storyteller. Detectives should not preface their questions with interrogatory remarks or a tone of disbelief (for example, "Do you seriously mean to say that . . . ?" would be unacceptable).

4. The umpire may intervene at any time to warn the detectives that their tone is judgmental or that they are violating any of the basic dispositions of good discussion.

5. The detectives then report to the storyteller the assumptions they believe are embedded in her interpretations or ideas. These are stated in a descriptive, nonjudgmental way. They are suggested tentatively, with no implication that they are right or wrong (for example, "Could it be that one assumption you were making was that . . ." or "One possible assumption I heard in your story was that . . .").

6. The detectives provide alternative interpretations of the story-teller's views. These could be readings that explain the experience in a different way or perspectives that throw a new light on the ideas expressed. In presenting these different viewpoints, the detectives must provide evidence or arguments substantiating their view. Again, they give these suggestions and opinions in a nonjudgmental, tentative, and descriptive manner (for example, "One different way of explaining what happened might be to see things from the following point of view" or "If you look at things from this perspective, you might conclude that . . .").

7. The storyteller gets a chance to comment on the detectives' alternative interpretations and to ask how they arrived at their positions. The storyteller is never expected to agree with the detectives' views.

8. Participants step out of role to do an audit of what was learned. They discuss the insights they gained from the conversation, the new assumptions and interpretations that have suggested themselves, how they might behave in similar future situations, how their ideas have broadened or modified, and so on. The umpire then sums up how well participants were able to give respectful, nonjudgmental, and descriptive feedback.

This is an elaborate and complex process for keeping a conversation going. It requires that participants, especially the detectives, think critically and creatively, but it calls on everyone to listen to all exchanges with great intensity. If the storyteller's viewpoint or experiences are too limited or uncontroversial or if the detectives are ineffective assumption hunters, this process won't get very far.

We usually introduce this exercise as a whole-group role play, with the teacher playing simultaneously the roles of storyteller and umpire. This lets us point out to students when they are asking questions, hunting assumptions, or giving alternative interpretations in a judgmental way. When it works, this three-role protocol helps people think critically by seeing that much of what they claim as truth is built on unchallenged or even false assumptions. It also discloses biases and prejudices that keep people from communicating despite their differences.

STAND WHERE YOU STAND

"Stand where you stand" came to our attention through Joan Naake (1996), an English professor at Montgomery College in Germantown, Maryland. It is another highly structured activity that encourages students to think critically, argue persuasively, and listen carefully to their opponents' points of view. It gives students practice in developing well-supported arguments, but it also challenges them to listen closely for the strengths of opposing views. A unique benefit is that it gets people to move around the room—literally to experience physically where they stand on a particular issue. Here's how the exercise works:

1. While studying a controversial issue, students read four essays as a homework assignment. Two of these support a particular idea or viewpoint, and two oppose it.
2. When the students gather in class, the teacher shares with them a claim that reflects one side or the other in these essays—for example, "Formal education is a waste of time and resources in nonindustrialized societies."
3. Students individually decide whether they agree or disagree with this claim and spend ten minutes writing down their position and their rationale for it, citing arguments, evidence, and quotes from the essays provided.
4. The teacher displays four large signs around the room, reading STRONGLY AGREE, AGREE, DISAGREE, and STRONGLY DISAGREE.
5. When they have finished writing down their views, students then stand in front of the sign that most closely reflects their position on the claim.

6. Students at each station take turns orally presenting arguments that support and justify the stance they have taken.
7. Students are then invited to move to another sign if the arguments they hear from peers at that sign persuade them that a different view is more accurate or defensible.
8. Students end the exercise by spending fifteen minutes discussing as a whole group how the activity altered their perspectives on the issue.

This exercise adds spice and variety to classroom discussion. It reinforces the importance of developing and articulating well-substantiated arguments, it motivates discussants to be as persuasive as possible, it encourages everyone to listen carefully to different arguments, and it helps students view each other as potential teachers. However, this exercise may bring about little or no change in the opinions of the participants, which makes it somewhat risky. While it sometimes helps students appreciate how complex most arguments are, it can also have the opposite effect of requiring students to take an artificial stand from four oversimplified possibilities, none of which truly captures their views. Of course, during the debriefing, students often point out the problem of being asked to choose an oversimplified view. This can then lead into a discussion of the difficulties of stating unequivocal positions or making strong arguments when you know the complexities of an issue. Students start to say, for example, that politicians who declare simple positions on issues or propose simple solutions to complex problems must be ignoring information inconvenient for their position or distorting the evidence that does exist.

INTRODUCING VERVE INTO DISCUSSION

In general, the more diversity a group of students exhibits, the more inadvisable it is to rely heavily on any one instructional method or strategy. Students from some cultures are reluctant to speak up in a large group or to have their words become the focus of everyone else's attention. Others find that their interest wanders when the same procedures are used repeatedly or when there are no visual or kinesthetic modes that allow them to move around the room. Still others are turned off by discussion that is merely an exercise in cognitive deliberation or critical thinking with no affective or expressive functions. If we want to get people to talk to one another irrespective of their differences, classrooms need to be structured to accommodate many different learning styles and many different modes of expression. Intimate dialogical pairs or triads should be alternated with larger discussion formats. At other times the chance to perform, to emote, even to elicit laughter should be given an important place. Classrooms may be primarily places for learning, but they can become as well places for living in all of its human richness and multiplicity.

This whole book is informed by the ideas that varying the pace of the class and using a multiplicity of methods are important keys to successful discussion. However, teachers must be particularly aware of two extremes when working with diverse groups of students. On the one hand, there is growing evidence that for some groups, "verve" is an especially significant concept, reflecting an important set of behaviors (Hale, 1994; Viadero, 1996). In essence, verve emphasizes movement, emotion, and performance. It indicates that discussion shouldn't be restricted to sitting in a circle and just talking but should embrace activities that encourage movement, intense feeling, and a certain amount of theatricality.

On the other hand, people in some cultures are extremely uncomfortable speaking before a large group and are reluctant to be the subject of their classmates' gaze (Swisher and Deyhle, 1992; Parsley and others, 1993). This doesn't mean, incidentally, that people from these cultures do not like to converse with others; they may in fact get great satisfaction out of discussion (Delpit, 1995). What it does mean, however, is that for these students, whole-class discussions are often not conducive to sharing ideas. Consequently, alternative formats must be found to give them opportunities to find their voice and express their views. This section explores two processes for incorporating verve into discussion.

DRAMATIZING DISCUSSION

Dramatizing discussion invites students to report their conversations through some sort of theatrical offering. Groups of six or seven students are asked to discuss a particularly provocative reading they have been assigned. An example might be one that uses narrative or drama to explore racial issues such as Derrick Bell's *Faces at the Bottom of the Well* (1985). The students discuss this reading for at least half an hour to identify important ideas and salient themes. Group members then have an additional hour to depict these ideas and themes through some sort of imaginative presentation. This could be a short comedic skit, a mock radio program, a song, a poem, even a short story that is acted out in pantomime. The challenge is to dramatize the themes uncovered in a playful and humorous way while remaining true to their underlying importance or seriousness. For this activity, we recommend six or seven students per small group, a larger number than usual. The rationale is that because this activity is risky and exposes students in unusual ways, larger groups are more likely to contain the exhibitionist core needed to help reluctant performers shed their inhibitions. After each presentation, the class as a whole reconvenes to discuss it.

As with so many of the activities we propose, the advantages and disadvantages of dramatizing discussions are sometimes different sides of the same coin. On the one hand, this exercise allows students to put aside the sedate manners and studied civility of most discussion, revealing their wild, raucous, and unrestrained sides. On the other hand, it may encourage students to do slightly crazy things for the sake of theatricality, yielding no educational benefit. This activity is also a big investment of time, taking a good two and one-half hours, with no guarantee of success. It may skirt the ideas and simply end up giving students license to let off some steam. However, sometimes a lot of good comes from letting off steam. It can create more of a sense of community in the classroom, reveal new sides of discussion participants, and allow the more dramatically inclined to contribute in important new ways.

When it works well, this exercise allows students to understand the material from a new perspective (for example, one that relies entirely on metaphor) that can be very revealing to everyone. Perhaps most important, it gives students who display verve, who love movement and emotion and drama, a chance to experience discussion in a way that is particularly well suited to their learning style. Furthermore, this activity can be a good way to put the spotlight on contentious issues such as race and racism without making participants feel accountable for the roles they assume or the words they use.

DRAWING DISCUSSION

Certain individuals and cultures (particularly Native American, Aboriginal, and First Nation cultures) tend to prefer interaction that does not rely too heavily on dialogue. They may discourage unnecessary verbal exchange and favor communication that emphasizes silence, emotion, body language, and behavior. The point is not that they do not value talk; it is rather that they appreciate the potency of words being used sparingly (Parsley and others, 1993; Swisher and Deyhle, 1992). In such cultures, actions speak loudly.

Since behavior and body language carry much of the burden of communication in these cultures, an alternative activity might involve kinesthetic and spatial abilities rather than verbal skills. Instead of dramatizing discussion, groups can come together to draw it. Instead of concluding a small group conversation with some sort of report, the group depicts the themes it wants to convey through some sort of visual representation. Here's how the process goes.

1. Groups of six or seven are formed.
2. Students are invited to identify three or four of the most important themes or ideas from a previously assigned reading. They have about thirty minutes to do this.
3. Once the themes or ideas are noted, groups have another hour to put together some sort of visual representation that communicates at least some of these ideas.
4. They are supplied with large sheets of newsprint to draw on and plenty of colored markers, pens, rulers, scissors, and tape to help them create fairly traditional two-dimensional drawings. They also receive magazine photographs, cloth scraps, and other textured materials for creating a mixed-media collage if they so desire.
5. Students are encouraged to be creative and playful while maintaining an underlying seriousness about the ideas they want to communicate. They are told that much of their time will be spent quietly sketching, drawing, and coloring their creation and that much of their interaction will be nonverbal. The teacher stresses that this is desirable because the intent is for people to work in a group where communication doesn't depend on words.

6. When all of the groups have completed their task, each group displays its work somewhere in the room for all to observe at their leisure. Keep discussion to a minimum; let the visual representations do most of the communicating.

Like dramatizing discussion, this activity requires a big investment of time with no guarantee of good results. Still, it has the special attraction of relying on skills that are very different from those that students are accustomed to using in academic classrooms. The exercise puts a premium on the sparing use of words and the productive use of nonverbal communication. It counteracts the freneticism of many discussions and underscores that there are many underused but powerful ways to convey ideas. It also gives more visual and less verbal learners a chance to contribute. As with drama, visual representations can be a way to convey ideas about contentious issues that cannot be communicated through speech.

E-MAIL DISCUSSION

A very different kind of process can be used to stimulate out-of-class discussion on topics that students may be reluctant to explore through direct speech. The electronic mail bulletin board procedure called NOTES allows participants to create a common yet private electronic space for sharing information. Students and teachers can raise issues and questions on this bulletin board that they were not able to address in class or that they would like to revisit because new perspectives have suggested themselves in the interim.

E-mail allows time for reflection and is a less anxious experience for many introverted or intimidated students. It also democratizes discussion. In cyberspace, everyone has the same opportunity to participate, no contribution can be made more loudly than any other, and no comment is privileged by the modulation or accent of the speaker's voice. Students who take more time to frame their contributions are not shut out of the dialogue by the speed of conversation. Quieter, more diffident students whose voices are lost in the hurly-burly of live conversation can be heard in an e-mail discussion. And because we have few or no clues as to the ethnicity, socioeconomic status, or sex of the writer, we are less likely to jump to interpretations of their words that are colored by stereotypes.

E-mail, of course, lacks the immediacy and spontaneity of face-to-face discussion; it can never replace conventional dialogue. But it can enhance and enrich the discussion that occurs in the classroom.

In one approach, the teacher explains to students that for each week that the class meets, they are required to use the e-mail NOTES bulletin board to make some sort of contribution to class discussion. The contribution could be a question that reflects genuine puzzlement or uncertainty about some material covered in class. It could be a paragraph summarizing what students consider the most important issues or ideas covered in the previous week's class. Or it could be a response to a comment made by the teacher or another student.

As the term proceeds, students must play the role of both initiator and respondent. If they tend to initiate questions or comments, they must on at least two occasions respond to other people's comments or questions. If they tend to respond to questions or comments, they must on at least two occasions raise a question or initiate a comment.

CONCLUSION

This chapter has shown that grouping students in clever ways can rejuvenate discussion and create settings and arrangements that give even the most hesitant participant a chance to be heard. We have stressed that students sometimes need the structure of assigned roles to help them attend more closely to their peers' contributions and to invite participation. There are no guarantees in discussion, but implementing processes like the ones described in this chapter should greatly improve your chances of keeping the discussion going.

CHAPTER SEVEN

DISCUSSION IN CULTURALLY DIVERSE CLASSROOMS

Diversity exists in every classroom. Even students who look and sound the same can have very different backgrounds, experiences, personalities, ideologies, and learning styles. Throughout this book we have encouraged teachers to view differences among their students as a source of dialogical strength, not a liability. In fact, one central purpose of discussion is to broaden horizons and deepen understanding by taking full advantage of the many differences that are inherent in any group. We would even go so far as to say that without a willingness to confront and exploit differences, very little of real value or meaning can emerge. As daunting as it may seem, at least initially, to address diversity, it serves no useful purpose to sweep it under the rug or pretend it doesn't exist.

Some people argue that by using good teaching practices and by showing respect for all one's students, the special problems of racial, class, and cultural diversity will take care of themselves. Perhaps. But in the new world order brought about by the information superhighway and the abolition of affirmative action, racial and class divides will continue to grow, and injustice will remain a source of enormous cultural tension. As one African American student said to us, "White people think they can forget color: treat everyone the same, and race will cease to be an issue. But for people of color it is always the issue. We see everything in the world through the lens of race." As Cornel West tersely stated, "race matters" (1993). Compounding the problem is the conjunction of class and race. Disproportionately large numbers of ethnic minority students come from either working-class backgrounds or the underclass. For them the worlds of pain (Rubin, 1976) and the injuries of class (Sennett and Cobb, 1973) documented in two famous American studies are felt at a level of deep hopelessness and alienation. When a group of Latino scholars analyzed the history of Puerto Rican students in the United States, they framed these students' experience as working class resistance (Nieto, Ramos-Zayas, Pantoja, and Associates, 1998).

So at least some of the special problems of discussion in culturally diverse groups must be confronted in a book like this. However, we want to acknowledge that we have written this chapter in an American context. The problems we address, and the exercises we suggest, spring from experiences in American university and college classrooms with students from diverse cultural backgrounds. Many of these students define themselves by their primary cultural allegiance first and their American identity second—as African Americans, Asian Americans, Native Americans, Hispanic Americans, and so on. The American aspect of their identity, and the way this identity intersects with the traditions, values, and behaviors of their primary culture, gives rise to particular social configurations and tensions that would not manifest themselves in the same way for, say, British Muslims or New Zealand Maoris. So readers of this book outside the United States may justifiably feel that some of our comments in this chapter fall well outside their own cultural framework.

All communication is hard, but communicating across racial and ethnic barriers can be particularly agonizing. For example, in the United States, many Americans of European extraction view genocide, slavery, and colonization as regrettable events of long ago that should be laid to rest. The same could be said of the attitudes of some European Australians and New Zealanders toward Aboriginal and Maori people. Yet these histories continue to cast a long and tragic shadow over all efforts to find common ground. Race-based intolerance has been so widely practiced and accepted that some people persist in the belief that it is not a problem that warrants any political attention or public debate. In their minds, affirmative action legislation has taken care of racist discrimination, and we can now move on with the project of building a color-blind society. To those who hold this view, people of color have ample opportunity to claim their share of society's benefits. If they can't get decent jobs, adequate health care, and safe communities (so this argument goes), it's because they still haven't learned how to work the system that's set up to help them or because they can't be bothered to make the effort. But for many nonwhites, racism and cultural bigotry remain pervasive.

Despite the fact that phrases like "equality of opportunity" and "fairness for all" have long been part of the American cultural fabric, minority groups' efforts to voice their concerns and to share power with the white majority have frequently been subverted and denied. Many people in the dominant culture believe that divergence from a white Anglocentric norm is a legitimate ground for expressing hostility toward the "other" and for repressing the other's opportunities to advance. Political and public debate on race has sometimes been little more than an opportunity for the white majority to silence and exploit the least privileged members of society, rather than the creation of a space where the right to speak was vigilantly protected for all. Today, as Ellsworth (1989) notes, many well-intentioned people who advocate dialogue as the basis of democratic education unwittingly use discussion to silence certain groups and bolster cultural divisions.

Race, class, and culture frame how people interpret, understand, and explain others' words and actions. The fewer values, assumptions, and beliefs shared by a group of people who gather to talk, the harder it is for them to understand one another. Although differences can to some extent be overcome, they present formidable obstacles. Discussions held in the face of such differences require participants to be unusually patient and sensitive. They need to be aware of the tendency to think that views diverging significantly from one's own are by definition wrongheaded or corrupt. This tendency must be fought if honest and probing discussion is going to occur among people from different backgrounds and cultures. When the approach to talking across difference is fraught with anxiety about what might happen, a productive exchange of ideas is almost impossible. So it's important to stress that talking across differences can be an enlightening and mutually satisfying experience, particularly when discussants come to it with hope. A realistic appraisal of the difficulties must always be balanced by a realization of the benefits such talk can bring.

At the same time as we acknowledge other cultures and worldviews, we must avoid stereotyping whole groups and the individuals that constitute them. Good teachers always respond to the individuals in their classes first, not the students' racial or ethnic groups. Although it's important to acknowledge that people often define themselves in terms of race or ethnicity, it is ill-advised and insulting to treat individual students from a particular group as if they automatically embody the tastes, ideological affiliations, and learning styles supposedly characteristic of that group. That is not only bad teaching but also a form of aggregate thinking that comes close to racial stereotyping. Assuming that all members of a given group think and learn alike ignores each person's individuality. As an African American student said to one of us, "Jesse Jackson doesn't speak for me, Louis Farrakhan doesn't speak for me, Toni Morrison doesn't speak for me. *I* speak for me."

Even when participants in a discussion make every possible effort to break through cultural and ethnic barriers, there will be times when these differences keep people apart and stall a seemingly good start. Failures and false starts happen in all discussions, but they are especially common when race and ethnicity stand in the way. But we shouldn't give up before we start. Attempts to keep the conversation going within diverse groups is a great challenge that must be aggressively yet tactfully pursued.

In one of our classes, a thoughtful African American student told the rest of the class (who were all white) that he could never trust a white person or what a white person said, no matter how respectfully that white person treated him. The others in the class were shocked and upset. But this statement was not uttered in anger or as a way of embarrassing the rest of the group. It was said nonchalantly, as a simple fact so obvious that it hardly needed stating. The reaction of one equally thoughtful white woman was, "So where does that leave all of us? Where we go from here?" These are the questions this chapter addresses.

HONORING AND RESPECTING DIFFERENCE

Who we are and how we see the world are substantially shaped by perceptions of our racial, class, and ethnic identities. Minority groups draw great strength and character from racial, religious, or national solidarity. So early in a discussion-based course, we need to introduce some exercises that seek to name, honor, and explore our differences. One of the cardinal rules for discussion across class and ethnic boundaries is to begin by acknowledging the fact of diversity. Honoring differences is a way of recognizing that racial, class, and ethnic identifications have greatly enriched many people's lives. As William Gudykunst (1994) says, "We need to respect the identities others claim for themselves if we want to develop a relationship with them" (p. 59).

Naming Ourselves

A good opening activity is to get people to talk about themselves as members of cultural groups or social classes. This means that serious dialogue doesn't begin until participants have shared not only how they want to be addressed as individuals but also the cultural groups and classes they identify with and the name they prefer for those chosen cultural groups. A black person might identify with African American culture and want to explain why this is meaningful to her. She should also be permitted to choose whether she wants to be known as African American, African Ameripean, Jamaican American, black, a person of color, or some other designation. A white person may identify with a European ethnic heritage or proclaim a strong class allegiance. He may wish to be known as Italian American, Breton, Scottish, Jewish, Celtic, or simply working-class.

In choosing how we wish others to think of us, we can explore how identifying with a particular class or culture influences our behavior, language, and attitudes. We start to think how we can show respect for different cultures and what words and actions might be interpreted as disrespectful. For instance, one of our students was a Native American woman who had a highly descriptive and traditional Indian name of which she was very proud. Yet she had to deal frequently with unthinking white people who found her name amusing and made it the butt of many jokes. Humiliated and saddened by this constant teasing, she refrained from using this traditional name for a long time. She endeavored to "fit in" by using a rather bland Western name, over time almost losing touch with her Indian roots. Finally, however, she realized she was denying her true identity and readopted her traditional Indian name. The jokes and teasing occasionally still occurred, but now they bothered her less. In reaffirming her Indian name, she gained the strength to rebuke those who continued to see humor in an identity that was so meaningful to her.

We must also be aware that people of color who prefer not to identify closely with any particular racial group have less choice in this matter than, say, European ethnics because their pigmentation, speech, or customs mark them as different. The revelation that some people in the group claim no particular cultural identity usually prompts some provocative discussion. Why it is that certain individuals tend not to experience strong cultural affiliations? Does it have something to do with the fact that white Europeans are not obliged, by virtue of their dominance and power, to identify with any particular group? Are they blind to their own whiteness and to the way whiteness constitutes the dominant cultural norm? When whiteness becomes named as one racial, ethnic, or cultural category among others, the way is open to investigate how it came to represent the standard against which other cultures were to be judged.

Here are the instructions we give out to describe the activity we call "naming ourselves":

> We want to begin the session today with an activity that may make some people feel uncomfortable. In the long run, though, doing this exercise improves our chances of enjoying relatively open and revealing exchanges of ideas.
>
> The exercise starts with each person spending five minutes in quiet reflection. Use this time to think about the cultural group or social class you most identify with. When time is up, gather in a circle. Your task is to introduce yourselves to each other as members of the cultural groups you see yourselves belonging to.
>
> One person will volunteer to begin the introductions by giving a name; the racial, ethnic, cultural group, or social class this person identifies with; and the label this person would like the rest of us to use in referring to that group. The person to the left of the first speaker will go next, giving the same information. The opportunity to speak will continue around the circle until everyone has had a chance to talk. Everyone's opportunity to speak will occur without interruption from anyone else.
>
> We will then go around the circle again, only this time all participants will briefly relate how their cultural identifications may have affected their language, their behavior, and their commitments—the things they care about most. What does it mean to you to be Navajo or Japanese, Cambodian or Irish, Jewish or Hindu, African American or Hispanic, Swedish or Ecuadorian, and so on?

The most frequent criticism of this exercise is that it may serve to drive students farther apart or overemphasize their differences. We acknowledge this risk but think it's worth taking. It seems to us that if one of our primary goals is to engage everyone in dialogue that is mutually enlightening, talking about our differences openly and unashamedly is unavoidable. Still, we sympathize with discussion leaders and participants who shy away from such an exercise, particularly if they sense that the group is not ready. One way to set the stage for this kind of openness is for the teacher to describe himself or herself in terms of ethnic, cultural, or class categories. Another is to expose students to historical figures who found it personally and politically important to refer to themselves in such terms. We have learned, though, that some students are more ready than others to speak this way. Those who are ready will often take the lead, without prompting, to introduce themselves in terms of ethnicity, culture, or class. When this happens, teachers can broach the topic of naming ourselves and invite others in the group to characterize themselves in this way.

Circle of Objects

The circle of objects is an exercise developed by the Fetzer Institute in San Francisco as part of its work on diversity dialogues (Harbour, 1996). These dialogues are kept as simple as possible with few expectations. They focus on key questions of identity that are constantly revisited. In the circle of objects, participants talk briefly about an object they have brought with them that reflects something about their ancestry. These artifacts represent some aspect of the culture or class they see themselves originating from. People talk about their objects without interruption but not in any special order. When "inspired" to speak, they rise and put the object they have brought with them on a table. They then talk about their object and its links to their culture and family history.

Because it is important for the discussion leader to model self-disclosure, this person goes first, speaking for no more than two or three minutes as a way of setting a time guideline. The circle of objects exercise requires everyone to learn respect for silence. Sometimes as much as a minute goes by between contributions, partly because people need time to find the words to express what they are feeling and partly out of respect for the often moving words that have just been said. The temptation to fill this void is great, but it is important to resist it. The discussion will be richer, more reflective, more truly an outgrowth of honest deliberation when silence is honored as an important aspect of this process.

As the objects are placed on the table, they are positioned in an arrangement that reproduces the circle in which the participants are sitting. At the end of the exercise, the objects on the table reflect the ancestries of all group members. When everyone has spoken, people may add comments about their objects. They may also comment on others' stories or ask questions of each other.

This activity is highly revealing. People share their hopes and dreams, their disappointments and tragedies. It can be overwhelming. A recurring theme is the limits and constraints imposed by racial consciousness. Native Spanish speakers frequently recall the expectation to reject their Hispanic roots, African Americans sometimes cite the social and economic advantages of acting or looking white, and American Indians often recount the painful stereotypes that were used again and again to stigmatize them. These recollections sting, but they are a bridge to authentic dialogue and an eye-opening experience for participants who have not faced such prejudice.

An important feature of this process is the way it acknowledges diverse learning styles. As we noted in Chapter Six, some research indicates that certain minority cultures prize kinesthetic and visual learning (Hale, 1994; Swisher and Deyhle, 1992). Although this research should never be used to stereotype, it can be assumed that a variety of learning preferences and styles are represented in any group. Having people bring objects to class introduces visual and kinesthetic elements to the discussion.

THE ENCIRCLED CIRCLE

An activity that the Fetzer Institute suggests as a follow-up to the circle of objects is to ask participants to grapple with the question "What is at stake?" This question is intentionally vague, though most groups find themselves interpreting it as "What is at stake when diversity is embraced?" Participants work in groups of three or four to give their responses. The facilitators warn people "not to go up into their heads" but "to stay with their heart" and allow themselves to be vulnerable during these conversations. These discussions are meant to be open. No guidelines are given other than focusing on the heart.

On returning to the large group, two members of each small group reprise the issues and themes they discussed. They do this summing up as an inner circle seated at the same table in the center of the classroom where the circle of objects is placed. The rest of the group listens and watches, forming an outer circle. The facilitators urge participants in the inner circle to avoid trying to distance themselves from their experiences. They are asked to monitor their own words and behavior so that they can catch themselves when they move from heart to head, or from the personal to the general. The idea is for members of the inner circle to focus on their own experiences and not to speak in abstract generalizations. They are thanked for being concrete, specific, and descriptive and for openly expressing anger, sorrow, and grief.

Finally, everyone in both inner and outer circles is invited to deal with the question "Is there something more?" By this time a sense of community has evolved that is often absent from groups that have been meeting for much longer periods. Consequently, people are usually willing at this point to consider some tough issues. Some of the themes that commonly arise from asking "Is there something more?" include racism's deep and seemingly ineradicable roots, the frustration and sense of futility experienced by those who have been promoting antiracist causes for some time, and the ways in which social class and economic inequality continue to intrude on efforts to promote democracy or increase civic participation. This is a time when frustration and anger are expressed. These displays of emotion should be respected by the group, with group members doing all they can to support their angrier peers.

AFFILIATION GROUPS

Classrooms are not inherently safe places for people to talk forthrightly about their cultural identifications and the differences among them. Ellsworth (1989) has argued that "dialogue in its conventional sense is impossible in the culture at large because at this historical moment, power relations between raced, classed, and gendered students and teachers are unjust" (p. 316). Although her conclusion may appear to be an extreme example of radical pessimism, it is crucial to keep in mind her caveat that even when dialogue appears to be equal and fair, this may be an illusion.

If we don't choose to bring our dialogical efforts to an abrupt halt, however, what alternative is left? One approach is to broaden the range of discussion forms available to us. White (1990) concludes a review of research involving different cultural groups in discussion by observing that "to achieve their academic objectives in classroom discussions, teachers need to be willing to adapt their classroom organization and management to incorporate aspects of participant structures found in the home community" (p. 170). Another answer may be found in Ellsworth's phrase "dialogue in its conventional sense" and her notion that we make use of the affiliation groups that form naturally outside of classrooms. Instead of relying exclusively on individuals to voice their experiences and knowledge in discussion, teachers can ask the cultural groups with which individuals affiliate to choose a spokesperson to express the opinion of that group. These spokespersons are charged to report what the group as a whole feels or believes. They are given periodic opportunities to speak out and talk back about such taboo subjects as institutional racism and sexism or the ways in which traditional, individualistic classrooms have a tendency to silence the least visible members of society—blacks, women, Native Americans, homosexuals. The relative safety and anonymity that one enjoys as a member of a group increases the likelihood that the discussion that ensues is honest, open, even defiant.

Affiliation group discussions are similar to circles of voices, only instead of individuals taking turns to speak without interruption, each group is allotted time to express its members' concerns and share their experiences of discrimination and injustice. Groups can prepare a presentation ahead of time, or members can all agree to speak about a particular theme. Either way, affiliation groups are an opportunity for people to be heard in an atmosphere that provides the support they need to express outrage.

But affiliation groups must always be balanced with an awareness of the potential they have for separating people and further marginalizing already excluded groups. Sometimes an overemphasis on affiliation can stall people's realization of their common humanity and interests. In one of his last books, Paulo Freire (1994) warned about the importance of creating unity in diversity. Finding allies and building common ground against oppression, he insisted, involves us in articulating differences while maintaining an understood commitment to solidarity and love. Freire is talking here about an armed, embattled, challenging love, not a sentimental, greeting card version. To him, unity in diversity is most effectively achieved when cultural groups assert their differences proudly while respecting the differences of others. Such a strain of respectful acceptance of other cultural identities was also woven through Alain Locke's ideas on Afrocentrism (Gyant, 1996). Open, inclusive, and sometimes fierce discussion is a way for different cultural groups to realize their common interests while retaining their sense of their own identities.

METHODOLOGICAL BELIEF AND THE FIVE-MINUTE RULE

In the documentary film *The Color of Fear* (Wah, 1994), a racially mixed group meets to discuss racism and prejudice in American society. One of the white members rejects example after example of contemporary racism from the people of color sitting around him and responds instead with these words: "You have no comprehension that the world is open to you. You have put up the dam and the block yourself." The others in the group grow increasingly frustrated and angry with this white male until, in an exasperated rage, one of the black participants erupts with a torrent of accusatory words directed at the white skeptic. He says he is sick of being told to live as white people want him to live because his skin and hair make that impossible. Why should he be the one to change? Can't white people be transformed by *his* experience rather than the other way around?

Despite the powerful words that fill the room, the white participant is unswayed. But then a little later the facilitator of the group asks the white man what he would say if everything the black man said was true. What if he could be black for a while and experience this racism as reality? How would he feel? The white man admits he would feel terrible. Somehow this simple moment of empathizing with the black man's plight breaks the dialogical logjam. Instead of relying on his habit of doubting, the white man experiences the habit of believing, of assuming for the sake of discussion that something is true.

This instance of what Peter Elbow (1986) calls methodological belief can be adapted to address some of the cultural differences that prevent discussion participants from engaging with each other. Elbow proposes what he calls the "believing game," the simplest application of which is the five-minute rule. This rule states that any discussion participant who feels that a particular point of view, however outlandish, is not being taken seriously has a right to point this out. The group then agrees to refrain from criticizing this perspective for five minutes and, in fact, to make every effort to believe it. Here are some of the questions people might ask to help them believe:

What's interesting or helpful about the view?

What are some intriguing features that others might not have noticed?

What would be different if you believed this view, if you accepted it as true?

In what sense and under what conditions might this idea be true?

Participants who are not able to answer these questions or to provide support for answers given in response to them must remain silent and attend to those who can muster responses. Sometimes unbelief turns into belief, at least for the duration of the discussion. More important, the habit of believing can help us take a more sympathetic stance toward controversial ideas and broaden our horizon of what is conceivable. Here's an example of how this habit might be applied to issues of diversity.

The Five-Minute Rule and Affirmative Action

During a discussion focusing on issues of diversity and multiculturalism, one participant notes that the policy of affirmative action as a safeguard against racial discrimination has been neglected in the conversation. Under the five-minute rule, everyone must believe that affirmative action policies are needed to combat racism. Participants begin brainstorming possible answers to three key questions:

- What's interesting or intriguing about this view?

- What would be different if it were true?

- Under what circumstances would this be true?

Only participants who can provide responses that support premises of these three questions are permitted to speak. No expressions of doubt are allowed. Anyone critical of this view must stay quiet and listen.

When answers to these questions are exhausted or when the five minutes are up, the answers are displayed on the chalkboard or in some other prominent way. Participants take another few minutes to reflect on the process, especially on how it affected those who initially did not take this view seriously.

As already suggested, this exercise can stretch students' capacity to engage seriously with seemingly implausible ideas. By providing a set of structured circumstances for empathizing with a believer, students are brought to appreciate diversity in some important new ways. The five-minute rule may, however, provide an excuse for sloppy thinking and permit students to believe, however temporarily, in some frightening things. For example, what if a student suggests we spend five minutes believing that the Holocaust never happened and that reports of it are a Jewish conspiracy to undermine the legitimate supremacy of the Aryan race? Does such an assertion deserve even five minutes of serious consideration? Will Humphreys, who is a colleague of Elbow's, notes that if we practice believing "things that are false we will end up with more false beliefs" (Elbow, 1986, p. 282).

Elbow points out, though, that it is not false beliefs that are the danger so much as unexamined beliefs. He argues that the believing game gives people a chance to try unfamiliar beliefs on for size as a way of preventing them from adopting unexamined beliefs. After the game is over, the thinking processes that are employed to promote belief can be critiqued and the beliefs put aside if they turn out to be unconvincing.

OUTLET FOR ANGER AND GRIEF

The scene we described from *The Color of Fear* brings up the issue of anger. Is it possible for discussion to provide an outlet for great anger or deep sorrow? Teachers sometimes think that classrooms are an inappropriate place for expressing anger or grief. But if we want people to express themselves honestly and openly, tolerating and even respecting expressions of strong feeling may be an important part of talking across differences. People who have not experienced day-in, day-out discrimination don't really understand its power to breed hostility and bitterness. Providing an outlet for anger about racism allows victims to reveal their honest feelings and gives witnesses opportunities to appreciate the impact of bigotry more concretely and deeply.

There are at least two ways to structure discussion to allow for the venting of strong feelings about race. One is to ask people to recount their own experiences of prejudice and discrimination or to relate examples in which they witnessed such cruelty toward others. The other is to invite them to read about historical events that were motivated by racial or ethnic bigotry. In both cases, the purposes are to help people learn more about the pervasiveness of racism and to give them a chance to experience it vicariously. The expectation is that group members will support each other in expressing anger and grief. The following are the instructions we give students regarding the expression of anger and grief.

Expressing Anger and Grief

Being the victim of racial discrimination is a terrifying and transforming experience. Those who face discrimination on a regular basis have a different attitude toward it than those who have witnessed only a few incidents. In general, though, we don't have many forums in which we can share these experiences or express our collective anger or sorrow. This exercise provides that opportunity.

1. Divide into groups of five.

2. One person, the storyteller, starts by briefly recounting a personal experience of cruelty motivated by racial, cultural, or class prejudice. This person talks about its impact on his or her feelings and behavior. If anger is felt, the storyteller is urged to express it openly.

3. As the storyteller speaks, the rest of the group listens sympathetically and intently as a way of conveying concern about the effects the incident had on the storyteller. In some cases, silence may be a way for members to convey solidarity. In others, righteous indignation or a few simple words of support may be appropriate.

4. When the story is over, each person then takes a turn to describe an incident of cruelty, being open about the feelings it elicits.

5. After everyone has spoken, the group takes a few moments to note similarities, differences, and recurring themes regarding both the incidents

themselves and the impact these had on storytellers. Look also for recurring emotions that were stirred by the telling of these stories.

6. After that, we will reconvene as a whole class, and each small group will be asked to recount a similarity and a difference and to reiterate a recurring theme or two. We will also consider the implications of this exercise for bringing about change in the future.

We are not accustomed to expressing ourselves in the open and unrestrained manner this exercise demands. Consequently, it can easily turn into a poorly facilitated sensitivity session in which emotions get out of hand and things are said that unintentionally hurt others' feelings. But because most of us have so little experience with the brute power of bigotry, the risks of this exercise are worth taking. It provides a way of gaining some idea of the impact racism and intolerance have on people's lives. Also, by collectively reexperiencing these incidents and actively supporting one another in expressing feelings about them, group members can attain a new level of trust and a deeper appreciation for how challenging it is to move toward a more inclusive and multicultural society.

As Harry Boyte points out in his book *Commonwealth* (1989), the etymological roots of the word anger "suggest grief—the sense that grows from separation, deep loss, failure to attain fundamental goals" (p. 132). History has been deeply scarred by racial bigotry and discrimination. To allow this anger and grief to go unacknowledged in a forum where cultural differences are the focus is a great error. But it is probably also a mistake to allow the venting of rage to stand on its own without trying to build on it in constructive ways. The culmination of this activity, therefore, is to find a way to use the experience of expressing anger to talk across differences more effectively and take action that will diminish future intolerance.

KEEPING RACIST SPEECH IN CHECK

One of the great challenges of cross-cultural communication is learning to say what we mean in a way that is not disrespectful or demeaning to those who hear our words. In diverse groups it is especially easy to choose words, use nonverbal cues, or develop arguments that are hurtful to others. We will examine two simple processes that can aid people to become more aware of how their comments are heard.

Monitoring Discussion

Regardless of the topic chosen, a panel of multiracial students can be appointed by the class to monitor the discussion for signs of racial or multicultural insensitivity. They note words, phrases, expressions, body language, assumptions, and arguments that may be insulting to one of the participants. However, they do not interrupt the discussion to raise these points. When the main discussion has ended, the multiracial panel, using detailed notes, gives its judgment on group members' use or avoidance of racist speech.

Anyone may participate as the panel airs its concerns, and anyone can disagree strongly with the findings of the panel. This second discussion has many of the same purposes as the first—to get people involved, increase understanding, clarify points of view, and even bring people closer together. However, it is meant especially to heighten awareness to the way race and culture frame, and sometimes distort, how we hear the words others use. Like many discussions with a critical edge, the atmosphere can become accusatory and raw. But if participants have gone through some of the preparatory steps we outlined in Chapters Three and Four, there is a good chance that this interchange will be enlightening.

Perception Check

We frequently assume that we know what others are feeling or thinking, but we rarely take the awkward step of probing explicitly and nonjudgmentally, "You seem upset? Are you?" or "I get the impression that this exchange has hurt your feelings in some way. Is that true?" Gudykunst (1994) suggests that one of the most important ways to improve intercultural communication is to introduce fairly frequent perception checks. In perception checks, we describe what we think a particular person is feeling or thinking and request that the person confirm or correct this description.

By using perception checks, you send a message to those with whom you are in conversation that you genuinely want to understand how they interpret your words. Perception checks are especially important in diverse groups. If it is true that people from different cultures interpret and understand the world very differently, perception checks can be a great aid in making communication less ambiguous.

As with the five-minute rule, perception checks take precedence over other discussion issues. When someone asks for a perception check (for example, "Are you saying that racism always has an underlying economic cause?" or "Did I paraphrase your last comment incorrectly?"), the discussion stops so that the person to whom the check is addressed may answer. Further exchanges are allowed that clarify what was said earlier or confirm the check. Only after both parties involved are satisfied that they have checked their perceptions and clarified their meanings does the discussion resume its normal course.

Although this process can interrupt the flow of discussion, it is probably worth doing to enhance communicative accuracy and improve mutual understanding. Perception checks help people ensure that they are interpreting intended meanings accurately. They also give those who may be chronic victims of miscommunication another chance to make their own views clear.

THE CONJUNCTION OF CLASS AND RACE

We want to say something specifically about the factor of social class and how this affects discussion. Class is the unspoken, invisible social factor in American life. Unlike Europeans, Americans generally do not like to talk about class. They believe that, with the exception of a few very rich and very poor people, they live in a classless society. Part of the democratic ethos is the insistence that class identity doesn't matter very much since in the last analysis we're all middle-class, or have the opportunity to become so. Of course, acknowledging that everyone can become middle-class implicitly acknowledges that class differences do exist.

We don't want to get into a detailed sociological definition of exactly what constitutes a working-class or middle-class identity, nor do we want to elaborate in any detailed way the characteristics of working-class or middle-class culture. But we do want to emphasize three things. First, working-class students do see a difference between their own class origins and identities and those of their teachers and many of their peers. As two anthologies of working-class academics demonstrate, even when working-class students become university professors, they continue to define themselves by their class of origin, whether or not they take on middle-class speech forms, interests, and affectations (Ryan and Sackrey, 1984; Dews and Law, 1995). Ira Shor (1987, 1992, 1996) has written evocatively of the attitudes of the working-class students he encounters in his life at a state college in New York. These students are "achingly traditional and proudly insubordinate at the same time" (1996, p. 2), are "often baffled at the language, requirements, and rituals of higher education" (p. 5), and are "largely unimpressed by professors and intellectuals, not easily persuaded, not pushovers" (p. 7). They expect "an authoritarian rhetorical setting: teacher-talk, teacher-centered standard English, an official syllabus with remote subject-matter, and unilateral rule-making" (p. 16).

Second, talking about "working-class culture" as a generic phenomenon displays the same kind of misguided aggregate thinking we warn against where ethnic stereotyping is concerned. Though we know that certain attitudes are more common among working-class students, we don't want to imply that they are universal. As Shor writes, "I would say that there is no *stereotypical* working-class student. Their typical traits and social conditions are identifiable, but this general reality does not exhaust their individual differences. Their diversity can produce a group personality in one class very different from the personality of another class" (1996, p. 7). To use cinematic and literary terms, working-class students can just as easily be from the pages of *Jude the Obscure* as from the cast of films such as *Blackboard Jungle* or *Dangerous Minds*.

Third, we want to stress that most teachers' idea of what constitutes appropriate forms of classroom discourse is much closer to middle-class than working-class speech norms. This is as true of working-class academics as it is of their middle-class counterparts. In her analysis of class differences in conversational style, bell hooks (1994, p. 186) observes that "students from upper and middle class backgrounds are disturbed if heated exchange takes place in the classroom. Many of them equate loud talk or interruptions with rude and threatening behavior. Yet those of us from working class backgrounds may feel that discussion is deeper and richer if it arouses intense responses." She describes a "collective professorial investment in bourgeois decorum" (p. 188) that shapes notions of appropriate tone and speech forms in class discussion. In Pierre Bourdieu's (1986) terms, middle-class students' greater linguistic competence constitutes a valuable form of cultural capital that they bring to college classrooms.

The research of sociologist Basil Bernstein (1977, 1986, 1990) has shown us how what he describes as "elaborated" codes of language are valued over more restricted codes that use a smaller vocabulary, frequently repeat colloquialisms, and prefer short, terse sentences. Ethnographic studies of schooling such as those by McLaren (1989) and Willis (1977) show how teachers use these ways of talking to distinguish the smartest students. Richness of language, precision of definition, frequent use of authors' names or of specialized terms, fluidity of sentence construction, and the use of subclauses are all taken as evidence of intelligence. Colloquialisms and the use of catch-all terms such as *stuff* or *neat* evince a lack of seriousness. Curse words are banished as the last resort of the unimaginative.

Talking of curse words and their prevalence in working-class speech brings us, naturally enough, to the ubiquitous "f-word." All social classes say "fuck" and "fucking," but middle-class students are likely to use this less and to banish it from formal classroom discussion. In working-class communities from Harlem to Glasgow, Detroit to Bootle, it attains near mantra status, being used in highly original ways every second or third word. If you stood on the now-demolished terraces of Spion Kop at Anfield (the home of the Liverpool football club) you would know what we mean. Mike Rose (1990) tells a story of how it was used to frame one of the highest pedagogical compliments a student ever paid him. When a Vietnam veteran wanted to show how Rose's teaching was affecting him, the man declared to Rose after class one day, "you-are-teaching-the-fuck-outta-me!" (p. 146).

Working-class students are usually smart enough to know that language used casually and colloquially in a bar or locker room will be inappropriate in a seminar discussion. This places an extra strain of self-censorship on them. Knowing that swearing offends "bourgeois decorum" (to use bell hooks's phrase), they have to monitor their discourse to purge it of a word that is used as an all-purpose noun, verb, adjective, and expletive. If it slips out in an exclamation such as "What a fucking brilliant idea!" it is usually treated as a slip of the tongue. The students either quickly apologize or remain studiedly defiant, daring someone in the room to challenge them. They know that cursing can easily lead to their being labeled unsophisticated, slow, and lacking diligence. This adds another layer of anxiety to the feelings of "impostorship" and cultural suicide they already experience. Impostorship is the sense among working-class students that they possess neither the talent nor the right to become college students. Students who feel like impostors imagine that they are constantly on the verge of being found out to be too dumb and unprepared for college-level learning. They imagine that once this discovery is made, they will be asked to leave whatever program they're enrolled in, shrouded in a cloud of public shame, humiliation, and embarrassment. Each week that passes without this happening only serves to increase the sense that a dramatic unmasking lies around the corner. "Surely," these students tell themselves, "sooner or later someone, somewhere, is going to realize that letting me onto this campus was a big mistake. I don't belong here, and I'm not smart enough to succeed."

The psychological and cultural roots framing impostorship are hard to disentangle, but most who speak about impostorship view it as having been produced by their awareness of the vast distance between the idealized images of omniscient intellectuals they attached to anyone occupying the role of student and their own daily sense of themselves as stumbling and struggling survivors (Brookfield, 1990). This distance between the idealized image of students' and professors' high-status discourse and the actuality of students' own conversations is so great that they believe it can never be bridged. Although many working-class students live with impostorship, it is usually kept private, masked behind a veneer of tough cynicism regarding all things intellectual. To admit to a sense of impostorship would be equivalent to admitting one cared about how one was perceived in a classroom, which in itself conveys that one takes education seriously as an important end in itself. Working-class students are willing to show that they take education seriously as a way of getting themselves out of their neighborhood and as a way of gaining work that pays better and has higher status than the work they do now. But showing that one takes ideas and educational processes seriously risks breaking with the "culture of cool," which mandates that extrinsic motivation ("I'm in it for the money") is OK but condemns as class betrayal any belief in the intrinsic importance or enjoyment of intellectual exchange.

The triggers that induce this sense of impostorship occur at distinct times in working-class students' lives. The first ordinarily occurs at the moment of public definition as a student. The news that one has been admitted into an educational program is greeted with a sense of disbelief and doubt that is not entirely pleasurable. Perhaps the acceptance letter was a fraud, or there has been a bureaucratic error in the admissions office. Another trigger occurs when the student gets to her first classes and is asked, along with everyone else, to introduce herself to the rest of the group. Teachers do this as a way of relieving students' anxieties and making them feel welcome. But this practice often seems to have the reverse effect of heightening the anxiety of many working-class students. Rather than affirming and honoring their prior experiences, this roundtable recitation of past activities, current responsibilities, and future dreams serves only to convince the student that everyone else in the class will succeed but she won't. Everyone else seems smarter, more articulate, more experienced, and more confident than she is. They have mastered the middle-class, elaborated speech code.

Of course, what students who feel like impostors don't realize is that this feeling is universal. It crosses lines of class, gender, and culture. Once one student talks about her own sense of impostorship, there is a domino-like collapse as, one by one, almost all the other students in the class admit to the same feeling. This is why it's so important to name impostorship early on in the course. A teacher can talk about his own feelings of impostorship as both student and teacher. After all, many college and university teachers identify themselves as coming from working-class backgrounds. The anthologies by Ryan and Sackrey (1984) and Dews and Law (1995) pay eloquent testimony to this feeling of being strangers far from home. The conventions and speech codes of academe are as exotic and intimidating to them as they are to many of their students. Speaking about the feelings of impostorship arising from their class identity can surprise and reassure working-class students.

Working-class and ethnic minority academics will also know much about the risk of cultural suicide run by many working-class students who learn a new way of speaking. Cultural suicide describes the process whereby families, peer groups, and communities exclude from their midst students whom they see as changing in front of their eyes as a result of their engaging in learning. The student who was formerly seen by friends and intimates as "speaking like us" is now seen as adopting an artificial and arrogant form of speech. She poses a real threat to those who see themselves as being betrayed. Her friends, colleagues, and family see her as taking on airs and pretensions, as growing "too big for her boots." She is seen as aspiring to the status of intellectual while those left behind feel that they are now somehow perceived as less developed creatures grubbing around in the gritty gutters of daily life outside academe. In the eyes of those left behind, the working-class student is perceived as having "gone native," having become a full-fledged member of the middle-class culture of academe. This is one of the central themes of Willie Russell's play (and later film) *Educating Rita,* concerning a working-class Liverpool woman who enrolls at the British Open University.

What does all this mean for the conduct of discussion? We wish to make three observations. First, teachers from working-class backgrounds can make their class identities public by talking about their own struggles as students and academics. This autobiographical disclosure will be welcomed by most students, particularly those from working-class homes. It is reassuring to know that the person in authority has walked in their shoes and is likely to be sympathetic to their use of nonacademic language. Second, teachers can acknowledge and encourage a wide variety of expressive forms. When students slip naturally into speech that teachers find annoying or unhelpful, they can hold their natural irritation in check unless they feel things have gotten completely out of hand. Mocking, however affectionately, a student's preferred way of talking is deadly to the development of trust. Third, any speech norms, ground rules, or codes of discourse the students generate should address explicitly the use of words people find offensive.

The problem is, of course, knowing in advance who will be offended by what. Most students can live with someone saying, "That argument is a crock." But someone saying, "that argument is a crock of shit" or "a fucking crock of shit" makes things much more tense and complicated. As with so many situations we've examined in this book, the CIQ will tell you the effect that different forms of speech have on different students. If some people's regular use of curse words offends others, that fact will be reported on the CIQ. This finding can then be turned back to the class, who will have to grapple, with the teacher's help, with what to do next. A discussion of what constitutes appropriate academic speech is not lightweight or idle. It cuts to several core issues: how we privilege certain ways of speaking and conveying knowledge and ideas, who has the power to define appropriate forms and patterns of communication, and whose interests these forms and patterns serve.

CONCLUSION

This chapter has provided just a few of the innumerable strategies for assisting people in doing a better job of communicating across differences. What we have tried to do is to present a few principles that underlie good discussions in general but that inform especially conversations involving cultural differences and feelings of racial intolerance. We have stressed that groups must openly confront racism, taking time to express anger and grief over the unfulfilled lives that result directly from bigotry. People must frankly assert their cultural identifications and the meaning these identities have for their lives. Teachers must try to create conditions that make people more comfortable with diversity, even as they use difference to generate greater respect for each other.

Doing these things is not an exercise in political correctness in which only the stories of those who feel themselves oppressed are told. Rather it is an attempt to offer as many different interpretations of experience as possible. A nation's story can be told many different ways, but it is really only recently that we have begun to acknowledge this. A Native American interpretation of U.S. history is going to be very different from an interpretation put forward by a Russian Jew, just as an African American's story will be starkly at odds with that of a descendant of a plantation owner, and an Aboriginal tale will be in stark contrast to that told by a European invader. The object of multicultural dialogues is to carve out spaces for many different versions of experience and to encourage people to cope with their complexity and to revel in their richness.

We do this not to impose equal acceptance of every story advanced but to create new appreciation for collective depth and diversity. We oppose the hegemonic intentions of those who claim there is only one, highly privileged American, English, Canadian, South African, or Australian story that must be protected and perpetuated. It is this hegemony of the official story, this enemy of pluralism, multiplicity, and complexity, that genuine dialogues about and across differences must be enjoined to combat (Bruner, 1996). When we honor a plethora of stories and interpretations and when we strive through discussion to find a place within our own stories for at least some of these other perspectives, we can begin to rebuild and reinvent commonalities. Unity does not entail jettisoning cultural richness and reinstating old, canonical models. This solution might seem neat and precise, unburdened by the messiness and turmoil of an ongoing conversation about our differences. But it is also blatantly undemocratic. It rejects the value of multiple stories and the importance of a cultural conversation that simply has no finish.

CHAPTER EIGHT

DISCUSSING ACROSS GENDER DIFFERENCES

The primary author of this chapter is our friend and colleague Eleni Roulis. It is based on her own experiences as well as on conversations and projects we have embarked on together. All three of us believe in the importance of teaching in a feminist key and that men as well as women can and indeed should work this way (see Digby, 1998). This means that college teachers who use discussion methods need to know something about the different ways in which female and male students talk to each other in discussion.

We want at the outset, however, to criticize the dichotomous assumption that women and men always have distinctly different, even contradictory, conversational styles. In widely read books such as *In a Different Voice* (Gilligan, 1982), *Women's Ways of Knowing* (Belenky, Clinchy, Goldberger, and Tarule, 1986), and *You Just Don't Understand* (Tannen, 1990), the authors maintain that although gender is of great importance, it is but one of many variables that shape how people talk to each other. Despite this caveat, many people now subscribe to the belief that all men always talk one way and all women another. Such a view is dangerous and simplistic, an essentialist form of reasoning akin to the "four legs good, two legs bad" sloganeering of the beasts in George Orwell's *Animal Farm*.

Over the past thirty years, the three of us have lived through the rise of feminist scholarship and feminist pedagogy. When we began our careers, we all noticed differences in the ways in which male and female students contributed to classroom discussions. Men spoke more often, and for longer periods, than women. The tone of male speech was also more confident and declamatory.

Women were more likely to adopt a tentative, hesitant tone when they ventured their contributions. These patterns pretty much mirrored our own personal experiences as college students.

Early in our careers, we lacked the language to name what we saw. But in the past decade, the feminist ethic of care and compassion has moved to center stage. Feminist concepts of voice, connected learning, constructed knowing, teaching as caring, and teachers as midwives have influenced cultural studies, developmental and cognitive psychology, linguistics, anthropology, sociology, and a host of related fields. These ideas have helped us understand why certain communication patterns between men and women are such a constant feature of the discussions in which we have been involved as leaders or participants. Yet as the following vignettes show, trying to unearth the role that gender plays in shaping communication between women and men is enormously complex.

HOW GENDER COMPLICATES DISCUSSION: FOUR VIGNETTES

A student wrote the following comment on a critical incident questionnaire (CIQ) sheet: "I'm sick of men talking across me. It doesn't matter how I try to get into the discussion, the men always interrupt or talk over me. You'd think by now they'd know better." This comment was reported to the class as part of the CIQ summary at the next meeting. At the end of that second meeting, one student wrote on that week's CIQ: "I am weary of male bashing. During the CIQ review one person noted that men were more forceful in getting into conversation. I don't know if the person who suggested it was male or female, but it triggered memories of past classes. I do not view myself as a cultural stereotype since I don't align my values with most men. In the classes I've had here, this is a pattern—usually one person makes it an issue because of hidden agendas. I know it is not politically correct to say this."

In a discussion among faculty on a search committee, a male teacher who was concerned about the gender imbalance in the department suggested that women candidates have the first crack at the job being advertised. Another female faculty member, who was known for her strong feminist views, turned to this man and said, "We don't need a woman—you're the best woman we've got." By this she meant that he worked from an ethic of care and compassion in making professional decisions, that he frequently deferred to others in discussion, that he modeled a self-critical and reflective stance toward his own actions, that he spoke softly, that he treated people with respect and care, and that in conversations it was obvious that he valued establishing warm relationships with the individuals involved.

One of the authors of this book pointed out in a discussion with students that the concept of "mastery" was an example of what Spender (1980) calls "man-made language," thinking that it showed the highly evolved state of his consciousness where gender sensitivity was concerned. After the discussion, two women students came up to him and said, "You know, you're taking this question of language too far. Mastery just means that you're good at something; it has no male or female connotations at all. Cut the crap—there's no need to be so politically correct."

In a class one of us taught, a male student had been waiting for some time to make a point in a discussion. Having raising his hand three or four times to indicate he wanted to speak, he smashed his fist on the table to stop the discussion. He followed this dramatic gesture by saying, "Now that I've got your attention, I can finally have my say." After he made his point, a white female student said his action had made her uncomfortable. It was a violent and offensive gesture, in her view. Another female student, an African American, came to the man's defense, saying she was glad he'd hit the table to get attention because that was the sort of thing she'd do.

These four vignettes illustrate the contradictory and complex nature of the issues at the heart of this chapter. The first opens by confirming the widely held view that men talk more in discussion and that they show no compunction in interrupting women students. This view is challenged by the second CIQ quote, which seems to record a male student's frustration at being stereotyped. Of course, things change dramatically if these quotes are written by female students. Changing the gender of these authors makes everything much more complicated!

The second vignette also challenges a simplistic analysis of gender characteristics. A strong feminist argues against the kind of aggregate thinking that presumes that men cannot talk in the same way as women. The third vignette is even more complicated. Are the women in this vignette pointing out a teacher's uncritical slide into politically correct speech? Or are they so inured to the masculine root at the core of the English language that they cannot see that defining excellence in masculine terms is a subtle form of hegemony? Is the way they express their criticism—"cut the crap"—a typically male form of communication, or is it an admirably direct and open judgment free of gender influences?

The fourth vignette shows how race and personality complicate the relationship between gender and speech. A white male's strong (some would say violent and hostile) gesture to grab the group's attention is defended by a black woman. Did she come to his defense because she had been forced to resort to the same kind of action to have her voice heard in discussions? Or was she just an extroverted personality who liked the fact that some spontaneous emotion showed up in class? And to what extent was her relief at a strongly expressed intervention the result of the speech patterns she had grown up with in her family, class, and culture? From these four examples it's clear that understanding how gender shapes men's and women's ways of talking is much more complicated than some would have it.

UNDERSTANDING MALE AND FEMALE SPEECH PATTERNS

That women's experiences are excluded or devalued in higher education has long been accepted by many progressive educators as the reality of most college classrooms. Maher's verdict that "women are silenced, objectified, and made passive through both the course content and the pedagogical style of most college classrooms" (1985, p. 30) is a judgment that has shaped how the three of us approach teaching through discussion. Maher argues:

> The dominant pedagogical style of most classrooms discriminates against women's experiences and participation in a variety of ways, all of which reinforce female passivity. Professors—male and, sometimes, female—tend to call on women students less in discussion, to ask them less probing questions, and to interrupt them more often. They make more eye-contact with men and are more attentive to male questions or comments. On a deeper level classroom discussions (as well as lectures) are usually conducted so as to reward "assertive speech," competitive "devil's advocate" interchanges, and

impersonal and abstract styles—often incorporating the generic
"he". . . . These modes of speech, while perhaps not inherently
"masculine," seem more natural to men in this culture; women
tend to be more tentative, polite, and hesitant in their comments
and thus are taken less seriously by teachers. Women who try to be
more assertive face a double bind, for they are perceived as "hostile" females rather than as "forceful" men. Perhaps as a result of
this treatment, as well as the subject-matter, women college students as a group are simply more silent than men. Like Freire's
"oppressed" they do not speak up; their experiences, their interpretations, their questions are not heard as often [p. 30].

Yet though some research into gender confirms the truth of this
perspective, other studies challenge this reading. Supposed distinctions between men's and women's talk sometimes reflect observers'
perceptions—their stereotypes and beliefs about gender variations—
rather than any actual differences. Crawford (1995) observes that
"despite many hundreds of research studies, there is little agreement
on the 'real' sex differences in speech style" (p. 3). She criticizes the
essentialism characterizing research on gender and language, arguing instead that we need to focus on the ways that any differences
noted between men's and women's talk reflect wider inequities of
power and status. Crawford argues that the essentialist line (women
talk one way, men another) moves the analysis of talk out of the
sociopolitical realm and away from the systematic exclusion of
women from positions of influence. She writes, "The rhetoric of difference makes everyone—and no one—responsible for interpersonal problems. Men are not to blame for communication
difficulties; neither is a social system in which gender governs access
to resources. Instead, difference is reified" (p. 106).
    Reviews of research studies of female and male communica-
tion styles illustrate Crawford's point. Two meta-analyses demonstrate that people refuse to conform neatly to generalizations about
gender. James and Clarke (1983) conclude that in the majority of
studies of male and female interruption patterns, there is no significant difference between the sexes. James and Drakich (1983)
argue that it is not gender that determines who speaks and for how
long but rather the specific cultural setting in which the conversation occurs, the participants' expectations in that setting, and their
perceived roles or status. So in some mixed-sex groups, women are

expected to talk more and males look to women for leadership, and in others the reverse is true.

When it comes to who talks more, Tannen (1990) suggests that men may talk more in public situations (such as college classroom discussions or faculty meetings) where they feel they are being judged by their peers or superiors. This is because they use talk to create and maintain a hierarchy in the group. But women often talk more in private situations (such as conversations among mixed-sex friends or small groups that form in larger discussion classes) because women are more likely to view conversation as crucial to maintaining close relationships with peers. Given that a great deal of small group discussion consists of private acts without the teacher present, we might conclude that women are more likely to play dominant roles in these conversations. On the whole we have found this to be true, and it's one reason why we like to use small group discussion as a regular feature of our classes.

You Just Don't Understand is one of the most popular analyses of male and female patterns of speech. In it, Tannen (1990) argues that many women approach the world as an individual in a network of connections: "In this world, conversations are negotiations for closeness in which people try to seek and give confirmation and support, and to reach consensus" (p. 25). She points out that when groups contain only women, the prevalent conversation is what might be called "rapport talk." Rapport talk is "a way of establishing connections and negotiating relationships. Emphasis is placed on displaying similarities and matching experiences" (p. 77). An example of how rapport talk can be misjudged when masculine norms of talk apply is the phrase "I'm sorry." To a male listener, a women saying "I'm sorry" means just one thing—she's apologizing for her actions. To a female listener, "I'm sorry" is recognized as carrying multiple meanings. It could indeed be an apology, but it could just as easily be an expression of regret or of sympathy for another's predicament.

When men form a discussion group, however, they adopt a "report" form of speech that serves to maintain their independence and helps them negotiate status. Report talk emphasizes participants' knowledge, verbal acuity, and ability to hold center stage. When men and women join in discussion, the norms of report speech, if not challenged, usually prevail. This tends to be especially true of discussion in college classrooms. Students assume that the quality and length of their participation are crucial to the teacher's opinion of their ability. This is underscored by teachers telling students that part of their grade is to be determined by their participation. If most classroom discussions do take the form of report talk, with students vying for status and "stage presence," men have a built-in advantage since they are experts in this conversational style.

We agree with Tannen that "when men and women get together in groups, they are likely to talk in ways more familiar and comfortable to the men. And both women's and men's ways of talking are typically judged by the standards of men's styles, which are regarded as the norm" (1990, p. 244). We are also impressed by the results of a study of women students in a master's counseling psychology program. Gawalek, Mulqueen, and Tarule (1994) report that women students felt more comfortable in classes in which a female instructor held a position of authority and was treated as an expert. They valued the pursuit of intellectual excellence in what was felt to be a safe environment, one where "mistakes" were celebrated as important moments for learning rather than penalized as evidence of inadequacy. They also preferred all-female classes or those in which females were in the majority.

Here is a rundown of the chief differential patterns of male and female speech we have noted in our own teaching.

- Men do tend to talk more often, though this is not a hard-and-fast rule. We have all had classes where two or three women were responsible for the great majority of the conversation. But given that the norms of report talk hold in most college classrooms, men generally take up the greater portion of airtime, even when they are in the minority.
- Men do tend to assume, or to be appointed to, the role of small group reporter when small groups are reporting to the whole class. If there are five males in a class and each one joins a small group, the reporting is frequently done by those five males. So the official record of each small group's conversation is filtered through the voice of the one male in each of those groups.
- Women are much more likely than men to preface their contribution to a discussion with a self-deprecatory remark, such

as "Of course, this is just my opinion," "Based on nothing but my own experience," or "This is probably a stupid point, but. . ."

- Women are more likely to show feelings associated with pain and suffering in a discussion. Sometimes this is pain associated with their own lives and sometimes an empathic living through others' experiences.
- All three of us can think of many female students who have wept when discussing an issue that affects them deeply but very few male students who have done the same. When we think of students who have displayed feelings of anger— hitting the table to silence the room, for example—male students come to mind much more readily than female students.
- Sarcastic comments in discussion emanate more often from men than from women. Comments that give praise, affirm the value of another's contributions, and express gratitude are made more often by women than by men.

But we emphasize that these differences are not carved in stone. Not all men subscribe only to the norms of report talk, and not all women find it difficult to comply with these. Gender must be considered in its larger social and cultural context. Factors of class and race are at least as important in determining who gets to speak and for how long and whose voice is taken seriously. Gender cannot be studied as a monolithic, unilateral construct that by itself shapes speech. Furthermore, it is inappropriate to generalize to all men and women any speech patterns noted in research conducted solely on white, middle-class North Americans and Europeans.

It is because of the complicated interaction between gender and other variables that we choose to distinguish between gender-specific and gender-related understandings of discussion. A *gender-specific* perspective reduces all discussion interchanges to examples of male and female communicative patterns. It implies a clear and constant inequity in terms of whose speech is encouraged and valued. A *gender-related* perspective (the one we hold) regards gender as an important variable but also acknowledges that factors of race, class, personality, culture, and age all determine who speaks up in discussion and how seriously their contributions are regarded. It allows for the possibility that what are proposed as female and male communicative modes often cross gender lines.

A FEMINIST APPROACH TO PEDAGOGY

In the remainder of this chapter we want to show how classroom expectations and rituals can be altered to help students find new ways of talking about and across gender. Some of what we advocate is familiar to individuals drawn to the ideas of feminist pedagogy and the feminist classroom proposed by Maher and Tetreault (1994), Weiler (1988), Lather (1991), Luke and Gore (1992), Gore (1993), McWilliam (1994), Diller, Houston, Morgan, and Ayim (1996), and many others. We believe that the central tenets of feminist teaching are constituent elements of good teaching. To be a good teacher means incorporating many practices labeled as feminist, whether or not one is female. The three of us all know men who have little knowledge of the literature of feminist pedagogy but who teach in ways that exemplify the best aspects of these practices.

What constitutes a feminist form of pedagogy, and how does this look in discussion-based courses? Generally, what is described as specifically feminist teaching parallels what this book advocates as respectful, responsive, and inclusive teaching. For example, one feminist who teaches African American women (Russell, 1985) slows down classroom processes to allow for a full consideration of each idea, uses a great deal of storytelling, grounds her classroom activities in the everyday experiences of students, and tries to develop a facility for understanding students' dialects, idioms, and colloquial language and communicating with them using this language. Feminist teachers studied by Sattler (1997) deliberately blur the distinction between teaching that happens inside or outside the classroom. They establish early on that there are no right answers that students are expected to discover, and they believe that students should gather in circles to engage in a process of inquiry. Using journals, a technique recommended by Roffman (1994) and Walden (1995), among many others, and affirming the personal, as advocated by Mattingly (1994), are also often proposed as defining practices of feminist pedagogy.

"Decentering the classroom" is how Woodbridge (1994) describes her practice of starting the class by asking students to fill in questionnaires, using the information gained from these to divide students into groups, and then giving each person in each group the chance to describe what he or she did for the last forty-eight hours before coming to class. In a class of thirty-five students, this creates thirty-five centers rather than one (the teacher). Woodbridge also recommends debate and theatricals to add spice and variety to her classes while urging discussion leaders to be restrained participants who use open-ended questions to invite spontaneous and exhilarating exchanges from students.

We believe that all these practices are at the heart of good teaching. To label them feminist is to risk partitioning off by gender the central features of good discussion leadership that male teachers need to adopt. We think it is accurate to say that more female than male teachers may tend naturally to gravitate toward these more relational ways of working. But all teachers should regard these procedures as central to good teaching.

BROADENING DISCUSSIONS TO INCLUDE FEMALE AND MALE WAYS OF TALKING

What are the implications of gender differences for teaching through discussion?

- *Relational talk.* If women are drawn to relational talk, regarding it as crucial to build the trust necessary for conversation, then discussion-based courses must begin with personal disclosure. Students need to get to know each other as people with idiosyncratic experiences, enthusiasms, and fears. Teachers can do a great deal to model this kind of disclosure, thereby setting a tone that the rest of the class emulates.
- *Safety.* If women value a classroom atmosphere that does not penalize verbal slips or errors, avoids seeing students as competitors, and regards teaching as caring (Noddings, 1984), teachers must do their best to ensure that such an atmosphere prevails. This can be accomplished by involving the group in determining ground rules for discourse (as outlined in Chapter Three) and by ensuring that these rules grant students license to stumble in conversation without feeling stigmatized. In addition, teachers can model a willingness to take risks and commit mistakes, both in discussion role plays with colleagues and in their own solo teaching.

- *Connected teaching.* If women value making connections between their own experiences and the discussion topic, teachers can call for regular time-outs in which all students try to create and discover these connections. They can also open the discussion by asking students to share critical incidents that illuminate the day's topic.
- *Rapport talk.* If female-only conversation is different from male-only conversation, and if women adopt the norms of male conversation when they talk in mixed groups, a case can be made for introducing periods of women-only discussion into the classroom. This could be alternated with a period of male-only discussion. Students could then reflect on what differences, if any, were evident in the two periods. After discussing these differences, the class could consider how elements from both periods could be incorporated into its ground rules and future conduct.

Again, these are all good discussion behaviors, appropriate for teaching classes with both male and female students. Although these approaches may be identified with research on women's communication patterns, we regard them as adult, respectful ways to approach teaching through discussion.

Let's turn now to some specific exercises we have found useful in broadening discussion to include female and male ways of talking.

STANDPOINT STATEMENTS

A standpoint statement is a good way to begin a discussion with some structured personal disclosure. Students begin by writing down perhaps five demographic facts that define who they are. These might be their ethnic heritage, gender, age, place of birth or residence, sexual preference, or educational level. For example, a student might write that she is a Jamaican American, second-generation, heterosexual woman with a college degree who lives in the Midwest and is in a long-term committed relationship. Another student might write that he is a Caucasian American of Russian heritage who earned his professional qualifications through night school, considers himself an exile from New York, and is in a same-sex relationship.

Each student is then asked to write down how these demographic factors have shaped their standpoint—their view of life and the preferred identity they present to the world. The Jamaican American woman might describe how some aspects of her demography (being a second-generation American rather than an immigrant, having academic success, and earning a college degree) have given her a position of privilege while others (such as her skin color, ethnic heritage, and gender) have caused her to be disregarded in certain situations. The male might describe how his Russian heritage is a source of both comfort and constraint and of how the regard in which he is held changes as he moves farther away from his childhood neighborhood.

The final written component asks students to consider three questions:

1. What parts of your standpoint do you think are shared by others with the same demographic characteristics?
2. Which parts of your standpoint are unique to you?
3. Of the demographic characteristics you mention, which are most important in determining your standpoint?

After writing their standpoint statements, students move to the discussion phase. In small groups they read their standpoint demographics and their responses to the three questions. They focus especially on how their standpoint has shaped what they think about male and female modes of communication. What gender stereotypes are embedded in their statements? How have the experiences behind the standpoint confirmed or challenged these stereotypes? Although this exercise focuses on gender, it could easily be adapted to discussion-based courses with a wide variety of student backgrounds.

DICTIONARY DEFINITION

This is another beginning exercise that shares some similarities with the standpoint statement activity. Here students write out a dictionary definition of who they are. It includes a phonetic respelling of their name and a description of the characteristics they possess that mark them as uniquely themselves. Volunteers,

including the teacher, go to the board to write out their defini-
tions. Class members then ask the volunteers questions about the
definitional characteristics that are most important to them. As
the volunteers' responses flow, the teacher highlights gender-
related characteristics and engages the class in a discussion of the
extent to which our gender defines who we think we are. Which
characteristics offered by volunteers seem to cross gender lines,
and which seem gender-specific?

Preference Lists

In this exercise students are given fifteen minutes to write down all
the things they most enjoy doing in their lives. These lists are confidential; there is no expectation that they will be shared with classmates. After the lists are written, participants are asked to write "A"
next to all the things they do alone, "OP" next to all the things they
do with other people, "A/OP" next to all the things they do both
alone and with other people, "N5" next to activities they weren't
doing five years ago, and "$" next to everything that costs $10 or
more to do. They then tally the percentage of their activities that
fall into each category.

Next the class moves into discussion of what people learned
about themselves, paying particular attention to whether or not
broad gender differences exist. Do the women in the class have
more friendship networks, in line with the collaborative, relational
style women are said to prefer? Do the men in the class follow
enthusiasms on their own, as the conventional wisdom would suggest? Do the women value more highly and take greater pleasure
from intimate relationships? Do recreational activities fall along
what are assumed to be gender lines, with men more likely to be
sport fanatics? And if certain taken-for-granted assumptions concerning gender are contradicted by these preference lists, what
does this say about our tendency to generalize about men's and
women's ways of being?

Commonplace Books

Efforts to make college classrooms more responsive to women's
ways of learning usually involve a substantial element of journal writing in which students are asked to disclose personal experiences.

One particular use of journals is based on the notion of journals as old-fashioned commonplace books in which lists, plans, projects, self-assessments, quotations, anecdotes, letters, invitations, and other materials are kept together (Murray, 1990). Students are given blank scrapbooks and asked to put in them any materials that indicate how their gender has shaped their lives. These materials often include pieces of writing that demonstrate how students, their parents, or friends were restricted in their career choices, recreational activities, or development of friendships by gender stereotyping. Students are asked to pay particular attention to including materials that help them develop a new sensitivity to the ways in which men and women talk to each other in discussion. Here are some of the things that may be included in commonplace books:

- Descriptions of memorable experiences that were influential in shaping students' perceptions of what it means to be female or male
- Descriptions of memorable experiences that showed how students became aware of the limits of male and female identity (for example, boys being called sissies for liking nice clothes or girls being called tomboys for excelling in sports)
- Statements that students have heard or read that summed up for them a powerful truth concerning gender
- Re-created transcripts of spontaneous conversations overheard in everyday settings—coffee shops, restaurants, bars, cinema queues, porches, theater lobbies, pool halls, school board meetings, friends' homes, locker rooms—that illuminate issues of gender
- Letters (or extracts from letters) in which a point is made that illustrates or challenges our assumptions about gender
- Newspaper reports written by men and women that illustrate how gender frames our perceptions of the world and our selection of what we consider to be important events
- Hypothetical projections of how authors' lives might have been different, or could be different, without the constraints of gender stereotyping
- Recollections of good and bad conversations across or about gender in which students have participated, accompanied by reflections on what made these conversations so good or so bad and how the features of the best conversations might be re-created

LITERACY NARRATIVES

A literacy narrative is a particular kind of story that tells how we create and learn the language we use to describe who we are. Students write a narrative of how they learned the specific words, concepts, and modes of expression that they use to understand and describe their experience to others. These narratives usually include explicit references to schooling, family life, coming of age, and important people in the writers' lives. Students are encouraged to experiment with whatever words really express their experience—slang, dialect, native language, colloquialisms, and so on.

When students share these literacy narratives, they are often amazed at how creatively and individualistically each person approached the assignment. Some tell stories of how they struggled to learn to read or write. Others recall reading certain beloved texts for the first time or the feelings of warmth they enjoyed while reading a favorite book by flashlight under bedcovers. And still others remember that gender stereotypes sometimes presented obstacles for both men and women. Males who loved poetry recall being teased by both peers and adults, and females remember how assertively their families and teachers sometimes attempted to quash their drive to probe the meaning and power of words. These narratives usually show that men tended to receive more positive reinforcement for their accomplishments in language learning in school but that they were also more likely to be rebuked if they fell short of family expectations.

As the discussion proceeds, a running list is kept of students' most salient and poignant experiences with literacy. Despite marked differences in the narratives, students tend to agree that learning to read, write, and speak eventually turn out to be liberating and transforming experiences. They declare passionately that the freedom to develop these skills must be given the highest priority throughout one's life and that every effort must be made to prevent gender from impeding a satisfying and enriching relationship with words.

ANALYZING CLASSROOM TALK

One obvious way to make students more aware of how gender influences discussion is to include an analysis of this factor in your own teaching. Students can spend five minutes at the end of a discussion writing down their observations of how the discussion went. These can be open-ended jottings, with no guidelines given, or students can focus on some predetermined aspects, such as differences in men's and women's questioning styles, other differences in conversational style, the gender of the most active participants in a discussion, whether men or women interrupted more (and whom they were most likely to interrupt), or gender differences in the length of contributions.

One variant might be to adapt the CIQ to focus on questions of language and gender. For example, students might be asked what specific words or phrases spoken by the teacher or by another student were especially engaging, distancing, affirming, puzzling, or surprising. Another extension of the CIQ might have students describe moments when the language directed toward them made them feel either included or excluded, acknowledged or discounted.

Reporting these observations to the whole class serves several functions. It helps people become alert to gender elements in communication, particularly the comparative aspects of female and male participation in the discussion. Students become more aware of any gender differences that exist in questioning styles and ways of responding to others' questions. Because observing gender differences in conversation is a lot to ask, you can assign a couple of participants to this task. It is clearly understood that these group members are primarily observers and not expected to play a significant role in the discussion.

TAPING DISCUSSIONS

To students who are skeptical of the existence of male and female ways of talking, viewing a videotape of their own class discussion can be highly revealing. When the tape is played back, students are often surprised at how frequently males dominate and females defer. They also become intrigued by who assumes the responsibility of connecting different people's ideas, who does the support work of keeping the conversation going, who focuses on detail, and which individuals assert themselves as voices of authority. Audiotaping can also be successful in revealing gender-based conversational dynamics. In fact, audiotaping is sometimes better when the purpose is to get students to focus on the words people use and the meanings invested in them. When watching videotapes, students are often fascinated with how they look as much as with what they say. They fixate on their clothes, gestures, nonverbal tics, and body language. Audio allows them to concentrate on language.

Because of the increasingly simple and unintrusive nature of video and audio technology, students are more and more able to experiment with different conversational styles. They can record a short discussion, listen to a playback, and then begin another discussion in which they attempt to change their patterns of interaction. Women in the first discussion may begin by making supportive and tentative statements, while men may speak more confidently and attempt to control the discussion's themes. In the second discussion these roles can be reversed, or both genders can decide to talk in more balanced ways.

TELEVISION AND FILMS

Because texts drawn from popular culture (television, movies, magazines, music videos) are familiar and accessible to most students, they are usually highly engaging, and their familiarity can be used to alert students to the ways in which these texts both perpetuate and subvert stereotypes about how men and women talk. For instance, by contrasting the ways in which mothers relate to their daughters in such films as *The Joy Luck Club, Terms of Endearment, A World Apart,* or *Secrets and Lies* with the manner in which fathers interact with sons in *Kramer vs. Kramer, East of Eden, American Heart,* or *Distant Voices, Still Lives,* students can witness significant differences in dialogue patterns and reflect on the ways in which parents condition their children to assume specific gender roles.

By viewing a quite different film, *Six Degrees of Separation,* students can see how differently a husband and his wife respond to a young black man who comes into their lives claiming to be Sidney Poitier's son. When their playful but confusing encounter turns into tragedy, the husband withdraws from the situation, denying responsibility for what has happened, whereas the wife finds herself unable to disengage, intent on trying vainly to maintain what has become an important relationship for her. How these different reactions reinforce gender expectations and roles can provide the basis for a provocative discussion.

Films can add immeasurably to what we can learn about gender, discourse, and power. Students can remove themselves from the action and assume a more critical stance toward the relationships and situations these films portray, even when these are similar to incidents in their own lives. This allows them to probe assumptions embedded in the film's scenes in a way that would be impossible with their own direct experiences. Interestingly, all of this can occur without students' losing the connection they have made with these films.

THEATER OF THE OPPRESSED

In Chapter Six we emphasize the value of theatricality in reviving discussions that have become flaccid and lethargic. Augusto Boal's groundbreaking "theater of the oppressed" is a highly provocative and engaging way of prompting students to uncover troubling assumptions and truths they hold about the world. Boal (1992) has developed imaginative exercises and games to stimulate debate and encourage performers and audience to explore untapped parts of themselves.

The process begins when participants act out on stage an unresolved problem in their lives and the audience is invited to suggest and enact solutions. The problem always involves a protagonist confronted by an oppressor. The initial scene or vignette (known as the model) is acted out; then it is repeated, only more rapidly. During this second performance, any member of the audience can shout, "Stop!" and replace any of the characters at any time, thereby changing the outcome of the scene. A "joker" presides over the action and ensures that the process runs smoothly by teaching the audience the rules of intervention. The rules can change, however, as different spectators intervene, and the scene can be redone an unlimited number of times. The result is a pooling of knowledge held by the participating spectators as they go up on stage to change the dialogue and alter the outcome.

This activity stimulates debate, shows alternatives, and illuminates our habits, rituals, and everyday assumptions. Through this theatrical process, people participate in observing and changing the entrenched rituals that surround how they live out their gender roles. It is great fun to watch normally shy individuals jump up enthusiastically and stop the action in order to effect change and find humane alternatives. The laughter of recognition is often heard as the familiar patterns, phrases, and intonations of male speech are portrayed and as women search for ingenious ways to skirt, subvert, and outsmart these machinations. Even more than film, theater has a power and an immediacy that can shed important light on the inequities of certain kinds of conversational patterns.

A variation on Boal's activity is to begin without a scene that has been developed in advance and simply to provide students with a situation for them to act out in a form of role play. One such situation is "The Weekend Dilemma." A couple are having dinner at home and begin discussing plans for the weekend. They can't seem to agree on how to spend their time. The husband wants complete peace without company; the wife has planned a variety of activities with friends, some of which take place at their house. The students assuming these roles are instructed to hold strongly to their original positions, trying to get the other to negotiate and change. Once both participants agree that the scene has been played out to their satisfaction and that they have stated their views as completely as possible, members of the audience are asked to comment on what they think they saw and heard. Almost invariably, each perspective offered is different, allowing the class to see the situation from multiple vantage points.

CONCLUSION

In this chapter we have affirmed as a tenet of good teaching the feminist belief that discussion is relational. We believe that building relationships is an important element of successful conversation and that participants in conversation need to feel they are respected, affirmed, and cared for. We want to stress that unless a deliberate attempt is made to break with the norms of report talk, discussion groups will automatically turn to a form of discourse characterized by showing off and competing for attention.

But while we affirm the importance of gender considerations, we don't want to slip uncritically into male bashing. The processes of relational talk, attending to participants' experiences, and expressing appreciation for others' presence are valued by many males as well as most females.

We want also to emphasize that respecting and incorporating relational, affirming ways of talking to each other in no way implies a rejection of critique. A balanced discussion involves critical analysis of one's own and others' ideas and a vigorous exploration of differences. But this critical analysis must be of ideas, not of persons. We need critique in safety—critique premised on affirming each other's personhood and respecting all experiences. Safe critique involves acknowledging what is meritorious and important in another's contribution. It requires that we thank each other for the act of speaking out, whether or not we agree with what is said.

We don't think critique is necessarily destructive or inherently male. We want to challenge the easy stereotypes that hold that women are concerned only with affirmation and men only with negative criticism. Critique is a process of inquiry into the accuracy and validity of our assumptions. This involves sorting out and naming which elements of our assumptions are accurate and which need further study. When female and male faculty teach a course together, they have a wonderful opportunity to model a respectful engagement in critique that acknowledges disagreement while affirming its value. When female and male teachers disagree in front of students, they can emphasize that the expression of a different perspective by a peer is a gift that requires thanks. It is particularly important for students to see male teachers consistently deferring to a female teacher's authority. A male teacher in a mixed-gender class should be aware that he sends a powerful message to students when he makes it known that it is only because of the presence of the female colleague's different views that an appraisal of his assumptions is possible. Grounding critical analysis in expressing gratitude for the way peers function as critical mirrors is safe critique—critique in a feminist key.

CHAPTER NINE

KEEPING STUDENTS' VOICES IN BALANCE

In this chapter we want to examine two common situations that teachers say hinder their attempts to use discussion. These are when a few students talk so much that they prevent others from talking and when students say so little that nothing of intellectual value occurs. Both of these scenarios demonstrate, in markedly different ways, what happens when the contributions of students to the discussion are out of balance. Discussions are out of balance when a substantial number of students feel excluded from the discussion for long periods of time. Discussions are in balance when students feel they have an equal right to participate but also feel comfortable with periods of prolonged silence. As teachers, we want contributions and comments to be spread around group members, but we also want one or two people to have the freedom to engage in an extended, focused conversation while others listen intently. Of course, we never reach a felicitous point of balance where all feel equally free either to speak or to listen during every moment of the conversation. There are always tensions between a commitment to democratic participation and a desire for intellectual depth or between affirming the value of individual contributions and introducing challenging but disturbing new perspectives.

This chapter is intended to suggest ways that these tensions can be felt as more, rather than less, congenial.

WHEN SOME STUDENTS TALK TOO MUCH

A common scenario in discussion happens when one or two individuals quickly establish their dominance in a group. Sometimes, because of their intelligence, verbal acuity, and self-confidence, the students step briskly into any early moments of silence and deliver a series of brilliant monologues. The other members of the group, confident that a couple of people can always be relied on to say something reasonably articulate, can settle back and let the confident students run the show. At other times, students want to contribute but are prevented from doing so because one or two talkative members are insensitive to the stifling effect their frequent contributions are having. Occasionally, an ideologue uses the group as a forum for conversion.

Garrulous students may seem to most discussion leaders to be a dream come true, rather than a problem to be dealt with. Most of us probably feel our chief difficulty in discussion lies not in people talking too much but in the opposite situation of working with students who resolutely refuse to say anything. But sooner or later all discussion leaders face the scenario where a few students unfairly claim the great percentage of the available time. Sometimes this is due to these students' simple enthusiasm and sometimes to their lack of interpersonal sensitivity. Sometimes the group is replicating political, cultural, and gender inequities that exist outside the classroom. The first step in dealing with this situation is to define what counts as talking too much. The next is to work out why some people are especially talkative while others are silent. Then, on the basis of this analysis, we can decide what we're going to do.

WHAT COUNTS AS TALKING TOO MUCH?

What counts as talking too much varies enormously according to who is doing the speaking and listening. Factors such as culture, gender, class, and personality shape our judgments on this matter. In Chapter Seven we noted that certain Native American cultures value silence over speech. A Zen Buddhist belief is "those who know do not speak; those who speak do not know." So judgments of whether someone is speaking too much are unavoidably cultural and always contextual.

It seems to us, though, that the following rule might be applied to determine appropriate levels of conversation. A member of a discussion group is talking too much when others in the group feel consistently that they are denied the opportunity to speak. According to this definition, a discussion that focuses on an extended interchange between two people is fine, provided that others don't feel excluded from joining in if they wished. Some of the best discussions are those in which two or three people spend a great deal of time probing an issue on which they hold differing views or trying to understand each other's contrasting opinions, experiences, and perceptions. Silent members of the group can listen carefully to this discussion and be stimulated by this exchange. There can then be a fruitful period of silence when all ponder their reactions and questions.

One of the most common mistakes discussion leaders make is to cut off prematurely an extended and ever-deepening conversation between two participants because the leader feels that some sort of democratic balance needs to be restored by having other people speak. Yet it may be that this extended, focused conversation between two people is exactly what is needed to take the discussion to a new level of complexity or to make group members aware of previously overlooked perspectives. If, however, this extended conversation is carried on while others are waiting, frustrated, for a pause so that they can jump in, something needs to be changed. Somehow, those who are dominating the discussion by talking too much must be made aware of this fact. The conditions for conversation must be changed to allow others to participate.

How do we know when some students feel that others are preventing them from speaking? One clear indicator is behavior. Students begin to speak but are cut off by others who refuse to give way and continue with their conversational steamroller. People raise their hands to indicate that they wish to join the conversation, but others ignore them and jump in to make their point. Sometimes nonspeakers roll their eyes or trade resigned glances when a particularly garrulous member gets on a roll. Sometimes the hostility is almost tactile as shut-out members glower, frown, feign sleep, refuse to make eye contact with the speaker, and carry on side conversations. In our experience, however, students will rarely protest directly to a teacher about another student's continued dominance of a discussion. It is as if in so doing they are betraying a kind of implicit tribal allegiance that marks the boundaries between students and faculty.

There is also the problem raised by the culture of cool. To complain to a teacher that one can't get one's voice heard in a discussion is to admit that one actually cares about the conversation. To want to be heard is to declare an interest in learning. In some campus subcultures, declaring this interest in learning is tantamount to committing cultural suicide. It means saying to your peers that you don't think all teachers are jerks or that all education is a con. Showing that you take learning seriously often isn't very cool.

The surest way we have found to determine when some students feel others are preventing them from speaking is through the critical incident questionnaire (CIQ), described in Chapter Three. The CIQ, you will recall, is the one-page form students complete at the end of each week's classes, on which they write about the moments they were most engaged or distanced as learners that week, the actions in class that most helped or puzzled them, and what surprised them most about the class. No names are allowed on these forms. The forms are then collected by the teacher, who prepares a report summarizing the main themes in students' responses. This report is distributed at the start of the next week's classes, and its content is discussed with the whole class.

Because anonymity is guaranteed through the CIQ, students are often willing to use it to raise issues that they would not speak about in public. If some people are unfairly dominating the discussion, comments will start to appear on CIQs. Students will express annoyance that a particular student or students dominated an issue, continued to speak when it was obvious that the rest of the group had lost interest and wanted to take the discussion in a different direction, or refused to let others get a word in.

Of course, one could claim that saying these things under the cloak of anonymity perpetuates a form of cowardice. Colleagues have argued that letting students hide their authorship of critical comments allows them to evade responsibility for their words. They can take potshots at other students and then leave it up to the teacher to sort out the problem. These criticisms are valid. But we continue to use the CIQ because, on balance, we believe that the honesty it elicits outweighs the potential for abuse. And when students use the CIQ to attack other students in personal or abusive terms, we reframe these complaints as general problems of the democratic process that the whole group must address.

Why Do Some Students Speak Too Much?

Most cases of overly talkative students can be traced to one of five sometimes interrelated causes. First, students expect that talking frequently and at length will win the teacher's approval. In thinking this way, they are conforming to that strand of academic culture that rewards speech. Without an explicit challenge to the norm that frequent speech signifies intelligence, diligent students will do their best to be noticed by getting their comments in speedily and regularly. When teachers tell students that part of their course grade will be based on class participation, students interpret this to mean that they should speak as much as possible. Whether their speech is part of an evolving conversation or whether it asks others to consider new and challenging perspectives is secondary. The task is to say something, anything, to get noticed.

A second reason why some students talk too much springs from a combination of personality traits that impels them into constant speech. We all know extroverted individuals who speak in groups as easily as they breathe. Most teachers are glad to have one or two such people in class because they are a kind of insurance against silence. We know we can rely on a couple of people to answer the questions we pose to a group even if everyone else stays silent. There are other garrulous individuals whose frenetic loquacity springs from a sense of insecurity. Their nervousness and fear manifest themselves in a desperate desire to be noticed by their peers. If they are not the center of attention, they feel they don't exist.

Among a third group of students, dominating a discussion reflects a desire to control and an automatic presumption of authority. Such desires and presumptions spring from a complicated mix of vanity and egomania buttressed by a social order that rewards these behaviors. The readiness to jump into speech and dominate discussions is behavior that is expected and legitimated by the wider society. As Ira Shor (1996) writes:

> While teachers tend to reward talkative students who respond to
> questions, society also rewards tough guys, operators, and empire-
> builders. As verbal bullies and discursive entrepreneurs, some talky
> students don't mind being impolite or aggressively competitive. In
> class, at work, and in daily life, men especially behave in the caste
> of "rising stars," "big shots," or self-impressed "honchos." The more
> aggressive male types tend to take over conversations, push their
> way to the top, or push people around. Others with something to
> say, who are less aggressive, less rude, less safe in public exposure,
> or less confident, like many female students and those of color in a
> white institution, will simply find it harder in a macho climate to
> take the floor if they have to start speaking without raising hands
> [pp. 69–70].

For the bullies that Shor describes, a discussion in which their voice
is not front and center constantly defining what's right and wrong
is a conversation that sadly has gone astray. Such people regard the
discussion group as a forum for the airing of their own views, which
they assume will be received with worshipful appreciation by
those they view as less intellectually endowed.

Fourth, we occasionally have in discussion groups fundamen-
talist ideologues from across the political and religious spectrum
who regard discussion sessions as strategic opportunities for the
conversion of others. Convincing peers of the accuracy and validity
of these ideologues' opinions becomes the criterion they use to
judge whether a discussion is worthwhile. Ideologues of any per-
suasion are hard-core opponents of democratic disciplines and
resist any attempts at self-critique.

Finally, overtalkative students are sometimes the direct result
of teachers' acceptance of an ill-conceived metaphor of free discussion. Some teachers recoil from intervening too frequently for
fear of distorting or unduly influencing the discussion. They
believe that the less they speak, the more authentic, democratic,
and free the discussion will be. But it is one thing to refrain from
setting out a party line of opinions that students should follow, and
quite another to refuse to get involved in regulating student-to-
student speech.

Indeed, allowing open-ended, unregulated discussion is the
pedagogical version of the free market ideal in which the fittest
survive. But the free market patently is not free if by free we mean

that everyone has the same chance to participate and succeed. The market frees those with the greatest resources, power, and privilege to maintain their position of dominance over others. So it goes with discussion. Free discussion seems a worthy libertarian ideal, but in reality this freedom simply allows the strongest to flourish. Those possessing the greatest cultural capital, as Bourdieu (1986) puts it, move to dominate in discussion. Students whose race, class, gender, or personality has helped them grow accustomed to holding forth outside the classroom will simply reproduce that behavior in class unless some preventive brakes are applied.

WHAT DO WE DO WHEN STUDENTS TALK TOO MUCH?

Throughout this book we have suggested ways of preparing students for discussion, getting them talking, and keeping them involved. Many of these same techniques address the problem of overly talkative students. To recap a few of these suggestions, the problem of some students' talking too much will be greatly diminished if the following six things happen:

1. Teachers model participation in discussion groups early in a course, trying to control how much they speak and making sure they give way frequently to other group members.
2. Teachers help group members research their past experiences as discussion participants so that they can use these to evolve ground rules for conversation. Guidelines are stated in which giving way to others and not holding court for too long are valued highly.
3. Teachers research constantly how students experience discussion and then talk with them about any problems that are emerging.
4. Teachers regularly assign roles to group members, making sure that some of these roles (for example, summarizer and detective) involve substantial periods of silence. They make sure these roles are rotated fairly and consistently.
5. Teachers call for regular periods of reflective silence (perhaps after every fifteen to twenty minutes) when group members think about the important points that have been made,

contradictions that have surfaced, omissions that occur to them, and where the discussion should go next. Students make a few notes on these matters, and teachers begin the next phase of the discussion by asking students who haven't spoken much to read out what they've written.

6. Teachers introduce regular exercises (such as circular response discussion and the circle of voices) and rules for discourse (for example, being able to talk only about other people's ideas or allowing others the floor before you speak a second or third time) that guard against one person's dominating the conversation.

But despite doing all these good things, there will still be times when students speak too frequently and too long. How should we respond? Does our role as teachers include trying to ensure some equity in participation? We believe it does. When we have found ourselves confronting this problem, we have found the CIQ to be enormously helpful.

If a student is unfairly dominating the discussion, this fact will inevitably emerge on students' CIQ forms. Students will comment on the domineering person's insensitivity or egomania, or express confusion over what this person is trying to achieve by shutting out others or surprise that anyone could be so enamored of the sound of his or her own voice. The students who are seen as unfairly dominating the discourse will be identified by name, dress, or reference to specific comments they made. These forms should tip teachers off that students, too, are aware that a problem of unequal discourse exists. Teachers can then act to bring participation into balance, knowing that they're tackling a group problem rather than pursuing a private vendetta against someone they feel is trying to gain control of the group.

Having been made aware that one or two class members are perceived as unfairly dominating the discussion, teachers have two action options. They can begin by addressing this issue with the whole class during the reporting phase of the CIQ. If they do this, they should frame the situation as a general problem of group discourse rather than a specific problem involving any particular student. The conversation that ensues will usually involve a strong reaffirmation of group rules that ensure equal participation. Sometimes this conversation is enough to keep the dominant student or students in check, at least for a while.

If the problem persists, the teacher needs to have a private talk with the person in question. In this conversation, the teacher should reveal that other students have reported on CIQs that this student is unfairly dominating discussions. Although these conversations are never easy, we have found that citing the CIQs strengthens the effect of the teacher's comments and at the same time precludes the student's raising objections. The CIQ comments serve as a body of unequivocal data that the dominating student must take seriously. Before we used the CIQ, we would both regularly take students aside and communicate our concern that they were speaking too much and preventing others from contributing to the discussion. We didn't do this together, as a pedagogical tag team, or as part of a "good cop, bad cop" routine. The conversation would always be between one student and one teacher, with the teacher expressing, as tactfully and respectfully as possible, some concerns about how the student's excessive talking was having a silencing effect on others.

But the dominant student could always counter with some very reasonable objections. They could ask, "How do you know I'm preventing others from speaking? Has anyone complained to you?" They usually hadn't. Or they could say, "If other students think I'm talking too much, all they need to do is tell me whenever it happens." They usually wouldn't. The talkative student could also argue that as teachers who were used to controlling our classrooms we were threatened by a strong student voice that served as a challenge to our habitual authority. Of course each of us would protest that this consideration had never entered our thinking, all the while being nagged by the suspicion that maybe the student was right.

Presenting to a student CIQ data in which his or her behavior is consistently noted by classmates as interfering with their education makes it much harder to dismiss the problem or rationalize it away. Also, the CIQ data help you avoid being perceived as trying to control a challenge to your power. Instead, you become the conduit of the entire class's concerns. Talkative students find it very difficult to ignore that their behavior is perceived a certain way by their peers, no matter how unfair or erroneous they feel these perceptions might be.

When presenting students with comments that reflect unflatteringly on their actions, it is important that they know the conversation is confidential. Reassure them that there will be no reference to the conversation in class and that other students will not know that their comments have been passed on. We don't want to shame dominant students in front of their peers, nor do we want students to think of the CIQ as a way to get at students they don't like. So the conversation remains private.

But this doesn't necessarily make the conversation easier. Students may react with a complex mixture of anger, embarrassment, and humiliation. They may deny that they are trying to silence others and maintain that their frequency of speech is just a sign of enthusiasm. They may feel that the teacher or other class members are out to get them. Sometimes resentment can be eased by suggesting specific things the student can do to remedy the situation. We might ask that after making a contribution, the student wait until at least three other people have spoken before speaking again. This focus on future actions gives the student a project to work at and helps save some shreds of self-respect.

In our experience, these conversations have often had very dramatic and positive effects. Students who consistently interrupted to "correct" other students have become more responsive group members who struggle to monitor their contributions judiciously. Of course, this doesn't always happen. There will always be students who remain unmoved by group ground rules, classmate complaints, CIQ feedback, and conversations with teachers. But the frequency of egomaniacal behavior tends to be much reduced when we have presented CIQ data to students.

WHEN STUDENTS TALK TOO LITTLE

The second discussion scenario we want to examine in this chapter is when students talk too little. A teacher thinks the students are ready for the discussion and throws out a provocative question. A long period of silence ensues, punctuated by much embarrassed shifting of bodies and aversion of eyes. The teacher, thinking the question was perhaps too opaque, rephrases it in a more direct way. Another period of silence descends on the room. Feeling that things are slipping out of control, the teacher counts silently to ten and then proceeds to answer the question himself. The teacher then presents a second question for discussion and follows this quickly with a lucid response or perhaps a short lecture. The teacher becomes increasingly frustrated by the lack of participation and interprets students' unwillingness to say anything as personal hostility or contempt for the class. Teacher and students are then sucked into a vortex of misunderstanding and mutual recrimination. Both are angry at the other for creating a situation that causes great discomfort.

HOW DO WE JUDGE WHEN STUDENTS SAY TOO LITTLE?

We argued earlier that the judgment regarding when some students are talking too much should reside ultimately with discussion participants. We feel that the same is true for times when students are saying too little. Students are saying too little when, in their own judgment, the level of silence or lack of participation in class represents a problem for their learning. It should be noted that teachers' and students' perceptions of what constitutes a comfortable period of silence often vary. The two of us are uncomfortable with silence that lasts longer than about twenty seconds. In a class time of fifty to sixty minutes, twenty seconds seems a drop in the temporal ocean. Yet to us, in the middle of a discussion, it can seem an eternity. Just try counting out twenty seconds in your head when you've finished this paragraph and you'll see what we mean.

Shor (1996) reminds us that students are usually given much too little time for thought in discussion. He writes, "In what often passes for classroom 'discussion,' students usually have only a few seconds to respond to the teacher's questions. . .. . . . It's not easy for students to think on their feet in class, especially when presented with unfamiliar subject matter in an alien academic idiom" (p. 78).

Knowing that students need time to think about what they're going to say, we try not to panic when silence lasts longer than twenty seconds. We keep reminding ourselves that silence is crucial to learning. Without periods of reflective analysis, when students are pondering new perspectives and making new connections, discussions can easily become unreflectively frenetic. Discomfort with silence is part of the reason why students and teachers (ourselves included) fall so easily into the trap of equating speech with intellectual engagement and silence with mental inertia.

Yet silence often enormously enhances learning. It provides students and teachers with time to stumble on relationships between previously disconnected ideas. It allows us to notice omissions or fallacies that we miss in the heat of speech. Silence represents a reflective interlude to "mull things over" that students say is crucial if they are to make sense of new information and unfamiliar perspectives. It also gives us pause to think before we speak out in frustration or anger, so that what we say comes across as a comment on ideas and not on personalities. If silence is serving any of these purposes, it is vital that it not be filled prematurely.

As with the judgment regarding what constitutes too much talk, we rely greatly on the CIQ for guidance. Students will use this form to tell us if and when they're bothered by silence. They will also use it to speak appreciatively of discussions where silence is encouraged as a necessary part of the conversational dynamic. Acknowledging the value of silence takes the pressure off students to act out the role of diligent and engaged participants always ready with an articulate contribution on every issue. In fact, silence bothers teachers much more than it bothers students. Far too many teachers think that if they're not speaking, they're not working. But if good teaching means helping students learn, staying quiet is sometimes the best thing we can do.

WHAT PREVENTS STUDENTS FROM TALKING IN DISCUSSIONS?

Let's now address the problem of unwanted quiet. Why won't students say anything even when they have ideas to express? The problem can usually be traced to one or more of the following factors:

- *Introversion.* Some students are so shy that nothing short of therapy will embolden them to speak.
- *Fear of looking stupid.* Students won't talk because they're afraid of making a mistake by saying something that's considered

daft, unintelligent, or awkward. This is particularly true if certain students or the teacher are models of confident loquacity.

- *Feeling unprepared.* Students feel they are being asked to talk about something about which they know nothing. They're reluctant to speak until they have had time for thoughtful reflection or research.

- *Fearing a trap.* Students won't speak if they sense that teachers are lying in wait for them, waiting to trip them up for saying something stupid; or teachers might be asking students to unveil themselves without teachers ever having spoken from their own hearts.

- *Feeling unwelcome.* Students feel alien in a new cultural landscape. The speech patterns and behaviors of academics are seen as strange, intimidating, deliberately hostile. In this situation, to contribute to discussion means you have sold out to the host culture, joined the enemy. Silence is an act of honorable resistance, a guarding of one's cultural identity.

- *Bad experiences.* Students may have learned from past experience that speaking out in discussions can trigger attacks by other students or teachers. A student who has been mocked and berated for expressing unconventional opinions, challenging groupthink, or contradicting professorial authority will think long and hard before speaking out in class again.

- *Maintaining one's cool.* Speaking up isn't cool. The culture of cool may be so strong in a group that breaking it by contributing seriously to a discussion means losing friends and status. Students sense that the price of talking authentically is an irretrievable loss of face in front of peers.

- *Reliance on the teacher.* If the teacher's doing all the talking, students won't bother to say anything. If you answer your own questions, interrupt students frequently, and jump in to fill silences, students will soon learn that they don't need to speak. Your conversation with yourself will be quite sufficient to fill up the class time.

- *Lack of reward.* If you say you value discussion but award grades based on students' performance on exams, students will put their energy into working to pass those tests. Preparing for and engaging in discussion will not be seen as worth the effort.

How do you judge which combination of these factors is stopping conversation in a given situation? One approach is to analyze the lack of talk through the four lenses of critically reflective practice (Brookfield, 1995). We can see the situation through students' eyes, we can consult our own personal histories as learners, we can talk to colleagues, and we can review the meaning of recurrent silence from different theoretical perspectives.

The most important lens is that of students' eyes. One way to find out why students aren't talking is to ask them. Of course, the contradiction here is that if they're not talking in the first place, they're hardly likely to open their mouths to tell you what prevents them from speaking! So two courses remain. First, the CIQ will probably be helpful since it bypasses some of the problems raised by students' talking publicly about their dislike of discussions. Asking a group of silent students why they're not saying anything is about as useful as asking rabid ideologues to set out the fallacies in their own thinking. Also, the cloak of anonymity provided by the CIQ allows students to express personal distrust of you and their fear of looking stupid without risking censure or being thought uncool. Second, you can consult students from earlier classes who somehow managed to get past the barriers to speech to become active talkers. Chances are that many of the factors that prevented past students from speaking in class are also present in the current situation.

The lens of your own history as a learner constitutes a second fruitful source of examination. If you're an introvert who has found it stressful to talk in groups and who much prefers to be lectured to, you have a wonderful vein of experience to mine. If you have ever felt the fear of looking stupid or uncool in front of peers or if you have ever mistrusted one of your own teachers, you will understand completely how these feelings kill speech. If you are an academic from a working-class background or from an ethnic minority, you will know from the inside the injuries of class and culture inflicted in discussions. If you are a woman who has spent most of her time learning in mixed-gender groups, you know that men often speak first and loudest and that teachers of both sexes tend to take male comments more seriously. If you are a faculty member who is told that teaching counts for tenure but you see abysmal teachers with good publication records being tenured, you know all about the need for reward systems to be consistent. If you are a participant in departmental meetings in which deviation from the party line is always punished, you will know how quickly people learn to express ideologically correct views. If you have ever been asked to give your opinion at a faculty meeting on a matter you have never thought about before and about which you have been given no information, you know how helpless this makes you feel. If you have ever wandered into a conference session expecting to hear a paper being read, only to be told by the leader that "the first thing we're going to do is break into small groups and share our experiences," you'll know how cheated students feel when teachers who refuse to disclose their own thinking ask students to reveal themselves to strangers. In consulting our own history, we relearn lessons that we knew rationally but have forgotten viscerally.

Third, colleagues' perceptions of students' silence can open up new perspectives on this situation. Both of us rely on our colleagues in the various "talking teaching" groups to which we belong to suggest explanations for students' silence that we hadn't considered before. Colleagues are especially helpful in alerting us to new perspectives on our own actions. When we complain about students' not taking discussion seriously and not being willing to say anything, our colleagues will often ask us questions that help us analyze this situation in a new way. By asking such questions as "How did you prepare students for the discussion?" "How did you make sure your voice didn't dominate?" "How did you reward students for speaking?" and "How did you earn the right to ask students to disclose something so personal?" colleagues remind us of important dynamics we may have ignored.

Finally, the lens of theory can help us read familiar situations in new ways. Theory can help us "name" our practice by illuminating the general elements of what we think are idiosyncratic experiences. It provides multiple perspectives on familiar situations. Studying theory can help us realize that what we thought were signs of our personal failings as teachers can actually be interpreted as the inevitable consequence of certain economic, social, and political processes. This keeps us from falling victim to the belief that we are responsible for everything that happens in our classrooms.

In her study of beginning teachers, Britzman (1991) comments that "because they took on the myth that everything depends on the teacher, when things went awry, all they could do was blame themselves rather than reflect upon the complexity of pedagogical encounters" (p. 227). This myth holds a particular power over discussion leaders. Teachers who subscribe to this myth believe that students are silent because teachers are not sufficiently animated or because they don't ask sufficiently provocative or interesting questions. It can be an enormous relief to read a theoretical analysis that helps us view the situation differently.

Reading critical ethnographies of schooling, for example, helps us realize that many students' unwillingness to talk seriously is the predictable consequence of a system that forces them to study disconnected chunks of knowledge at a pace prescribed by curriculum councils and licensing bodies. Reading developmental theory in psychology gives us a new appreciation for the risks students perceive when they have to conduct a critical discussion of previously unquestioned assumptions and perspectives. Reading cognitive psychology reminds us that while some people interpret new information verbally and prefer social learning settings, others are more visual learners or like to exercise self-direction.

RESPONDING TO STUDENT SILENCE

To consider this question, let's take each of the possible causes of silence noted earlier and suggest ways of responding to it.

RESPONDING TO CRIPPLING PERSONAL INTROVERSION

There's probably not much that teachers can do about this, since a class that meets for an hour or two a week over three or four months hardly provides much scope for substantial developmental change. However, two small steps are possible. One thing you can do is make clear at the outset of the course that talking is not the only way students contribute to discussion and that if students choose to stay silent, they will not be penalized or viewed as mentally negligent. An example of this speech policy is given in Chapter Four. The relief this announcement induces sometimes emboldens very shy students to speak. If students still feel too shy to speak after such a declaration, at least they don't feel so inadequate and ashamed about their silence.

The other possibility is to make sure that some sort of electronic discussion is part of the course. Students who are too shy to speak up in groups may find it much easier to make their point on a class bulletin board, chatroom, or listserv. The Internet allows students the time and privacy (though not anonymity) to say what they want to say in the way and at the pace they want to say it. Broadening discussion to include e-mail discourse can bring the most introverted students into the conversation.

Reducing the Fear of Looking Stupid

The fear of looking stupid is a milder form of the kind of crippling introversion discussed earlier. This fear is culturally learned. Students whose past attempts to speak in discussions have been met with ridicule will quickly learn to avoid this embarrassment by not risking any contributions. Four specific steps can help allay this fear.

1. Make sure you begin each discussion with the reminder that in your class there are no stupid questions. Publish the speech policy in the course syllabus, and repeat it regularly in class.
2. If faculty conduct a discussion in front of students at the outset of a course, make sure a debriefing is included. If any of the faculty felt the fear of looking ignorant or unintelligent in the discussion (and chances are they will have), help them talk about this. If students see that the faculty "experts," who supposedly know everything and are possessed of supreme self-confidence, also suffer from this fear, it loses some of its power to stifle speech.
3. Begin a discussion-based course by convening a panel of former students. The panel members are asked to pass on to the new students the best advice they can give on how to survive and flourish in discussions. Chances are good that the theme of looking unintelligent will emerge strongly. Panel members can describe this feeling and talk about how they dealt with it. The new students will feel that their fear is universal, not unique. Knowing that others have shared this feeling and have managed to pass the course will ease their anxieties on this matter.

4. Make sure that before holding a discussion, students are assigned specific tasks or roles that they are to perform in the discussion. Knowing that one has a specific task to perform in the discussion and being able to prepare properly for it before-hand gives a sense of security. It helps reduce the fear that one will be surprised by being asked to speak extemporaneously in the middle of a discussion.

HELPING STUDENTS FEEL PREPARED FOR THE DISCUSSION

If students don't feel prepared to talk intelligently on a discussion topic, they will generally keep their mouths closed. Who wants to risk saying something foolish, thus earning the teacher's disap-proval and the ridicule of one's peers? Chapters Three and Four contain many suggestions for helping students prepare for their conversations.

COUNTERING STUDENTS' MISTRUST OF YOU

This problem cannot be dealt with quickly or easily. Mistrust of teachers is learned early in many students' lives, and it is reinforced by their experiences and confirmed by their peers' comments. It may be that students won't trust you no matter what you do. But some things are possible.

Conducting a faculty discussion and starting with a panel of former students—both mentioned earlier—also work well to build trust. Modeling your own engagement in discussion earns you the right to ask students to do this. Having previous students talk about the feelings of mistrust they had for you demonstrates that you mean what you say about honoring all voices, no matter how critical.

When you report on students' CIQ comments at the start of a new class, make sure you give full public acknowledgment to crit-icisms made of your own conduct in and contributions to last week's discussion. Seeing you do this nondefensively, week in and week out, will convince some students that you mean what you say about welcoming criticism. Modeling self-critique this way helps students believe that you can be trusted not to penalize them for saying something that contradicts your own opinion.

Also, if you're asking students to discuss something that involves them in any kind of self-disclosure or personal revelation, make sure you go first. Speak from your own experience about things that are highly personal, that make you squirm with embarrassment when made public, and that part of you would rather keep secret. If teachers give of themselves first, they stand a better chance of breaking down students' fears that their self-disclosures will not be matched by a similar openness on the part of teachers.

Helping Students Feel Welcome

Feeling unwelcome and not trusting faculty are undoubtedly linked. However, the sense of exclusion we're talking about here involves feeling separated from other students as well as from faculty. Students who feel that their class, culture, or race marks them as different from the majority often feel surrounded by alien and hostile speech and behavior. We have dealt with this situation at some length in Chapter Seven. Beyond what we said there, we suggest the following actions:

1. In any comments you make about your own expectations of discussion participants, make it clear that you will monitor and act against any speech that is hostile to persons who are not part of the dominant culture. If you are a member of the dominant culture (as many college teachers are), acknowledge your position of privilege. But don't do this in a guilt-induced display of self-abasement. You shouldn't feel ashamed of your class or ethnicity.

2. If you open your course with a panel of previous students, make sure you choose as participants some who will act as cultural brokers. These are minority group students who are trusted by members of that group. Such students perform several functions: they communicate students' concerns to the teacher, they interpret the teacher's behaviors and requests to other students in comprehensible ways that keep the teacher informed about how her actions are being perceived and about how the students are experiencing their learning, and they vouchsafe the teacher's honesty and sincerity to students who would otherwise be skeptical or hostile.

3. If the subject matter allows for this, try to ground the discussion in students' personal connections to the subject itself or in their experiences as learners in this area. An example of this would be to introduce the sociological and anthropological concepts of class and culture to working-class students by asking them to contrast what they consider to be examples of working-class behavior or thought with what they define as middle-class conventions and norms.

DRESSING WOUNDS THAT BURN

The wounds inflicted from being "put in one's place" in a discussion (whether by a teacher or a group of one's peers) take a long time to heal. Repeated assurances from new teachers that any and all views are welcome and that anyone can say anything without repercussions will be viewed skeptically by anyone who has been chastised in the past for speaking "too frankly" in a discussion. Over time, however, five factors may help assuage this skepticism.

1. If you start a course with a panel of former students and (when you're out of the room) these former students assure new students that you won't penalize them for dissenting or critical views, this goes a long way toward emboldening those new students to risk speaking out.

2. If you as a teacher model your acceptance of critical comments by quoting students' criticisms of your views and actions that have been recorded on the CIQ and if you respond nondefensively and openly to these criticisms, you will gradually convince some people that you mean what you say about welcoming challenges to your ideas.

3. Any time a student makes a comment that's critical of you, thank the person for the comment; if other students jump in to save you, intervene immediately. Say that a commitment to open discourse is indivisible and that you are trying to preserve the critical student's right to voice an honest alternate view. Point out that without critical voices, people get caught in groupthink and teachers get comfortable with their image of their own competence. Ask the critical student to say more about the expressed criticisms and let other students know that you are trying to guard all viewpoints.

4. At the start of the course, you will have developed ground rules
   for respectful discourse. If a rule requires that dissenting views
   and critical comments be heard, enforce it. Call a time-out
   every twenty to thirty minutes, and ask students to do some
   structured devil's advocacy, arguing against the prevailing tenor
   of opinion in the discussion.
5. If students are unwilling to offer alternative or challenging perspectives, make sure that you do this yourself. In lectures and
   in the discussion itself, make sure you regularly argue against
   your own ideas or against an emerging consensus in the group.
   Point out ideas and information you have omitted, ethical and
   moral dilemmas you have glossed over, contradictions in your
   position you have ignored, and questions you have chosen not
   to address because you don't have answers to them.

Making Talking Cool

The culture of cool can be so ingrained in some students that there
is often little a teacher can do to overcome this. However, three
things are worth considering. First, allowing students to make their
comments through e-mail may persuade them that the privacy
this affords allows them to contribute without destroying their
image. Any behavior that leaves you looking like a teacher's pet in
front of your peers can seem uncool. But when peers are present
only electronically, the importance of being cool is greatly diminished. You can't hear anyone snicker or see them roll their eyes at
your comments when you're sitting alone at a keyboard. And given
the curious inversion of status whereby computer proficiency is now
actually considered cool, some students may be much more
inclined to contribute electronically.

Second, you can try to include on the panel of former students
that are brought in at the start of a course some members who are
generally regarded as cool. (This presumes, of course, that you
are able to identify these people.) The presence of these students
does a lot to reassure new students that participating in discussion doesn't blow one's cool. Third, teachers can make clear that
the ultimate price students might pay for their coolness is failing. If
you truly believe that students who never speak are in some way in
dereliction of their responsibilities as discussion group members,
you need to make that fact clear early in the course and repeat that

message regularly. You can provide a midterm review of students' performance or some interim evaluations of their progress that makes the consequences of their not contributing very clear. By telling students halfway through a course that if this were the end of the course they would fail because they have never spoken in discussion, you bring home to them the consequences of their silence. Of course, students may choose to continue to stay out of discussions. But at least they can't turn around at the end of the course and complain that they didn't know that speaking in discussions was necessary for a passing grade.

MAKING SURE TALKING IS REWARDED

We emphasized the importance of creating a reward system for discussion in Chapter Two. Here we would just add the recommendation that you check early on that students understand the reward system that is in place. One useful way to do this is to ask students to write down their responses to sentences like the following:

I know I've contributed usefully to the discussion when I . . .

The best way for me to show I take the discussion seriously is for me to . . .

Professor X will know I'm participating in the discussion when I . . .

If you ask students to complete one of these sentences at the start of the course, in the middle, and toward the end, the responses should tell you whether or not the students understand how discussion participation is defined and rewarded. If there are discrepancies between students' understanding of what participation looks like and what you're expecting, these need to be publicized and discussed with the group concerned.

WHAT TO ASK YOURSELF WHEN STUDENTS DON'T SPEAK: A CHECKLIST

To end this chapter we would like to propose a list of questions you can ask yourself in the event that discussions are faltering because no one is speaking.

Did students complete preparatory tasks, essays, and other reflective assignments before the discussion began?

Have you built a case for the importance of speaking in discussion by arranging for a panel of former students and cultural brokers to testify to the value of participating in discussion?

Have you modeled public critique of your ideas?

Have you held an opening faculty discussion replete with silence, halting speech, and colloquial language? In the debriefing to this discussion, did faculty acknowledge their fears of looking foolish?

Have you created possibilities for students to participate in the discussion through electronic means?

Have you helped the group set ground rules that deal with hate speech?

Is the part of the grade given for discussion participation defined by specific indicators that acknowledge silent contributors?

Have you checked that students understand these indicators?

Is the discussion focused on an open-ended question of sufficient complexity and ambiguity?

Have you ensured that you've avoided answering the question you've posed, either implicitly or explicitly?

Have you allowed enough time for silence and acknowledged its value in your opening speech policy?

Have you assigned tasks and roles to the group members, especially the rotating role of critical opener?

Have you tried to link the discussion topic to a critical event in students' previous experiences?

Have you researched the causes of the silence through CIQs or some other form of classroom research?

If you have answered all these questions in the affirmative and students still won't talk, perhaps it's time to retreat, temporarily, from your commitment to discussion. A sustained refusal by students to participate in discussion is a message to a teacher to regroup and rebuild. It's their way of telling you to back off, one of the few forms of sabotage available to disaffected students. You should not construe their silence as a personal failure (though we guarantee this is exactly what the great majority of readers of this book do). Instead, you should realize that practicing the art of democratic discourse is demanding and difficult. There is no shame for them, or for you, if people are not ready for this task. Better for you to take a step backward and work on providing the cognitive and behavioral scaffolding that will help students learn democratic talk. If this means you lecture more, give more directions than you would like, do some intentional education about democratic processes, and work on assigning students simple speech tasks, so be it. You are still engaged—in the early stages—in the project of critical conversation.

CHAPTER TEN

KEEPING TEACHERS'
VOICES IN BALANCE

In this chapter we turn our attention to the roles, responsibilities, and actions of the discussion leader. If students are going to feel that discussion invites them to develop and express their ideas in an unpressured way, the discussion leader must find a way to teach that is neither too dominant nor too reserved. Although discussion leaders sometimes interject new material or introduce leading viewpoints from current scholarship, this should be done as sparingly, dialogically, and concisely as possible. As we stress in Chapter Three, lectures can be delivered in a way that discourages students from merely echoing the views of the teacher. Teachers should share their knowledge and understanding in discussion only to help students gain a personal and critical perspective on what is learned, not to show off in front of them.

At the same time, the leader should not be so reticent that the students lack any basis for understanding new ideas or are constantly attempting to second-guess the leader's outlook and beliefs. Democratically inclined teachers are frequently silent in discussion, curbing the compulsion to say all they would like to say in the interests of promoting engagement and participation. Still, they do have a responsibility to teach—to guide the process of conversation, to invite student involvement, to express a point of view, to foster critical commentary, and to model the dispositions of democratic discussion. Whether actually speaking or not, discussion leaders must remain alert and active, constantly on the lookout for ways to encourage students to contribute and to help them make comments that respond to their classmates' observations. No matter how sensitive or careful we are as teachers, however, the problems of speaking too much or too little, too forcefully or too tentatively, are always there.

Before going any further, though, we wish to issue one strong caveat. We believe that achieving the perfect balance of teacher talk to student talk is impossible. We can never reach a point of exact equilibrium where everyone feels that all participants are speaking for just the right amount of time. However, we do think it is possible to gauge how close or far we are from this ideal position. Our voices can definitely be out of balance. This chapter will examine some of the assumptions and practices that help teachers keep their voice closer to the balanced ideal.

WHEN TEACHERS SAY TOO MUCH

One of the authors of this book is known for being an especially passionate teacher. His eagerness to share his knowledge and to stimulate lively exchanges of ideas is evidenced in his loud and enthusiastic voice and excited, even zealous reactions to his students' contributions. Many of his students profess to enjoy this sort of teaching, favorably citing in course evaluations his enthusiasm and obvious love of the subject matter. In recent years, however, it has come to his attention (primarily through CIQs) that although this kind of teaching is appreciated by some students, it tends to discourage the participation of others. They are intimidated by his loud, brash manner and are inhibited by an enthusiasm that strikes them as forced or artificial. They also find it difficult to contribute their views because the discussion moves too quickly or because the teacher seems intent on filling up all the available talking space by reacting to virtually every student comment.

This example goes right to the heart of the problem of when discussion leaders' voices are out of balance. In many cases, teachers dominate quite unintentionally and with the approval and collusion of students. They receive praise from many students for exercising a high degree of control over what and how the students learn. This kind of control emerges instinctively and naturally, without much reflection or scrutiny. Teachers teach the way they were taught, and often their most fondly recalled classrooms were dominated by charismatic and passionate teachers. Such teachers offer high entertainment value and expect their students to emulate them. They are less focused on helping students develop their own understanding of the subject matter and are rarely willing to share the spotlight with others in the classroom.

In what ways does too much commentary on the part of teachers limit learners' participation? Under what circumstances does too much enthusiasm actually constrain some students? And how can the instructor's passion and knowledge be used as a bridge to student participation and engagement, rather than as a barrier to involvement?

There is no simple resolution to these questions. It is undeniable that teachers possess knowledge, expertise, and experience that the students frequently lack. To this extent, we have power. As hooks (1994) points out, power itself is not by definition negative, coercive, or abusive—it depends on how it is exercised. In students' eyes, teachers have attained their position by virtue of their erudition and scholarship in a particular field. To pretend otherwise is seen by students as false humility, naiveté, or an abdication of one's professorial responsibilities. But a teacher's knowledge and power can be used in a variety of ways. Certainly, it can distance the teacher from students and underscore the teacher's superiority. Sometimes, however, it can be used to enlighten students and arouse their interest in the subject matter. At other times it can be a springboard to a more collaborative and student-centered learning process. We believe that the teacher's authority must be viewed as a means to promote student growth. It can be employed most constructively to inspire students, to help them find their own voices, to model a commitment to critical conversation, and to honor the individual and collective knowledge that students invariably hold.

We also believe that enthusiasm is generally desirable as long as occasionally it's balanced with periods of calm restraint. Teachers who are unremittingly ebullient about everything that transpires in the classroom come across as affected and undiscriminating. To more introverted students, this constant display of enthusiasm is insincere and exhausting. Since they can never match this Robin Williams–like level of improvisational energy when they come to speak, and since it requires a degree of strength and confidence to interrupt a teacher who is bouncing off the walls with enthusiasm, students slip easily into the role of passive audience. Struggling to find a balanced voice involves teachers in researching when this kind of high enthusiasm is appropriate and desirable and when silence or a subdued tone is more suitable. Furthermore, being responsive to the diverse personalities and learning styles that are encountered in classrooms requires teachers to vary their ways of communicating.

One reason we commit ourselves to democratic discussion is because we think it helps students find their own voices and develop their own understanding of the subject matter. One of the first steps teachers can take in the pursuit of balance is to recognize student knowledge and experience. By drawing on the collective wisdom found in all classrooms, everyone benefits. Students learn more, develop appreciation for how widely knowledge is distributed, and come to understand that learning is a social process. Although education may take many forms, we believe that the most meaningful and memorable learning occurs when people have a shared, communal experience, guided by teachers who are at least as interested in getting to know their students as they are in helping them master the subject matter.

WHY DO TEACHERS TALK TOO MUCH?

Why do some teachers feel compelled to speak so much in discussion? Let's look more closely at the unwitting tendency of some teachers to dominate the discussion. We think there are five reasons why this happens.

TEACHERS MISUNDERSTAND THE NATURE OF KNOWLEDGE

Teachers are socialized to believe that they have acquired valuable information and understandings that must be passed on to students through lectures, articles, books, and other means. Didactic transmission to students is frequently the only teaching method they employ. Of course, good lecturers and authors can be highly engaging and interactive, and what they do remains an indispensable part of teaching. However, it is our contention that in everyday life, knowledge is not so much given and received as constructed by people individually and collectively (Bruffee, 1993; Stanton, 1996; Tarule, 1996; Maher and Tetreault, 1994). Even the most familiar material is renewed through questioning, criticism, discussion, and deliberation. In fact, education is not so much an accumulation of knowledge by students as it is a "process of acculturation into an interpretive community" (Damrosch, 1995, p. 135). It entails students becoming familiar with the language and procedures of various disciplinary communities and the development of the critical skills needed to define the boundaries and limitations of those communities.

But education also involves illuminating these disciplinary discourses by connecting them to the everyday experience of people from diverse communities. This means specifically that we don't really understand a topic until we have had the opportunity to see how our own experiences—our personal troubles, C. Wright Mills (1956) called them—intersect with what are perceived to be the wider society's public problems. Although we shouldn't allow our personal experiences to define our understanding of the issue or topic, neither should we allow received research or theory to determine our approach to the subject matter. Knowledge is not something that is held by individuals regardless of context and relationships. It is shaped and altered by the different environments in which it is constructed. Far from being acquired by autonomous agents, it is made cooperatively and held in common (Davis and Sumara, 1997).

Since learning conceived this way is largely a social process, pedagogies that take the social nature of learning seriously tend to be more successful. Students report that when they have opportunities to discuss, critique, and relate the material to their own lives, it becomes more meaningful and memorable, more connected to their understanding of the world. They also tell us that when learning is social and discussion is widely used, their educational experiences tend to be more satisfying and regarded as things they would enjoy reexperiencing in the future (McKeachie, 1978; Bruffee, 1993).

TEACHERS ARE UNCLEAR ABOUT THE PURPOSES OF EDUCATION

An important purpose of higher education is to help students see the link between their current experiences and understandings and the ideas they encounter in college. They can make this connection only if time is set aside for them to articulate who they are and what they believe and to have these identities and beliefs count for something. The implication of all this is clear: teachers need to take time to reflect on the purposes of education and on the degree of consistency between their avowed purposes and their actual practices. Many teachers, even those using largely didactic methods, say that students should acquire a new appreciation for the subject matter as well as an increased ability to write, speak, and think clearly and critically about this material. Yet classrooms that are teacher-centered are unlikely to allow students to wrestle with new understandings.

Deborah Meier has said that a good education and a good life can be conceived similarly (Wiseman, 1995). Both entail the desire and ability to participate in an increasingly more complex and engaging conversation. If this is so, then giving students the opportunity to sharpen their conversational and deliberative skills is one of the most important things we can do. This means that teachers must frequently step aside to allow students to construct their own knowledge and understanding. They must reflect continuously on the educational outcomes they seek, ensuring that their practices are consistent with their deepest hopes for their students.

TEACHERS SUCCUMB TO THE EXPECTATIONS OF OTHERS

Sometimes instructors dominate classroom interactions because they think they're supposed to—it's what the institution expects, it's what their colleagues do, and it's what the students demand. After all, if a student has signed up for the class because of the instructor's expertise (so the student's argument goes), that instructor should make every effort to display that expertise and have learners emulate and acquire it. Teachers are socialized early in their careers to believe that they must take responsibility for maintaining the pace of the class, for keeping up student interest, and for enlivening things when the proceedings become too dull. In this conception of teaching, everything revolves around the teacher. If learning doesn't occur, it's the teacher's fault. If it does occur, the teacher also gets the credit. This is the myth that "everything depends on the teacher" (Britzman, 1991).

This myth is so widely held that it will probably never be entirely overturned. Even teachers who have a less authoritarian view of the instructor's role are frequently conditioned by the "collective patterns of expectation and behavior" of their students (Davis and Sumara, 1997, p. 114). When teachers attempt to set a new standard for learning and teaching, the expectations held by colleagues and students inevitably constrain their freedom of action. Our actions are not wholly determined by these expectations, but they often constitute a formidable barrier to changing norms and expectations for classroom interactions.

Our view is that teachers who dominate the class by filling every vacant conversational space with the sound of their voice prevent students from learning. A skillful teacher uses both voice and knowledge to enhance students' participation and understanding. Conceived this way, skillfulness means working tirelessly to get students talking to one another. There is nothing passive about this role. It requires teachers to be active listeners and participants, constantly on the lookout for new connections, new understandings, and new constructions of the familiar and the obscure.

Both of us are occasionally criticized by students for not speaking up more in class. They tell us, "You have so much to share, and yet you contributed so little. I'm all for student participation, but you know more than me. I think you cheat me by not interjecting more of your ideas." Although we are probably guilty of being too absent from some discussions, we think this criticism also indicates that we have done a poor job of communicating the facilitative role we are attempting to play.

We do not see ourselves as the class's repository of knowledge. Our responsibility is to model the dispositions of critical discussion while assisting the class in collaboratively exploring the material to be learned. We want students to speak and think with as much clarity and rigor as possible and to accomplish this in a setting that is collaborative and deliberative. How much we actually contribute to the discussion as individuals is not the issue. Our voices are not, by definition, the most important. They are but two of many that are heard in the complex mix of contributions that constitute the discussion. Until teachers, students, and other community members understand the need to blur the distinction between teaching and learning, viewing them as part of a continuous whole, it will be difficult to challenge the dominance of the teacher's voice.

TEACHERS UNDERESTIMATE STUDENTS

Teachers sometimes underestimate their students, assuming that students are poorly prepared, unaccustomed to thinking critically, and unable to learn difficult material. Teachers who assume these things at the outset of a course usually conclude that the greatest service they can render their students is to lead them by the hand, telling them point by point what they need to learn. This leads directly to didacticism or to discussions that are carefully directed and controlled by the teacher.

These assumptions about students can be badly misguided. First, students may know a lot more than they're given credit for. Adult learners in particular have a vast storehouse of experience and a reservoir of practical wisdom that can add immeasurably to any class. The point is that teachers must leave plenty of room for students to show what they know. Second, even when students are poorly prepared or seem to lack knowledge, what they need more than anything else are opportunities to hone their skills of speaking, listening, writing, and thinking. They will miss these opportunities if the instructor attempts to do too much of the speaking and thinking for them. Furthermore, as we noted in Chapter One, when people come together to explore complex issues, they often reveal a depth of knowledge and a collective wisdom that greatly exceeds what they might have appeared to be capable of as individuals.

What we're really advocating here is that teachers adopt the kind of methodological belief, in this instance about students' capabilities, that we described in Chapter Seven. As we approach a new course, let's assume that students do know, and can do, a great deal. And let's ask ourselves what it means for our teaching if we credit students with ability and skill.

TEACHERS OVERESTIMATE THE VALUE OF THEIR OWN CONTRIBUTIONS

This is a tricky one. By asserting this, we may be undermining the value of the very book you hold in your hands. So be it. Teachers have accumulated a lot of knowledge. Some of it is useful to people, and a lot of it isn't. Our contention is that no matter how much teachers know, only a small part of it can be usefully and effectively conveyed to students. Teachers should confine themselves to a reasonable quota of lecturing minutes per class, preferably at the beginning or the conclusion of a class. These brief lectures should be prepared thoughtfully to make the most of this time and to capitalize on the students' undivided attention. If the rest of the class is devoted to discussion, teachers must select their conversational openings with care. When to respond to a student's comments, when to ask a question, when to move the discussion in a new direction, when to alter the discussion format from large to small groups—these are difficult decisions that should be made thoughtfully and sensitively.

In general, reticence on the part of the discussion leader is a virtue. The leader's contribution can interrupt the momentum of a stimulating exchange or get in the way of a student who is speaking up for the first time. It can also effectively steal the spotlight away from a student who has worked through some difficult ideas. If the teacher is an active but relatively nonverbal participant, the discussion can become focused on the ideas of the students and their struggle to make meaning. This goal is almost certainly more valuable than whatever the teacher might want to say. It takes work to know when to maintain silence, and sometimes it's necessary to intervene. But if the focus of instruction is really on the students' efforts to learn and understand, deference to their ideas and opinions, by staying silent, is one of the discussion leader's greatest strengths.

When Teachers Say Too Little

In general, saying too little is a much less common problem among teachers than saying too much. Teachers' professional socialization and students' expectations make it far more likely that teachers will dominate classroom discussions. But sometimes there is a tendency among teachers striving to encourage greater participation among students to become overly passive. Teachers who are excessively reserved can cause students to feel that they are losing their intellectual bearings. This badly undermines the inclination to learn and leads students to become obsessed with second-guessing the instructor's beliefs. This can be discouraged by teachers' being forthright about their intellectual positions and ideological stances. But there is one major proviso to this. When sharing our ideas with students, we must model a rigorous critical scrutiny. Students must see us consistently applying the same standards of critical analysis to our own ideas as we expect them to apply to theirs.

Why Do Some Teachers Say Too Little?

As in the case of teachers who dominate discussions, teachers who are overly reticent share some mistaken understandings about the conditions that promote learning.

Teachers Assume They Belong on the Sidelines

With a certain level of ambivalence, we have stated that when in doubt, teachers should keep silent. However, we have also argued just as strongly that this does not imply passivity. Teachers must be active listeners, carefully tracking what students say so they can intervene when necessary to keep the discussion moving. This intervention may be a simple one-word prompt or nonverbal gesture. It may call for a question or a supportive comment. Or it may mean doing nothing more than continuing to be an alert member of the group. However, if the criteria for judging whether or not good conversation is occurring include the amount of participation on the part of students, their willingness to be constructively critical, or their ability to make claims that are supported by evidence, teachers will have to model these behaviors. Students need to see teachers taking responsibility for getting participants talking and thinking, collaborating and critiquing.

Benjamin Barber (1993) writes about three forms of leadership—founding, moral, and enabling—that have relevance for teaching through discussion. Although enabling leadership is closest to the sort of teaching we have advocated (and the kind Barber most strongly endorses for a democracy), we believe that founding and moral leadership must sometimes precede more participatory approaches. Founding leaders establish a structure or introduce a process that makes broad participation possible, but in doing so they initially play a quite active role. They do this to help others become able and willing to contribute. Moral leaders model behaviors conducive to democratic participation and enact what they later ask their students to do. Moral leaders also inspire people to get involved and to develop such a strong commitment to participation, cooperative deliberation, and mutual respect that they eventually cannot imagine participating in a class that is structured in any other way. So although an important goal of discussion is to promote student participation and group problem solving, the means to that end may at different points require instructors to take strong pedagogical leads.

TEACHERS FAIL TO MODEL EXPECTATIONS FOR STUDENTS

We have said it repeatedly, but we will say it again: whatever students are asked to do must first be modeled and demonstrated by the teacher. This responsibility requires teachers intermittently to dominate the proceedings. When students are called on to share their stories, critique their own work, or summarize what has been said so far, these skills must have been demonstrated—often repeatedly—by the teacher. Doing this establishes credibility with the students and lets them see what a reasonably good performance looks like. If we expect students to do something capably, we should be able to model it capably. We know that students learn from us, but we also hope that in emulating us, the quality of their work will surpass our own.

TEACHERS ARE UNCLEAR ABOUT THE PURPOSES OF EDUCATION

Embedded in the two points just discussed are claims about the proper purposes of education. As important as it is to get students talking, especially to one another, just doing this is not the end of the story. We believe that discussion groups are crucibles for the democratic process. They help students learn to think through problems collaboratively, to work with others so that the group's interests transcend those of any one person, and to encourage their peers to grow as members of a deliberative community.

Unless teachers are clear about these purposes, they may be inclined to remove themselves prematurely from the discussion, particularly if student participation is high. Although it is desirable for teachers' voices to be less and less present in discussions as the semester progresses, they must look for signs that the discussions are truly productive before absenting themselves too much. These signs include a willingness on the part of students to critique their own and others' ideas; a tendency to use both personal experience and scholarly authorities to support their claims; a habit of posing questions to their peers for clarification and elaboration, rather than waiting impatiently to add another comment; and an inclination to use discussion to show appreciation to others and to affirm the willingness to participate.

TEACHERS UNDERESTIMATE THE VALUE OF THEIR OWN IDEAS

As radical educators have acknowledged (Gore, 1993; Shor and Freire, 1987), there is nothing inherently wrong with lecturing. Teachers have scholarly knowledge that is useful to students, and there should be a way, either through occasional short lectures or in the course of interactions with students, to share this knowledge concisely. Teachers experienced in democratic theory and the democratic process can be very effective in using this knowledge (for example, by asking provocative questions at key moments) to create the conditions for highly participatory discussion.

Finally, we know that one of the reasons people go into teaching is because they can't wait to communicate what they've learned. They take great pleasure in sharing important ideas or telling a story that has meant a great deal to them. Although it's very easy for teachers to overdo this and to satisfy their performative impulses by turning their students into captive audiences, there should be a place in even the most democratic and open of classrooms for teachers to share their knowledge. However, this expression of knowledge should always serve to foster student participation, group deliberation, and communal learning.

THE RIGHT BALANCE: NEITHER DOMINANCE NOR ABSENCE

Here are some suggestions for achieving the right balance in your use of discussion.

AVOID IMPROMPTU LECTURETTES

Many—perhaps even most—teachers in discussion-oriented class-rooms think nothing of interrupting conversation to launch into a ten- or fifteen-minute oration on a topic that emerges from the group's exchange. This impulse to deliver impromptu monologues should be avoided at all costs. Because they are extemporaneous, they tend to be bad lectures. It takes a great deal of skill to lecture dialogically in the manner described by Shor (1992). You must be well versed in the subject of the discussion, have listened very care-fully to what students have said, and be able to draft an outline of your comments in your head while still facilitating the discussion.

Impromptu lecturettes also interrupt the flow of the conversa-tion, inhibiting some students and intimidating others. If you want to address a point that arises in discussion, control the impulse to respond at length and instead make a note to yourself that you will deal with it later. Keep a notebook with you in which to jot down your reactions to the discussion so that you can organize your thoughts for a presentation of these reactions at a more appropriate time. Inci-dentally, in calling on teachers to avoid impromptu lecturettes, we want to repeat that we are not saying they should refrain entirely from participation. Intervention is sometimes necessary to move the dis-cussion going, but it should be done as succinctly as possible.

USE CRITICAL INCIDENT QUESTIONNAIRES

As we have shown throughout the book, the CIQ is a useful way to get information about classroom processes. If students think the leader is dominating discussion or staying too removed, they will say so in the CIQ. Since the CIQ is anonymous, it is the likeliest source of frank information about your dominance or reticence. But even in the CIQ students are sometimes reluctant to be critical of their instructor. The fact that the CIQs say nothing about your voice being out of balance doesn't rule out the possibility that this is a problem.

VIDEOTAPE YOUR TEACHING

Having their practice videotaped feels artificial to some teachers, who freeze as soon as the VCR record button is pressed. If you can't stand to look at a video recording of yourself, an audio recording will probably do just as well. The point is to be able to see or hear for yourself how much you control the course of discussion or how much you remove yourself from the exchange of ideas. Look for the relative percentages of student-to-student talk and teacher-to-student talk. Watch out for times when you interrupt or stall conversational momentum. Are there moments when your reluctance to intervene actually prevents students from keeping the discussion going or from making sense of difficult concepts? When does your silence strengthen the interchange, and when does it get in the way of constructive engagement?

KEEP TRACK OF WHO PARTICIPATES

Another tactic that may work when you fear you are dominating is to maintain a written record of who speaks. This keeps you so busy that you are less prone to excessive participation. It also alerts you to how many students speak between your own comments. If you like to intervene, try making one comment of your own for every four or five that students make. Of course, how much you participate depends not just on the number of students who get involved but also on the thoughtfulness and continuity of their collective deliberations. Interestingly, one of the residual benefits of this strategy is that you end up with a permanent record of the class's discussion, which you can analyze to improve subsequent discussions.

If you don't like the idea of keeping this written record yourself, you may want to ask one or two students to do it for you. This actually presents a number of advantages. First, it frees you of the responsibility to maintain this record. After all, monitoring and facilitating discussion is very hard work even when you don't say anything. Being able to give your full attention to the course of the conversation and to attend carefully to the substance of what individuals say is a real plus. Second, students who assume this responsibility (which should be rotated) are sensitized to the conversational dynamics of the classroom. It helps them see who is dominating and who is silent and how the teacher's participation affects these variables. Third, putting students in the interesting position of enlightening you about your tendency to be too controlling or laid back shows how much you respect and depend on their judgment.

Still another variation on this strategy is to ask a colleague to observe a class and check for participation patterns. Of course, this should be someone you trust, as you may well have to face data that are painful to confront. Observers should be familiar with the tensions of keeping the teacher's voice in balance. The best observers are probably individuals struggling with this in their own practice. The advantage of this method is that when complete outsiders keep a record of the participation patterns in the class, they are unlikely to be biased by particular personalities or preexisting class dynamics.

Written Minutes of the Class

With the help of the record created in the preceding suggestion, minutes of each class can be generated. Students can take turns writing up and photocopying these minutes for the rest of the group. If the minutes are distributed on a regular basis, they can contribute to the group's sense of continuity. Notes from previous discussions become the basis for new conversations. Minutes can be used as a substitute for in-class summaries, since they eliminate the need to spend class time recalling previously covered material. If teachers keep the minutes, they can add written responses to student questions or elaborate on some of the topics raised in the discussion. Although teachers may still want to give brief lectures, minutes provide a space for them to write what they were going to say, leaving more time for the students to grapple directly with the readings or the ideas explored in the minutes.

Call Periodic Time-Outs

As mentioned in Chapter Nine, it is often a good idea to take a break from general discussion to give students a chance to reflect silently on what has been said. A reflective interlude allows students and teachers to note problems or contradictions, to consider unarticulated points of view, and to identify new directions for conversation. Students take a few minutes to jot down their thoughts about these matters, and when everyone is ready, the teacher reopens the discussion by inviting people (especially those who have not yet participated) to read some of what they've written. This slows down the often breakneck pace that heated discussion can activate. It gives students time to think about the ideas that have been exchanged, and it reminds teachers to curtail their participation for the sake of the least aggressive members of the group. It is a helpful check on discussions that are limited to only one or two perspectives and that are dominated by only a few people, particularly if one of those people is the discussion leader.

USE SMALL GROUP EXERCISES

Of course, the surest way to prevent teacher dominance is to remove the teacher from the discussion altogether. This is most effectively done by dividing the class up into the kinds of small groups we discussed in Chapter Six and by giving group members two responsibilities: to stimulate as much participation as possible and to hold each other accountable for mutual comprehension of the topic. What this does not do, however, is address the issue of teachers who are perceived to be too reserved. One way to handle this is to encourage the teacher to migrate from group to group, spending at least a few minutes with each one.

THREE SCENARIOS OF BALANCE AND IMBALANCE

What follows are three short discussion scenarios that focus on how the leader's role affects the course of events. They show a teacher who exerts too much control over the discussion, a teacher who is too aloof, and a teacher who comes close to striking roughly the right balance.

SCENARIO 1: TOO MUCH TEACHER CONTROL

Teacher: The assignment for the day was to read the conclusion of teacher Mike Rose's remarkable autobiography, *Lives on the Boundary* (1990). Rose not only concludes his story with some very concrete examples of how to cross cultural and class boundaries but shows us as well the implications of these examples for shaping educational policy. One of the strengths of the book is Rose's ability to move back and forth between the worlds of classroom practice and national policymaking. What do you think of the way Rose handles this?

Student 1: I guess I didn't notice what you're talking about, but I was really impressed with what he says on page 222 about being hopeful and assuming that good teaching can make a big difference for students.

Teacher: Yes, that's important, but almost the whole chapter that includes the quote you cite shows Rose going back and forth between practice and policy. Let me show you what I mean. *(Reads about a page of material)* Isn't that impressive? One of the things that makes this book great is that the implications for reform emerge from the particulars of everyday teaching. Anybody want to comment on that?

Student 2: I think Rose is a great teacher, but does he really think that every student can learn? Where did he get that faith in everybody?

Student 3: I have the same question, and I'm also disturbed by the fact that this is a story, that it necessarily has a plot. Doesn't the need to have a plot affect the incidents Rose relates and how they get resolved? How much does this really help us understand the messy world of day-in, day-out teaching?

Teacher: I think you are all missing the point. This is a great story about one person's successes and failures in teaching. It has a plot, sure, but that plot can still be translated into proposals for reform. I mean, what do you think Rose's reform proposals would look like?

Student 4: I don't know about school reform, but could we talk about the episode when Rose helps that student make sense of the standardized test she took? With just a little help, she's able to figure

> most of it out. How often do you think that
> happens with our students who regularly do
> poorly on achievement tests?
>
> *Teacher:* Let's take a look at that a little later. I still want
> to know what you think Rose can teach us about
> school reform. *(Long silence)*

The teacher in this excerpt is much too dominant and controlling. He insists on sticking to his own agenda despite his students' resistance. Moreover, he ignores the excellent questions his students raise, each of which could have led to a productive exchange. The teacher clearly likes the book and wants his students to like it too. He is also intent on exploring the "big" issues of policy and reform. His students are much more interested in discussing and questioning its specifics. The potential for enlightening discussion is enormous here; students are taking a lot of initiative, and there is a great deal of participation. Unfortunately, the teacher is just too self-absorbed to see it.

SCENARIO 2: TOO LITTLE TEACHER PARTICIPATION

> *Teacher:* What do you think of the last section of Rose's
> *Lives on the Boundary?*
>
> *Student 1:* I liked it, especially what he says on page 222
> about remaining hopeful and using good
> teaching practices to help even the most poorly
> prepared students.
>
> *Student 2:* I'm not sure why he's so hopeful. Where does
> that faith come from? I've been in lots of situa-
> tions where even the best and most dedicated
> teachers couldn't help their most difficult
> students.
>
> *Student 3:* I have too. Also, even though I liked the way
> Rose tells his story, I'm not sure there's much
> to learn from it. Stories are not like day-to-day
> teaching. There's no plot or climax in real-
> life teaching. Just plugging away and trying
> to make the best of it.

Student 4:   But aren't some of the incidents revealing? What about the example of the student who at first does poorly on the achievement test and then does much better with a little coaching from Rose?

Student 5:   I think Rose knows about underachieving students because he was there once himself.

Student 6:   But he also became a scholarship student. I don't think he does know what it's like to struggle with poor preparation, limited skills, and especially racial discrimination.

Student 7:   Does he still teach writing to students at UCLA, or is he doing something else now?

Teacher: He still teaches writing, but he also has an appointment in the School of Education.

This scenario seems, superficially, an improvement. Seven rather than four students have spoken, so the level of participation is higher. However, although there is enormous potential for discussion in the issues students raise, there is almost no continuity, no attempt to build on individual comments. Instead, the teacher responds to only one question—the one that is the least interesting and least likely to go anywhere. If the teacher had intervened just once or twice, each of the issues raised by students could have been considered and developed much more fully.

For instance, the teacher could have asked the first two students, who appear to disagree, to talk to each other about the citation from page 222. Questions she could have posed are "Does page 222 give any clues to the source of Rose's hope and faith?" and "Where else would we look in the text to support one view or the other?" The whole issue of plot and story also seems rich. The teacher could ask, "In what ways do stories help us understand everyday experiences and practices?" and "In what ways are stories a flawed source?" The point here is not for the teacher to give her own views but for her to ask a question or raise an issue that gets students talking to one another. One final comment: although this discussion is flawed, it is significantly better than the first one in which the teacher dictated the issues to be covered.

SCENARIO 3: A BETTER BALANCE

Teacher: The assignment for today was to read the conclusion of teacher Mike Rose's autobiography,
Lives on the Boundary (1990). Rose not only concludes his story with some concrete examples
of how to cross cultural and class boundaries
but also shows us some of the implications of
these examples for shaping educational policy.
Could you comment on some of these examples and their value for promoting educational
reform?

Student 1: The quote on page 222 was especially important. We must assume that students have potential and ability and then act accordingly. That
should be the basis for all educational change.

Student 2: Maybe, but what makes him so hopeful? Where
does that faith come from? I've seen lots of situations where even the best and most dedicated
teachers couldn't help their most difficult
students.

Student 3: I have too. Although I like the way Rose tells his
story, I'm not sure there's much to be learned
from it. Stories are not like day-to-day teaching.
There's no plot or climax in real-life teaching.
Just plugging away and trying to make the
best of it.

Student 4: But aren't some of the examples revealing?
What about the student who at first does poorly
on the achievement test and then greatly
improves with a little coaching from Rose?

Student 5: I think Rose knows about underachieving students because he was there himself.

Student 6: But he also became a scholarship student at
UCLA. He may have lost touch with those roots.
I don't think he knows what it's like to struggle
with poor preparation, limited skills, and especially racial discrimination.

Teacher: I wonder if we could pause here for a moment and try to bring these interesting and diverse observations together. A number of you characterize Rose as sensitive to the needs of the poorly prepared students. Others question whether the way he tells his story or his position of privilege puts him in a position to understand the most marginalized students. Is there reason to think that both claims are at least partly true?

Student 7: Is he still teaching writing to students at UCLA, or is he doing something else now?

Teacher: He's still teaching writing, but now he has an appointment in the School of Education. But I want to get back to the other point. Can Rose teach us some valuable things about educational reform, or is his stance too idealistic, too removed from the realities of real classrooms?

Student 5: I still think his background as a student who was mistakenly put in the vocational track gives him a valuable perspective on injustice and on the failure to realize the promise of educational opportunity.

Student 6: You know, I forgot about that incident. It probably still has an important impact on his thinking and practice.

Student 3: I just don't trust the story format. He makes it all come out so neatly in the end.

Student 1: Does he? I think he's quite realistic about how much can be accomplished with students who have been neglected and oppressed. All those years of bad education are a great burden, but progress can be made, especially when we retain hope.

Student 3: But his determination to create a narrative of hope frees him of the obligation to recount all the failures, all the partial successes.

Student 2: And why be so hopeful? What's the reason for keeping the faith?

Teacher: I think there may be at least two reasons for doing so, both of which are in Rose.

Student 5: May I?

Teacher: Please, go ahead.

Student 5: Rose is hopeful because there is no other choice. Despair is not a good basis for change.

Student 2: What about revolution?

Student 5: Perhaps, but while we wait for the revolution, Rose shows that if you're patient and try hard to cross boundaries, if you keep looking for ability where others have only seen deficiency, great strides can be made.

Teacher: Rose is like Dewey in a way. He can't imagine being anything but faithful, but it is not a blind faith. It emerges from experience.

Student 2: Well, could we talk about some of those experiences specifically? What are the concrete bases for his educational faith?

Teacher: Let's do that.

Perhaps the thing that most clearly distinguishes this scenario from the others is that here the discussion builds. At first students aren't really conversing, but with a little prompting from the leader, they begin talking and responding to each other. There is clear disagreement, which is tolerated and even encouraged, but with assistance from the teacher, there is also some basis for agreement. The teacher makes seven brief comments in this dialogue, but all but two (first and second to last) are intended to foster increased interaction and continuity. The scenario ends with the promise of much more discussion based on close attention to the text. This probably wouldn't have happened without the teacher's contributions.

Of course, this scenario may come across as a bit too idealistic; good discussions don't materialize as effortlessly as this one seems to. But it is surprising what a difference a few well-placed questions and comments can make. This scenario shows that teachers don't have to intervene constantly or absent themselves entirely to make discussion work.

CONCLUSION

Balance is one of the keys to good discussion. When one or two people dominate the exchange of ideas, the benefits for the whole group are greatly diminished. Similarly, when groups identifiable by gender, race, class, or ideology completely withdraw from the discussion, the range of ideas being explored is greatly reduced. Of course, perfect balance is impossible, but attention to who's speaking and who isn't is one of the crucial elements in making discussion work. The teacher's first concern, however, should center on her own patterns of participation and how these are contributing to or detracting from the efforts of students to deliberate together. Here is a checklist of questions to keep in mind as you continue the struggle to keep your voice in balance.

Is my participation preventing students who want to speak from making a contribution? Have I interrupted students in mid-sentence?

Have I made more comments than all of the other students combined? Do I respond to every student who speaks? Do students pause before responding to each other because they expect me to make a comment after every student speaks?

Am I sticking to my preset agenda for discussion despite alternative suggestions and even resistance from my students?

Are my teaching practices in discussion in contradiction with my goals for the class?

Am I discouraging student participation because I think the students lack knowledge or experience?

Is the discussion faltering because of my own lack of participation?

Does the discussion lack focus because I have contributed so little?

Have I neglected to interject any comments that help students see how their ideas are related?

In general, what am I doing to build continuity and a sense of collaborative engagement?

What am I doing to assess and evaluate the degree to which my voice is in balance in discussion?

CHAPTER ELEVEN

UNDERSTANDING THE DYNAMICS OF ONLINE DISCUSSION

Since the first edition of this book appeared, online education has exploded. Many colleges now offer whole degrees online and, whether they like it or not, most faculty are now having to integrate online teaching into their courses. The two of us were initially very skeptical about this trend to commodify learning and market courses stripped of the presence of a particular teacher. We felt such courses embodied the worst of what the critical theorist Erich Fromm criticized as the alienating features of higher education. Writing of higher education in the twentieth century Fromm argued that the education system equates knowledge with content, with "fixed clusters of thought" (p. 37) that students store. In this system teachers are reduced to "bureaucratic dispensers of knowledge" (1968, p. 120). This disembodied content, transmitted mechanically, is alienated from learners' lives and experiences. To us this captures precisely what we imagined to be the depersonalized nature of online teaching.

We also assumed that the increased institutional enthusiasm for online teaching indicated how cost effectiveness, institutional convenience, and competitive advantage were now driving the engine of higher education reform. We doubted whether online courses could be taught with intellectual integrity and feared for the disappearance of discussion-based teaching altogether. Online environments seemed impersonal and alienating, threatening our wish to form collegial relationships with students. In brief, we were sure that online instruction would take all the spontaneity, personality, and serendipity—all the fun—out of teaching. When online teaching was presented to us as a way to reach students in remote settings, however, our resistance weakened. It seemed to us that we couldn't forgo our responsibility to work with students in hard-to-reach geographic, occupational, or social locations who need education as much as do students who are well placed to attend regular classes.

We suffered the usual precourse jitters before teaching online, this time magnified by the intimidating variable of technology. Would there be enough time to gain all the technical knowledge needed to be successful and to avoid looking foolish? Would we be able to organize the course so that students could easily navigate it? How would we build in opportunities for discussion and leave room for improvisation and spontaneity? What would happen when the computer crashed, when the university shut down its server for maintenance (usually on Sundays when many students working full time relied on completing assignments), when students couldn't access electronic materials or make their required postings? In an online course it also seemed that everything had to be painstakingly planned beforehand and dutifully posted on the class Web site. Nothing, it appeared, could be left to chance.

As it happens, planning and teaching online does have its difficulties. However, though it is time consuming it is also quite manageable. Although some of our initial concerns about teaching online remain, we have been for the most part pleased with how well it can support discussion-based teaching.

The Architecture of a Typical Online Course

Perhaps a useful place to begin is with the typical way in which an online course is organized. Figure 11.1 shows the Welcome Page of one of the courses we have taught.

The Welcome Page is the learner's first contact with the course and accessing it is the equivalent of students walking into the room on the first night of class wondering what awaits them. The Welcome Page typically displays all the links that are available in a course and provides a place for periodic announcements. On the Welcome Page shown here there is a place to learn how to navigate the online

Figure 11.1. Welcome Page

College of Education
Welcome to Ed Lead 501!

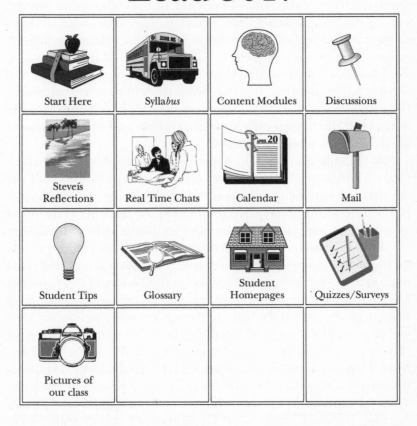

Start Here	Sylla*bus*	Content Modules	Discussions
Steve's Reflections	Real Time Chats	Calendar	Mail
Student Tips	Glossary	Student Homepages	Quizzes/Surveys
Pictures of our class			

course ("Start Here"), a location to review the syllabus ("Sylla*bus*"), and a link to begin to access the course content ("Content Modules"). This third link tells students how they should respond to ideas in the readings and how to engage with each other and the instructor. The fourth link ("Discussions") is where students go to post thoughts with respect to the assigned discussion topics. Although most of the discussion topics for this course were predetermined by the instructor, students may also initiate their own discussion themes within the same link.

Moving down one icon, the next link ("Mail") allows students to exchange e-mail messages with one another and the instructor. To the left of the "Mail" link, the "Calendar" shows most of the course activities and indicates when assignments are due. Next left is the "Real Time Chats" link, the sole outlet for synchronous discussion. Through this link students, as well as the instructor, can meet at agreed upon times to engage in real-time conversation. Left again, "Steve's Reflections" offers another avenue for students to communicate about the content of the class. Here the instructor models the journal keeping that he has asked the students to do, puts forward additional thoughts on the course content, and reflects on the themes emerging from student postings. Although the communication here is largely one way, we have found that students read the instructor's journal carefully and often comment on the most provocative entries.

By clicking on "Student Tips" (located directly underneath "Steve's Reflections") the instructor can record pithy quotes of the day that pop up when students access the Welcome Page. Although this feature was originally designed to expose students to inspiring epigrams, we use it more as an outlet for student ideas. Instead of employing the more typical "quotes from famous people" approach, we highlight "quotes from students in the class." The sayings that pop up each day when students access the Welcome Page are not axioms from remote scholars and pundits but quotes from students that are gleaned from discussion postings, e-mails, journals, and formal papers. The "Glossary" (to the right of "Student Tips") is a list of important terms that are cross-referenced with content modules. Next along the "Student Homepages" link contains individual pages that display images and words composed and posted by students. These are intended to communicate something about students' interests, personal concerns, and professional commitments. Essentially they replace the brief ice-breaker introductions that students are sometimes asked to give at a first face-to-face class meeting. The "Quizzes/Surveys" link to the right of "Student Homepages" is for students to record their reactions to class activities and assignments. This is also where they complete periodic course evaluations such as Critical Incident Questionnaires (CIQs). The final link in the bottom left-hand corner is "Pictures of Our Class." This holds pictures taken of each student during the mandatory face-to-face class orientation. Until students complete their Web pages, this is the only way for the instructor and the members of the class to match student faces to names.

As students make their way through online courses like the one illustrated, they find themselves turning to the "Content Modules" link most frequently for instruction, guidance, and directions about next steps. They are instructed at various times to undertake certain tasks that constitute the learning activities of the course. These include posting a message on the discussion board, participating in a live chat, sending an e-mail, logging a reaction or observation in their journal, or writing a short reflective paper about their understanding of the content presented. Except for the live chats that, by definition, only work if students are online at the same time, all of these activities are undertaken asynchronously; that is, at any time that is convenient for the individual student.

Interestingly, while live chats are the mode of communication that most closely resembles face-to-face discussion, there are enough drawbacks with live chats to relegate them to a subordinate position in most online discussion-based courses. Just like face-to-face discussions, real-time or live conversations exhibit dynamics that are sometimes problematic. At a very basic level, fast typists enjoy a distinct advantage over those with little keyboard experience. Also, unlike a live conversation, there is a delay (sometimes rather prolonged) between the individual typing the words she wants to convey and all other chat participants seeing the words projected on the computer screen. Such delays often result in responses that overlap with each other, leading to multiple lines of communication that can be confusing and disorienting. Since chats cannot work at all unless the group of participants is small, the instructor who decides to rely heavily on them may find herself, particularly in a large class, committing to as many as five or six one-hour chats a week. In Palloff and Pratt's (1999) opinion, live chat "rarely allows for productive discussion or participation and frequently disintegrates into simple one-line contributions of minimal depth" (p. 47). It should be noted, however, that some online instructors have found the strategic use of chat to be an effective way to motivate and energize learners and to "develop a sense of 'social presence' and group cohesion" (Berge, 2000, p. 27). We will have more to say about some of the possible uses and benefits of live chat at different points in this and the following chapter.

Almost by default, then, the primary mode of student-to-student and student-to-instructor interaction in an online course occurs through asynchronous discussion. The advantages of this kind of interaction include its flexibility and convenience, the time it affords learners to reflect and think things through, and the large number of participants that can be accommodated. The instructor can also do a lot to make asynchronous discussions work better. Asking interesting and intriguing questions, responding quickly to student thoughts and questions, and encouraging students to respond to one another's postings are all ways the instructor can integrate asynchronous discussions into the course.

Practicing the 4 Rs in Online Discussion

Virtually everything we know about good face-to-face discussion also applies online. For us teaching online means employing the 4 Rs of discussion-based teaching: research, responsiveness, respect, and relationships.

Research

One of our axiomatic beliefs is that good teachers continuously monitor their teaching practices to assess the impact of these on students. This applies just as much in cyberspace as it does in face-to-face classrooms. Hence, a central feature of online teaching should be the use of classroom assessment procedures such as the CIQ (described in Chapter Three) to solicit information from students about how they are experiencing the class. After collecting students' opinions, instructors regularly report a summary of these to students and consider what they mean for the online environment. Sometimes teachers change features of the online class to make it more satisfactory for students. At other times they have to rejustify and reexplain why they can't change the course organization and why activities that are disliked by learners are integral to students' intellectual development. It is essential that this feedback from students be captured in the form of anonymous, written responses, and securing this anonymity initially posed problems for us in our early efforts teaching online. However, two ways to address this problem are available. First, students can go to the Discussion Postings of WebCT and check a box that automatically records all responses for that particular posting as anonymous. An alternative is to have a students-only course list serve where students post their CIQ responses to each other and then have one of their number compile these and post the summary to faculty.

Since most of the online class activities are asynchronous, it is important to specify on each CIQ the inclusive dates that constitute the "week" in question. Otherwise the questions are the same as for the face-to-face version:

1. At what moment during this week of online class were you most engaged as a learner?
2. At what moment during this week of online class were you most distanced as a learner?
3. What action that anyone took during this week of online class did you find most affirming or helpful?
4. What action that anyone took during this week of online class did you find most puzzling or confusing?
5. What surprised you most about the online class during this week?

After analyzing the CIQ responses using the same procedure outlined in Chapter Three, we report the results in a prominent place on the Welcome Page to ensure that students read them. We also invite students to offer written reactions, questions, and elaborations regarding the CIQ summary that all students in the class can view and consider. Then, based on what is received, we propose, if necessary, a course of action to address the concerns raised.

As valuable as the anonymous CIQs are, they are not the only form of research an instructor might employ. Following Brookfield's (1995) analysis of critically reflective teaching, discussion leaders can also use their autobiographies as learners, their colleagues' perceptions, and educational theory as lenses through which to view their practice. When teachers use the first of these lenses—their autobiographies as learners—they reflect on how it feels to negotiate the strangeness and anxieties of online learning. The intent is to experience what their own students are going through. Before teaching in cyberspace for the first time it is a definite advantage if you can take an online class. Noticing what affirms or demeans you, what helps or hinders your learning in an online environment, helps you understand what will make for a supportive learning environment in your own online course. A minimum recommendation we make to all teachers working online is to secure a special ID that will allow them to view their class through their students' eyes. To enter your own course as if you were a student, without the capacity you possess as the instructor to manipulate and alter the online environment, provides a valuable new perspective on the course. It also brings to the surface the learning approaches you most favor and the knowledge and skills you most value which may, or may not, match those favored and valued by your students.

As an example, entering the online course illustrated in this chapter shows that the instructor emphasizes the close reading of the texts, requires students to show that they understand the key ideas, and uses them to illuminate and problematize students' experiences. Students are clearly expected to respond, almost exclusively, in writing to the questions posed and the assignments required. There is little call for students to use the Internet to gather resources or accumulate relevant images. There are no hands-on projects to do and little or no group work to complete. In other words, this course is almost stodgily traditional in its approach. Despite being online, it makes few allowances for the unique environment in which students find themselves. We often miss such obvious biases until we have the opportunity to see the course from the student's vantage point. Incidentally, Palloff and Pratt (2003) devote an illuminating chapter of their book, *The Virtual Student,* to the importance of creating online courses that appeal to a wide range of student learning styles.

The lens of colleagues' perceptions operates when colleagues observe our teaching or when we ask them for new perspectives on our problems. We have found it helpful while planning our own online courses to have access to similar courses taught by online veterans. Being able to access a colleague's class while it is in progress, see how she organizes the course and handles student-to-student and student-to-instructor interaction, is enormously helpful in putting your own course together. Once your own class is up and running, it is equally valuable to have an experienced colleague sign on as a student or teaching assistant, something that can be easily done through Web-CT. Your colleague can take a quick peek at the class as though she were a student (much more easily and conveniently than is the case in a conventional class) and offer observations about the course's content and organization. It is especially helpful for a colleague to review the discussion postings or the chat records to assess how well class conversations are deepening students' understanding and promoting student participation. Finally, the opportunity to make use of theory as a useful lens on online teaching is the same as it is for conventional teachers, though it should be noted that as more and more research articles are made available online, the best place to access a wide variety of scholarly materials is probably on the Internet.

RESPONSIVENESS

Instructional responsiveness is central to the creation of an effective online learning environment. Such responsiveness is evident when instructors seek out student concerns, share those concerns publicly with students, and take action to address them. Examples of such action are building on students' comments to reorganize the course for ease of navigation or addressing what students say in online discussions. These actions underscore that student issues are heard, taken seriously, and acted upon. We believe that responsiveness more than any other factor contributes most decisively to the success of a discussion-based, online class.

It is important to acknowledge, however, that it is neither possible nor desirable to give students feedback every time they contribute to an online class. First, there are not enough hours in the day to make this work. Second, such an obsessive level of responsiveness only teaches students to become more dependent upon the instructor's comments and approval. Yet if we were to err on one side or the other in an online environment—toward participation or reticence—we would err on the side of high instructor participation. We endorse Fein and Logan's (2003) observation that "From the very beginning of the course, the instructor should foster a high-quality feedback environment by establishing an expectation around the importance of instructor-student and student-student feedback" (p. 53). The reason for this is simple. Learning online can be a lonely, unrewarding experience. It can also breed uncertainty and loss of confidence. When instructors are relatively absent from discussion, students begin to wonder: Why aren't I hearing more from the teacher? What is she doing as I slog my way through these learning modules? What does she think about the quality of my work? Why should I be taking so much time to express my ideas when she takes so little time to acknowledge them?

In our experience the number one complaint from online learners is the low level of instructor responsiveness. Students clearly need to hear from us on a regular basis. In a class one of us conducted while writing this chapter there were some 1,800 discussion postings in all. The instructor was responsible for about 300 of those. The number of postings varies tremendously, of course, depending on how active individual students are. Some post ten or twenty times a day (something they should probably be discouraged from doing), while others post less than once a day. For those who tend to be less engaged, or at least less participatory, we urge frequent responses from the instructor, often in the form of simple acknowledgments or requests for further information. One advocate of online discussion (Bender, 2003) urges teachers to be up-front about their likely level of participation. She writes "making explicit the frequency of your participation in class helps students to anticipate when they will be hearing from you, and also will not give false impressions that just because the class is available 24 × 7, that you are, too" (p. 57).

The following anonymous comments made by students in end of semester evaluations of an online course one of us taught recently illustrate this point:

"The course is much better than I expected. I've mastered the IT challenges and the readings are excellent. The instructor is very interactive. I appreciate the comments he makes to me and what he says to others. I'm impressed that he's able to keep up with four discussion groups. I'm also impressed at how he will respond—he rarely says that someone is wrong—he just presents another view. I look forward to taking another course on line."

"Great online experience because of the sense that the teacher was constantly present and available."

These comments exemplify what the literature concerning online teaching calls the "social presence" of the instructor, which is closely tied to the principle of responsiveness. In one prominent study, Gunawardena (1995) defined social presence as the extent to which someone "is perceived as a 'real person' in mediated conversation" (p. 151). Gunawardena and Zittle (1997) also argue that social presence has two major components—intimacy and immediacy. Both have to do with bridging the physical and psychological distance that exists between instructor and students in online environments. The evidence is fairly strong, according to Gunawardena and Zittle (1997), that "social presence is a strong predictor of satisfaction" in computer-mediated conferencing environments. Drawing on the research of others, Aragon (2003) claims "that social presence facilitates the building of trust and self-disclosure within an online learning context" (p. 61). He asserts that instructors enhance social presence by involving themselves heavily in discussion board exchanges, by balancing their own contributions with those from students, and by providing timely individual feedback (perhaps by responding to student e-mails within a day of posting). He also suggests that instructors chat informally with students who arrive early for live chats with the intent of getting to know them better, and that they include their own personal experiences in any responses they post to students' stories. Instructors who are highly responsive to students in some of these ways can make the difference between an online class that is personable, engaging, and vital and one that is lackluster and uninviting.

RESPECT

Practicing and modeling respect is essential in any learning environment, especially those that are discussion-based. Yet respect is a term so widely employed that it has degenerated into a cliché. Everyone seems to recognize the importance of respect, and yet it has come to mean so many things that it has lost its impact. What does it mean to show or practice respect in online environments in ways that deepen the concept and that do justice to its significance and magnitude?

The root of the word respect is to regard, to look at again, to see discerningly. When we show respect for others we work diligently at seeing them clearly for who they are. We avoid labels and categories, stereotypes and stigmas. Bill Ayers (1993) writes that respect is evident when we ask ourselves certain questions about the people with whom we work. These questions include: "Who is this person before me? What are his interests and areas of wonder? How does she express herself and what is her awareness of herself as a learner" (p. 29)? Respecting people means treating them as unique, distinctive individuals with experiences and interests that set them apart from others. William Isaacs (1999) defines respect as being able "to see a person as a whole being" (p. 110). He refers to a Zulu phrase that people use when they greet one another, *Sawu bona,* meaning "I see you." In Zulu tradition, this greeting brings people more fully "into existence by virtue of the fact that they are seen" (p. 111). To say "I see you" is to affirm another person's being and presence, to acknowledge her as important. It means honoring whatever is unique about someone and finding out all we can about them, without, at the same time, intruding on their privacy. After all, another dimension of respect is learning to accept and recognize boundaries. Only when we are doing these things can we say that we are showing people the respect that they deserve.

One of the ways in which we show respect for our students is to provide a space for them to tell their stories, to share their passions and commitments, and to reveal, if they so choose, little seen parts of themselves. This can be done in an online environment by inviting students to compose their own homepages that tell something of their personal lives and their professional commitments. We have tried to encourage this kind of student participation by producing our own simple homepages as a both a model of what a homepage might be and as a stimulus to those with far greater creative powers to post pages that excite the imagination. We do not suggest that students always recount their personal stories in lengthy prose online. But by utilizing the multiplicity of images that are widely available through the Internet, and by accessing simple and easy-to-use tools that can add color and flair to any Web page, stories can be told dramatically with just a few words and images.

We also try to practice respect by conducting online discussions that take into account the everyday experiences of our students. We do this by pairing questions about the text or the content of the course with questions that ask students to share their individual experiences around a topic. Sometimes we invite them to think about the special challenges that content poses for the professional contexts in which they find themselves. A discussion about organizing for democratic governance, for instance, might take into consideration the special challenges of a school that faces severe overcrowding, or a university whose top-down administrative structure is ineradicably entrenched. A conversation focusing on educational reform might emphasize innovations that occurred in the particular region in which the students find themselves and perhaps even in schools with which they are familiar. Of course this honoring of student experience must ultimately be accompanied by the habit of critically examining and problematizing that experience. A key part of any discussion-based class, whether online or not, must be maintaining a constructively critical dialogue between the direct experience of the students and the theories and wider perspectives found in research papers and texts.

RELATIONSHIPS

There was a time earlier in our careers when we thought it was OK to meet our classes, deliver our lectures, conduct our discussions, collect our papers, and administer our tests without getting to know our students in any significant way. One of us can still remember the epiphany he had in the middle of presenting a lecture to a class of about thirty students. It went something like this:

> There is no question that my lectures are well researched, cogently argued, compellingly and interestingly delivered. I have worked hard to provide these students with the latest and best thinking on this topic. Yet I can't help thinking that despite all the good things that are happening here this is a missed learning opportunity. One person is talking, albeit a well-informed and experienced speaker, but what is being said could be presented to these students in written form without losing all that much. But what is irretrievably lost are the voices, ideas, and experiences of the students themselves.

There are thirty people out there that I am not learning from, thirty
people whose ability to teach everyone else is going untapped.
There is something sad, even tragic about this situation. The only
way to redeem this class is to alter completely the way in which it is
structured, so that the voices of the students count at least as much
as my own.

Since that epiphany the class experiences that have meant the
most to us, and about which we retain the strongest memories, are
the ones where we have formed long-term relationships with students. Those relationships have emerged from our commitment
to show respect for students' experiences and knowledge, and our
recognition that teaching and learning don't end at the conclusion of class or when we step outside the classroom. However, relationships with students don't just exist for their own sake, but
because they enhance and deepen the learning we enjoy together.

How do we begin to build such relationships online? In part by
taking seriously the 3 Rs already mentioned. We stay curious about
our students by continuing to *research* how they experience our
teaching and their learning. We practice *responsiveness* by staying in
close touch with them and by replying promptly to their inquiries
and concerns. And we *respect* our students by seeing them in all
their uniqueness and complexity and by taking seriously the ways
in which they understand the world. The fourth R—*relationships*—
obliges us to go farther, particularly when we teach online. This
need impels us to create multiple ways for students to get to know
us and for us to get to know them.

As unwieldy and difficult to arrange as live, online chat can be,
it is one of the best ways to build relationships. It works best with a
very small group of two or three students, or even just one-on-one.
The competition for airtime largely becomes irrelevant in such a
situation, and the problem of fast versus slow keyboardists fades
away. The logistics of scheduling such chats is probably the biggest
problem, and the challenges for an instructor with a large class can
be particularly daunting. But if we can address these organizational
problems, an occasional live chat is most likely time well spent.

Telephone office hours can also be a useful alternative in relationship building. Phone chats can be held at designated times each
week when students can confer with instructors. As impersonal as

telephone conversations might be, the ability for instructors and students to hear each other's voices and to have a relatively normal or synchronous conversation is a huge bonus for everyone online. One-on-one telephone conversations—where tone, tenor, and attitude count as much as the words exchanged—are an obvious and important way to build and deepen relationships.

It is also important to try and find time for periodic face-to-face meetings, either at the university or at the student's worksite. Of course, a major reason for resorting to online classes is to support students who are unable to travel to campus. This option is attractive, then, only to those students who have the capability to visit campus, or to instructors who have the time and support for travel to visit remote sites that are convenient to their students. At the same time, it is probably true that the best way to optimize online teaching and learning is to build in time for face-to-face meetings, both with the whole group and individuals. We strongly believe that a live, face-to-face orientation at the beginning of any online class lays the groundwork for relationship building. If possible, midterm and culminating face-to-face classes should also be scheduled. There is no substitute for live interactions as a way to build and sustain long-term relationships and to make the online experience less lonely and alienating.

This chapter has argued that the dynamics of good teaching online are essentially the same as those in the face-to-face classroom. Online teachers should treat students respectfully, conscientiously research the online learning environment, make responsiveness a cardinal value, and pay attention to building relationships both with, and among, students. We have tried to show that the online environment does not present insuperable obstacles to any of these dynamics, but that its own internal features need to be recognized and worked around.

The one complication we acknowledge is that most of the teachers we know (including the two of us) who teach online have spent most of their years as elementary, high school, and college learners in conventional face-to-face classrooms. This learning history inevitably frames the approach they take to teaching in an environment fundamentally different from the one they know as learners. This is why we advocate taking a class online before teaching one. In an ideal world we would insist that any enthusiastic dean, vice president, or president who urges an expansion of online education in their institution provide at least two course releases; one in the semester or quarter prior to beginning online teaching so that the prospective teacher may take an online course as a learner, and one in the semester or quarter that the course is being taught to take account of the large investment of time needed to do online teaching well. But since we don't live in an ideal world we have to work with what we have—and the next chapter examines how teachers new to online teaching can create the conditions for good discussion.

CHAPTER TWELVE

CREATING THE CONDITIONS FOR ONLINE DISCUSSION

As we suggested in the previous chapter, online environments are sometimes experienced by learners as sterile, unfriendly, and alienating. In our view, however, online education is particularly well suited for enhancing meaning-making. It can provide students with the opportunity to undertake a reflective, solitary exploration of real problems or experiences and then to write about this process in an environment untainted by peer expectations, opinions, or ideological pressure. Teaching for meaning-making online emphasizes the learners' experiences and their interpretations of those experiences, not the teacher's. It stresses the praxis of reflection on experience, sharing of interpretations, and then further reflection. For teachers, this means developing the habit of focusing more on what students offer for consideration and less on what the teacher as expert regards as significant.

Online instruction for meaning-making must try to provide multiple outlets for students to make sense of and critique their experience. Every content module should include questions that ask students to relate the course content to their own experiences. These thoughts can be posted on a discussion board, recorded in a journal entry, noted in an e-mail, or explored in a live chat. Formal papers should also include opportunities for students to consider and to problematize those experiences that are germane to the course content covered. Some prominent commentators have argued that online interaction lends itself more to meaning-making and the serious treatment of subject matter than does face-to-face interaction. Palloff and Pratt (1999) write: "The ability to think before responding and to comment whenever the student wishes helps to create a level of participation and engagement that goes much deeper" (p. 31). They furthermore note that because online courses are a text-based medium, "participants focus," with an unusually high level of intensity, "on the meaning of the message conveyed" (p. 32).

For us the privacy, relative isolation, and reflective space associated with asynchronous online learning enhance the development of genuinely individualistic, critical thought. In face-to-face discussions the phenomenon of groupthink, of everyone moving toward the consensual mean, is a constant danger. Few want to risk being the odd person out by expressing a contrary view. In cyberspace, however, the pressure to move quickly toward a shared point of view under the eyes of the teacher is felt much less strongly. With time, space, and the freedom (within limits) to post whenever one is ready, students are more likely to articulate a view that reflects their own individual thought-out position. From this perspective online discussion can sustain more of a genuine intellectual struggle on the part of students.

Two critical theorists we mention in the following two chapters deal with this particular dynamic. Marcuse (1965, 1970) argued that a period of separation from cultural and social influences was vital for people to develop independent, critical thought. When we spend the majority of our lives in an administered society, he maintained, the pressure to conform to common expectations means the chance for individual thought is lost. In his analysis, the only way people can come to a truly critical perspective is by distancing themselves in some manner from the stupefying influence of commonsense ways of thinking, feeling, and speaking. Hence, in Marcuse's view isolation and separation—the conditions of true autonomy—are potentially revolutionary, the precursors to a commitment to social change. As such, educational formats that involve substantial amounts of independent study, such as online education, and that emphasize periods of learner isolation and separation from institutional services and peer interactions (again, online education) can actually offer more, not less, opportunities for the development of critical awareness.

Analogous to this argument is Erich Fromm's thesis in *Escape from Freedom* (1941) that experiencing freedom in the contemporary world "means growing isolation, insecurity, and thereby growing doubt concerning one's own role in the universe, the meaning of one's life" (p. 51). The individual attempts to escape this burden of freedom by trying to cede to others the responsibility for developing individual judgments and opinions. People try to discern what the commonsense, majority view on an issue is and then ape it as fervently as possible. This is what Fromm calls the process of automaton conformity. When she succumbs to automaton conformity the individual feels that "if I am like everybody else, if I have no feelings or thoughts which make me different . . . I am saved; saved from the frightening experience of aloneness" (Fromm, 1956, p. 13). The automaton conformist's credo can be summarized thus: "I must conform, not be different, not 'stick out'; I must be ready and willing to change according to the changes in the pattern; I must not ask whether I am right or wrong, but whether I am adjusted, whether I am not 'peculiar,' not different" (1956, p. 153).

One of Fromm's critiques of American higher education was that it did not encourage students to fight the temptation to succumb to automaton conformity. He felt that traditional education's emphasis on extended periods of teacher-directed group discussion ran the risk of strengthening the power of automaton conformity. In his view it sometimes takes a temporary separation from this face-to-face learning modality for people to stand any chance of developing a critical stance. Although he did not specifically address anything like online learning formats, the logic of Fromm's analysis of automaton conformity is clear. Extended periods of face-to-face learning constitute an ideal crucible for the successful perpetuation of automaton conformity. For genuinely independent, critical thought to occur a separation from face-to-face discussion can be very productive. Discussions that involve extended periods of individual, private reflection are less tainted by the pressures to automaton conformity we observe in face-to-face discussion groups. Students in such groups hear peers sighing in annoyance, see them rolling their eyes or nodding their heads in approval or disagreement. These gestures and aural clues then guide them toward articulating the majority viewpoint. When these cues are absent, as is the case with online discussion, automaton conformity can be more easily held at bay. Hence, Fromm, like Marcuse, believes that the conditions of online discussion can be very conducive to developing individual intellectual judgment.

The more we observe and participate in online discussion that links theory to practice and content to experience, and the more we seek to develop independent critical thought online, the more we are convinced that certain conditions for online discussion should be in place. Such discussions should be participatory, thoughtful, and disciplined.

CREATING PARTICIPATORY DISCUSSION ONLINE

Meaningful, sustainable discussion is highly participatory. Roughly speaking, participatory discussions may be defined as those in which most learners participate, in some form, at least part of the time. Without broad participation, students do not get the practice they need in expressing their ideas cogently, and the group lacks the diversity of viewpoints it needs to make multiple connections effectively. One strategy we have tried to increase participation online is to begin real-time conversation by giving each person in the group, in turn, a chance to make a comment about the topic under discussion without interruption from anyone else. This is an online variant of the circle of voices exercise discussed in Chapter Four. Once all the participants have had an opportunity to post their initial responses, more free-flowing conversation ensues. Each person's contribution, however, must somehow refer to what someone else has said during the first round. This has helped us ensure wider online participation, but it does create two additional problems. First, the discussion sometimes becomes rather stilted and can sap energy as the group waits for each person to post. Second, once the more open dialogue resumes, the same problem can arise of a few people dominating the exchange.

Despite these drawbacks, circle of voices may offer a partial solution to some of the problems presented by live chats. By keeping the group small, and by beginning the chat with the ground rule that each person will present her or his ideas, without interruption, each person gets a chance to participate. Circle of voices avoids the pressure to type fast and the problem of overlapping dialogue. By employing it a group can enjoy the energizing "social presence" that live chat affords, while avoiding its most frustrating tendencies.

We also have found that adapting the technique known as circular response (also described in Chapter Four) prevents a few people from dominating the exchange and helps bring focus to participants' contributions. Circular response requires all speakers to begin their remarks by commenting on the previous participant's observations and to use those observations as a springboard for their own contributions. Once again, online environments are particularly conducive to this process. Contributors to the conversation can actually see and read what the previous speaker has said, and thus more easily frame their comments to explore the themes that were raised. Indeed, circular response is so well suited for online discussion that it would be quite appropriate to require that all online exchanges begin with a reference to a previous contribution.

One of the most important lessons teachers must learn, whether face-to-face or online, is not to participate too much. Finkel (2000) writes of the value of *Teaching with Your Mouth Shut* and questions the assumption that the good teacher teaches primarily by telling. He argues the contrary view that the teacher's chief responsibility is "to create a classroom environment that both invites and promotes democratic participation" (p. 116). We have seen many potentially rich exchanges undermined by teachers who ventured their own views too frequently, thereby removing from the students the responsibility and the opportunity to keep the dialogue going. Yet it is also true, as we have already indicated, that online instructors need to be present and participate more than instructors who are live. The crucial variable is the manner of the instructor's participation. Declarative statements, lecturettes, overly extensive and lengthy corrections of students' misguided understandings are all to be discouraged and kept to a minimum. A wide variety of brief, concise observations, questions, clarifications, affirmations, and acknowledgments are the best ways for teachers to maintain "social presence," while keeping students coming back for more conversation and participation.

We want to end this section by supporting the contention of Palloff and Pratt (2003, p. 25) that participation in online courses is enhanced when the instructor models good participation herself. This can be done when she contributes frequently to the discussion and when she contacts nonparticipating students to invite them into the conversation. The instructor should also be ready to intervene when participation drops off, when conversation veers off into unproductive tangents, and when certain students are dominating by taking up more than their fare share of air-time.

Creating Thoughtful Online Discussion

Thoughtful discussion is conversation that is quite literally full of thoughts, overflowing with ideas and concepts. Discussion is not particularly effective for disclosing new facts or for arguing over something that can be checked out by consulting an almanac or dictionary. Discussion *is* ideal, however, for exploring complex ideas and entertaining multiple perspectives. It is almost never suitable for reaching definitive solutions or putting forward a single, indisputable answer. This is not to say that definitive solutions and single, indisputable answers do not have a place in education. It is only to assert that discussion, as we understand it, is best employed when an intriguing ambiguity prevails, and when it is particularly profitable for learners to consider a wide range of experiences and viewpoints. We agree with Duckworth (1996) that some of the most intriguing opportunities for learning arise from situations in which the teacher lacks the answers and an atmosphere of "not-knowing" prevails. Such an atmosphere gives teachers and students reason to create new understandings and knowledge.

A stance of "not knowing" creates a state of readiness for learning. It stirs in learners and teachers a wide-awake expectancy, a mindful openness to new possibilities that helps encourage disciplined inquiry. Experienced online educators Palloff and Pratt (1999) observe that "Questions posed in the online environment need to be the jumping-off point of a discussion promoting deep exploration of a topic and the development of critical thinking skills. There are no right or wrong answers to these questions. . . . What is important is to provide a kernel or a nugget of a question that serves to begin a dialogue and empowers students to pursue the issue at hand" (p. 119). It is important to state for the record that the teacher's "not knowing" is not the same as a self-deprecating admission that one is completely clueless and has nothing to offer the discussion. It is more to acknowledge that even with a history of learning and teaching in the area concerned, there are still questions to be answered, imponderables to be considered, mysteries to be solved. In this state of "not knowing" the teacher still knows a lot—about protocols for finding answers, about how others have sought previously (and often failed) to find answers, or about the relative importance of asking good questions as against finding answers in the wider scheme of things.

Discussion works best when students who are somewhat knowledgeable about a topic are prepared to apply that knowledge to untried areas or to explore questions that take them beyond the simple information given. Lectures and other kinds of didactic instruction (including reading of texts) work best when imparting information and knowledge. Coaching is particularly appropriate when teaching skills. But when the goal is to enlarge the learner's understanding, to gain greater insight into oneself and the surrounding world, then thoughtful dialogue and shared inquiry are called for. Using discussion frequently helps increase the depth and complexity of student knowledge and gives students practice in using that knowledge to tackle difficult questions and problems. Of course it also does the same thing for the teacher—it challenges her to investigate new, unexplored questions and possibilities.

Thoughtful discussions happen when the questions we post on discussion boards, the topics we select to discuss during live chats, the areas we invite students to explore in their journals, and the papers we assign, all include frequent opportunities for students to connect learning to their own lives and work. At their best, then, thoughtful questions should do two things:

1. Invite students to show what they have learned and what they understand from texts, lectures, and other didactic online materials, as well as from ongoing online discussions
2. Encourage students to explain how this new learning might influence their thoughts and actions at home, work, and in the larger community

For us, then, the most thoughtful online questions ask learners to demonstrate their knowledge of content and to explore critically the implications of that content. What follows are three examples of questions from one of our recent online courses designed to address both of these objectives:

- How convincingly does Spring (2003) demonstrate that American schools from the past were intent on denying and even destroying the home cultures of their students, especially students from minority groups? Tell two brief stories about your own school or a school you know today: one that shows how the history Spring describes still affects us, and one that shows how things have changed.

- What in your view are the most important indicators of a democratic school as cited by Glickman (1997)? Give an example of how one of these indicators can be found in your school. If it is not observable, provide an example of what factors are preventing democratic forces from emerging at your school.

- Why does Barth (2001) claim that the most effective schools support everyone's learning—both students and staff? Why isn't it enough for the students alone to be learning well? Consider your own school from this point of view. Whose learning does it support—everyone's? Just the students? No one's? How do you know this?

Questions like these not only assess what students know, they also require students to think deeply about the ways knowledge of content confirms or alters their opinions. As we have tried to show, online environments are particularly supportive of thoughtful discussion. They provide outlets for carefully crafted written statements and observations. Except in the case of live chats, they don't require immediate responses to complex questions. They allow students time to reflect on what the instructor and other classmates have said, thereby increasing the likelihood that new comments will be linked to previous contributions as well as to the texts. Furthermore, when prompted by thoughtful questions, online environments support students who want to dig deeper and probe challenging questions more carefully. They allow students the opportunity to consult additional research or to re-read relevant texts, and they encourage students to review the records of earlier online conversations to make connections and identify important recurring course themes.

CREATING DISCIPLINED ONLINE DISCUSSION

Discussion is disciplined when participants stay focused on the topic, offer evidence to support their point of view (or somehow explain the basis for that view), recall and summarize some of the multiple viewpoints that have been shared, attempt to identify connections between contributions already made, and show how the discussion has changed their thinking or added to their knowledge. The initial responsibility for creating such discipline lies with the instructor. She can work to keep students connected to the topic by inserting questions and comments such as

How does your observation relate to the topic of discussion?

What is the connection between your comment and what was just said?

Can you explain how your idea is helping us make sense of this subject matter?

We seem to have wandered away from the main topic. What do we need to do to get back on track?

Who has a comment or question that can help us regain our focus?

We have found that modeling our attempts to keep discussion focused, and letting students know this is what we're doing, is crucial. In different ways we have found it both easier and harder to encourage these behaviors online. It is easier because students can read comments the instructor has made and see clearly how the instructor has responded to their ideas. What makes it harder is the fact that the instructor often cannot intervene in the middle of an exchange, and may even find that once she has responded the rest of the group has moved on to another topic or issue. There are two ways to deal with this problem. One is to orient students from the outset toward the idea of disciplined discussion by including references to it in the syllabus and deliberately attempting to practice it during a required face-to-face orientation. The other is to be persistent and consistent in asking the kinds of questions that are listed above while letting students know your purpose is to keep the discussion as focused as possible.

Roughly the same strategies should be tried in fostering dialogue that is evidence-based or clearly grounded in some explicit reasoning. Again, teachers must initially model questions and comments such as the one's below to get students in the habit of thinking through and supporting their responses:

How do you know what you say is true?

What evidence do you have to support that claim?

What is the source of that point of view?

Whose work that we have studied confirms what you are saying?

By what process of reasoning did you reach that conclusion?

Students should be supported when they pose such questions to their classmates and hold one another accountable for backing up comments with evidence, logic, experience, justifications, rationales, and so on. An important indicator of success is when students apply these same standards to assess their own teacher's contributions. Online instructors can help this process by subjecting their own comments to these focusing questions. Even more powerfully, they can critique comments they themselves have posted that clearly do not meet the standards they are requiring of students.

Discussion is also disciplined when participants can summarize what they have learned from the conversation. One way to encourage summaries is to pose a final synthesis question to the group. The synthesis question offers the added bonus of creating a thinking pause in the conversation. Once the final synthesis question is posed, everyone must withhold comment until a minute or two has elapsed. Participants are invited to write their final thoughts as a way of slowing down the pace of the discussion, thus giving participants more time for reflection.

Examples of synthesis questions are

How has this discussion changed the way you are thinking about this topic?

What is the most memorable thing you have heard here today?

What question or questions does this discussion prompt you to ask?

What is something that you learned or relearned here today?

What do you know now that you did not know before this dialogue began?

What assumptions you had about this topic have been confirmed or questioned for you by this discussion?

Note that these synthesis questions are not summarizing questions in the sense of giving a précis of the discussion. Instead they provide a final reflective moment to think about what has been learned and what new learning projects have been suggested. Once the habit of responding to final synthesis questions becomes ingrained, learners often develop greater proficiency in commenting on the discussion as a whole. Synthesis questions also heighten the feeling that the effort participants have put into the dialogue has been worthwhile.

Online environments are especially well suited to practicing this kind of disciplined dialogue. Unlike live, face-to-face conversation, asynchronous exchange permits learners a relatively leisurely review of everything that has been said. This makes it easier for them to look for recurring themes, essential questions, and emerging understandings. The challenge is to build in ways to redirect students to previous discussions, so they can review everything that has been said and record their reflections. In courses we have taught the assignments have sometimes been so numerous that there hasn't been time to revisit previous postings. Johnson and Aragon (2003) note that one of the biggest problems with online courses is a tendency toward "information overload" (p. 37). The solution is, of course, to slow the pace and require fewer assignments.

The learning pause that occurs in the wake of the synthesis question has special value in addressing the problems of live online chat. Instructors who are interacting in real time online with a small group of students can leave ten to twelve minutes at the end of the chat for responses to a final synthesis question. When the question is posed all activity in the chat is suspended and participants are asked to spend the next two or three minutes scrolling back through the whole dialogue. Each student in turn then offers a response, taking about a minute to address the synthesis question. Some sort of rotation should be worked out ahead of time—assigning of numbers may work best. Each respondent attempts, in some manner, to take account of the content of the dialogue just reviewed. This has three advantages. First, participants have the opportunity to review the entire dialogue that has occurred. This helps produce more focused, disciplined, and thoughtful comments. Second, this procedure avoids the problem of overlapping dialogue. Third, it brings a more relaxed sense of closure to what can sometimes be a disorienting and frenetic experience.

Organizing the Online Course for Discussion

In order for an online class to work it must be well organized. Good course organization is evident when (1) students understand clearly from the beginning the expectations for the class, particularly how and when assignments are due, (2) students are assigned to small, deliberative groups to promote interaction in discussion boards and live chat, (3) students see clearly how the opportunities for interaction are linked to the content modules of the class, and (4) ground rules for participation on discussion boards and chat rooms are public, openly discussed, and subject to change based on CIQs and other ongoing course evaluations. Let's talk a little more about each of these in turn.

Clear Expectations and Requirements

Online learning can be a bewildering experience, particularly for first-time learners. Consequently, instructors need to create and maintain a sense of stability and order from the very beginning. In any teaching situation, it is disconcerting when the instructor is constantly shifting the requirements and expectations. In an online environment this is doubly distressing. We believe strongly that the construction of online courses should be completed by the time of the initial course orientation. In this way, students are not "ambushed" by additional assignments and can map out their time for the run of the course. They can read the syllabus, access the online calendar, and review all the content modules to find out when everything is due and what criteria are applied to evaluating learning. If online participation is graded the criteria for this should be stated up front.

As a rule we discourage grading class participation. It is difficult to do fairly and, in our experience, it tends not to raise the quality of contributions. When discussion participation is graded it can easily undermine the quality of class exchanges, as the focus shifts away from developing shared understanding and toward making sure that individuals get full credit for what they say. In other words, grading participation tends to encourage students who talk a lot and penalizes those who contribute sparingly or selflessly but who add a great deal to group cohesion. Given our assumptions about discussion, we believe that the only reasonable way to grade participation is by assessing the group's ability as a whole to advance the conversation.

In the course shown earlier in this chapter, students were informed how many discussion postings, chat room contributions, e-mail messages, journal entries, and papers were required. Although we would be the first to admit that in this course we probably asked the students to shoulder an unreasonable burden, it helped them to know exactly what was coming.

ASSIGNING STUDENTS TO SMALL GROUPS

It is not uncommon for us to teach thirty or forty students in an online course. Although we dislike having such large enrollments it is a reality we, and many others, face. Given such a large class size, it is essential to assign students to smaller, more manageable groups for many of the interactive opportunities online. For example, the instructor can divide a class of forty into five groups to make chat work. Alternatively, students can assign themselves to a group discussing a topic (from a list suggested by the teacher) that interests them. If all the students opt for only one or two topics the instructor obviously has to intervene to distribute students more equitably.

Posting messages on an asynchronous board works best if there are no more than ten or twelve students per group. Though it might seem best to maintain the same groups for all forms of discussion, we have found it is actually rather stimulating and broadening (and only a little confusing) for students to be assigned to one group for the asynchronous discussion board and a different group for live chat. However it is done, students should know when they are to participate in their groups and what their individual roles are. The responsibility for facilitating small group discussion can be rotated so that each member of the group has this opportunity at some time during the course. The instructor usually suggests how to do this and checks in occasionally to ensure this is happening.

LINKING INTERACTION TO CONTENT MODULES

Whenever we pose questions as prompts for discussion postings or chats, we try to show how these emerge from the course content. The ability to answer such questions depends on how carefully students have reviewed and understood the content. Discussion questions are also sequenced, so that issues explored in one posting are the basis or prompt for subsequent conversations. Consequently, students gain a sense that although many of the topics assigned are challenging, none is arbitrary or viewed as "coming out of left field." The course content may be perplexing but the organization of postings and required assignments is seen to have a logical structure.

EVOLVING PUBLIC GROUND RULES FOR DISCUSSION

The value of evolving ground rules for classroom discussion noted in Chapter Three also applies online. Online learners have best and worst face-to-face discussion experiences that suggest ground rules that are clearly transferable to online situations. These ground rules can then be supplemented by instructors who have accumulated a rich store of "letters from online successors" (see Chapter Three). Such letters are likely to suggest that contributions to online discussion should:

- Be concise
- Leave room for others to contribute
- Include plenty of responses that affirm and build on what others have offered
- Combine personal stories and anecdotes with broadly applicable conclusions and generalizations
- Focus on questions as much as answers
- Emphasize responding as much as initiating
- Build in time to circle back and revisit discussion postings which participants have contributed days before
- Look for recurring themes and overriding issues

These are only examples, of course. But the opportunity to agree on some ground rules for how students will interact online can be invaluable in building richer, more inclusive, and more collaborative conversations. Of course these ground rules are not fixed and can be revised in the light of CIQ feedback.

CONCERNS ABOUT ONLINE TEACHING AND LEARNING

We hope we have been clear about our enthusiasm for online teaching and learning. We think it has tremendous potential for accessing hard-to-reach students whose geographical, social, and occupational locations make it impossible for them to attend regular college classes. We also find it provides opportunities for more learners to participate in discussions that deepen their engagement with complex questions and challenging topics. However, online formats, like face-to-face ones, are far from perfect. We dislike entire degree programs done online since the spontaneity of live instruction can contribute so richly to student learning. Also, we have always believed that building relationships is a key part of effective discussion and that there is a limit to how well this can be done online. In general, we worry about online courses being abused by institutions wanting to capitalize on their cost effectiveness and convenience for students. Also, instructors who are not interested in, or comfortable doing, online teaching are increasingly pressured to create Web-based courses, as such courses appear to be so financially advantageous to their home institutions.

Instructors who habitually teach online often have less time to chat informally with their students and may therefore overlook the personal and professional challenges their students are experiencing. Also, since instructors cannot physically see how students are reacting to what they say online, they may ignore the impact of the tone or choice of their words on students. Furthermore, because there is so much preparation that goes into an online course, there is a tendency to believe that, once the course design is in place, that the bulk of the work has been done. This can make frequent participation on the part of the instructor seem unnecessary.

Other problems with online courses are largely logistical. It is, for instance, very difficult to ascertain exactly who is actually assuming responsibility for doing students' work in cyberspace. There is virtually no way to know when students designate someone else to do a particular assignment for them or even to take the entire course in their place. In addition, online courses are not a good environment to develop the ability to think spontaneously on one's feet or to practice and hone oral communication skills. For someone who likes to use films in teaching, the online environment remains technologically ill equipped for such media, and securing copyright permission for airing films continues to be prohibitively expensive.

None of these problems are, however, insurmountable. We want to reemphasize that we don't regard teaching through discussion online as qualitatively different from teaching through discussion in more traditional face-to-face classrooms. Certainly, online teaching exhibits its own particular features that need to be recognized. Because students and teachers can't see and hear each other speak their words, the ability to write clearly and appropriately becomes doubly important. Stripped of tone and gesture some comments can seem abrupt, confrontational, rude, or disrespectful. But such comments are hardly a rarity in face-to-face classrooms. What is crucial is that teachers take the lead in modeling contributions that are thoughtful, disciplined, and self-critical.

CHAPTER THIRTEEN

HOW THEORY CAN INFORM DISCUSSION PRACTICE

The bulk of this book is aimed at practice—specifically at how we plan for, conduct, and evaluate discussions, and how we negotiate the ways race, gender, class, and teacher power frame the dynamics of group conversation. In the first edition we strenuously avoided any extensive theoretical analysis in the belief that this would get in the way of this practical focus. We wanted to produce a helpful resource that could be used immediately in the classroom. In the six years since the first edition of the book appeared, however, several readers have told us they noticed, and regretted, our omission. Although they appreciated the practical nature of the book they felt we had cheated them by not placing our understanding of discussion in a wider theoretical context. They wished to know which theoretical perspectives framed our understandings of the process. Frequently they would ask us how we felt discussion dynamics looked from one or other theoretical viewpoints. And often we would be asked directly what was our own theoretical "take" on discussion and whether or not a specific exercise we liked was grounded in a particular theory. This chapter attempts to answer these questions by exploring how three complementary theoretical concepts have been especially important in informing our understanding of discussion processes. It also explains how several of the practices and exercises elaborated in the previous chapters flow from these theoretical perspectives.

The first intellectual tradition we examine is that of neo-Marxist structuralist analysis. This perspective focuses on the ways in which education serves as a sorting device that mirrors and preserves economic relations in the wider society. In Althusser's (1971) formulation educational practices (including discussion) comprise ideological state apparatuses (ISAs). ISAs help ensure that the logic of capitalism, prevailing relationships of authority, and dominant belief systems are widely accepted as normal by the population. This perspective examines how discussion reproduces the dominant ideology of capitalism so that its practices and values are left unchallenged. A second perspective is that of poststructuralism, represented chiefly by Michel Foucault's (1980) analysis of the way power relations are inscribed in the specific practices of everyday life (such as classroom conversation). This perspective examines the way in which students in discussion groups work to reproduce invisible norms of what they imagine to be "good" participation and to survey themselves and others to monitor their discussion performance. The final perspective reviewed is Herbert Marcuse's analysis of tolerance. Marcuse (1965) warns that attempts to widen the scope of discussions by including a diversity of viewpoints and positions often backfire. Dominant ideology has so penetrated students' interpretive synapses that when a new perspective is introduced into a discussion its very unfamiliarity serves to reinforce the legitimacy of the mainstream view. Instead of core ideas being de-centered their centrist position is confirmed. The contradictory logic of this practice is described by Marcuse as repressive tolerance.

STRUCTURALIST ANALYSIS

Structuralist analysis is a perspective much favored by teachers who are influenced by neo-Marxism and critical theory. This intellectual tradition investigates how social structures that are manifestly unjust maintain themselves. People are born, live, and die, yet a clearly iniquitous system stays relatively unchanged—how can this be? Shouldn't humans' ability to change their lives—their sense of agency—mean that each generation creates a new world? Why doesn't this happen? Macro-sociological studies of schooling by Carnoy and Levin (1985) and Bowles and Gintis (1974) show how education functions as a sorting device for the economy, socializing students to accept their class-determined occupational roles as white or blue collar workers, service personnel or self-employed professionals, owners of capital or sellers of their labor power. Schools reproduce the hierarchical organization of factories and supply the different kinds of mental and physical labor that the capitalist system needs to function. In Willis's (1981) terms, this perspective explains why working class kids get working class jobs.

Structural analysis views education as an ideological state apparatus (to use Althusser's [1971] term) that works to ensure the perpetuation of dominant ideology. It does this partly by teaching values that support that ideology, and partly by immersing students in practices that are ideologically determined. Prime among such practices is the conduct of discussion. When they choose discussion topics, delineate acceptable "boundaries" of analysis, and select who is to speak (and for how long), teachers function as ideological managers. In the ways they respond to different comments teachers ensure that certain perspectives are marginalized and discredited while others are portrayed as "common sense," the clear choice of those with intelligence and discernment.

The sorting process described above pervades all educational activities, including discussion. To help us understand how this happens the concept of cultural capital proposed by the French thinker, Pierre Bourdieu (1986), is useful. Cultural capital refers to the style and patterns of speaking, dress and posture, the command of language, and the knowledge of cultural matters that one brings to an educational situation. Differences in the amount of cultural capital people possess explain why students from middle and upper class homes consistently do better in school than working class students. Learners from middle and upper class homes bring culturally approved ways of speaking, writing, and thinking into higher education discussions. To many teachers these students appear smarter, quicker, and more knowledgeable. Just as in a capitalist economy resources accrue to those who already possess capital, so it goes in discussion. Students with substantial cultural capital—who speak the right way, use academic terminology correctly, and make their arguments with confidence—quickly come to be regarded favorably as academically able.

The research of British sociologist Basil Bernstein (1990) briefly alluded to in Chapter 7 extends our understanding of how cultural capital manifests itself through class-based speech patterns in discussion. Over the past three decades Bernstein has drawn an oft-quoted distinction between elaborated and restricted codes of communication both in education and the wider society. The *elaborated code* is a broadly middle class form of speech comprising a wide vocabulary, the giving of reasons and justifications based on argument or appeals to evidence, and frequent use of clauses, sub-clauses, and qualifiers. The *restricted code* is a broadly working class form of speech comprising a smaller vocabulary, an appeal to authority rather than giving reasons ("why should I do this?" . . . "because I'm telling you to"), shorter, terser sentences, and frequent repetition of colloquialisms.

What implications regarding the conduct of discussions can discussion-based teachers take from structuralist analysis? First, it is clear that they can explore ways to decrease the negative effects caused by the disproportionate distribution of cultural capital among students. In Chapter Six we explore two such approaches in our sections on "Drawing Discussion" and "Dramatizing Discussion." Both activities ask students to present the themes of their small group conversations visually or theatrically instead of orally. The newsprint dialogue exercise described in the same chapter also deliberately challenges the privileging of speech by having small groups post the results of their initial conversations and then placing a blank sheet of newsprint next to their postings to receive the written comments of individuals in the class. When we have used these techniques we have noticed that they draw strong reactions—both positive and negative—with some students saying this is the first time their voices have been "heard."

A second implication concerns the teacher's conduct. Discouraging students from using complicated terminology only to impress their peers (and the teacher) is difficult but there are some steps we can take to stop this from happening. We can make it clear from the outset that speaking this way is not what we regard as good participation. We can add to the speech policy described in Chapter Four a sentence or two making it clear that using complex terminology for its own sake is discouraged. This can be underscored in the "truth in advertising" statements mentioned in Chapter Three as part of a course syllabus. In addition, when groups are generating ground rules as described in Chapter Three the teacher can reasonably add one of her own to the effect that anytime an example of unfamiliar terminology is voiced by a student, the teacher, or another student, should request a definition, clarification, or illustration. This gives pause to students who just want to mouth concepts, names, and terms as a way of being noticed. The "Conversational Moves" exercise in Chapter Five offers another opportunity for teachers to reduce the destructive influence of unequal cultural capital. Most of the moves we have included in this exercise are deliberately written to stop students showing off by voicing complex terminology and to emphasize instead that good discussion participation involves strong elements of showing appreciation, drawing others out, and making synthesizing and integrative observations. Finally, an additional role—the clarifier role—can be added to the conversational roles exercise in the same chapter. The student who is the clarifier has the role of asking participants to provide an illustrative example of a new concept or term at the point at which it is introduced into the discussion. Again, this helps ensure that if difficult language is introduced into the conversation it is done to enhance learning rather than to show off.

Poststructuralism

The second theoretical perspective to be explored is poststructuralism. Poststructuralism also investigates the reproduction of dominance, but its proponents argue that people themselves, rather than a ruling class or elite, are the chief agents responsible for this reproduction. This perspective examines how people learn to internalize norms (including norms governing discussion participation) that serve to maintain the status quo. We feel this perspective is relevant to any teacher who fears (as we do) that students embrace an unspoken, invisible norm that equates good discussion participation with frequency of contribution. Our concern is that students bring to class certain expectations regarding participation that are drawn from a dominant ideology that privileges speech. This norm may well have been learned in school and then reinforced by popular culture and peer pressure. The norm that popularity equates with extraversion, and that intelligence equates with an articulate command of academic jargon, will, if unchallenged, quickly introduce an unequal pecking order of contributors and a superficial level of conversation. In their efforts to exemplify the norm of talkativeness, students who want a good grade will do their best to exemplify this norm and will monitor themselves, and others, to gauge how they are doing in the discussion performance stakes. In effect, they will exercise disciplinary power on themselves; that is, they will watch themselves to make sure they are behaving in the way they feel the discussion leader (the judge of what constitutes good participation) desires.

Disciplinary power, self-surveillance, invisible norms, and judges of normality are all ideas associated with the French cultural critic Michel Foucault (1980). Foucault was a poststructuralist theorist who posited that in modern society sovereign power (power emanating from a clearly discernible central authority) has been replaced by a different kind of power—disciplinary power. Disciplinary power is power exercised by people on themselves to make sure they stay in line. In a society subject to disciplinary power we constantly watch ourselves. Hence, self-surveillance is the most important mechanism of disciplinary power. Because we live in a society characterized by constant surveillance we learn to interiorize (a term Foucault often uses) this feature to the point where we assume the responsibility for monitoring and censoring our own thoughts and behaviors in discussion groups and elsewhere. When this happens there is no need for the state to spend enormous amounts of time and money making sure we behave correctly, since we are watching ourselves to make sure we don't deviate from the norm.

Self-surveillance in the sphere of everyday conversation begins with surveillance by representatives of the larger society, individuals referred to by Foucault as judges of normality. Examples of these judges are psychiatrists, counselors, therapists and, of course, teachers. We watch ourselves because we know that we are being watched by these regulating presences. Over time the norms enforced by these judges become internalized to the point where the judge's presence becomes unnecessary.

Adapting Foucault's analysis to understanding learning through discussion we can surmise that students experience discussion as an activity in which their behavior is constantly watched by a judge of normality (the discussion leader). The discussion leader monitors the extent to which students are participating in the conversation in a suitable manner. Discussion leaders as judges of normality tacitly reinforce the power of this participatory norm by operationalizing how it will be recognized. They establish rules to determine who is to be allowed into the conversation, for example by acknowledging those who have raised their hands to signify they wish to speak. Through the judicious use of invitational eye contact they confer the message that now a particular student can make a comment. With a nod of teacher approval they register that a particularly insightful comment has been made, and with a grimace they condemn another comment as obviously asinine.

Whenever teachers assign part of a grade for discussion "participation" they activate the norm's tacit influence over participants. Learners immediately interpret the teacher's injunction to participate as meaning that they (the students) should do their best to exemplify this norm. So they jump in at every opportunity to capture the teacher's attention and register the fact that they are frequent contributors. They throw into the discussion terms, concepts, theories, and names in a desperate effort to sound knowledgeable and profound, irrespective of whether or not these contributions actually enhance the conversation. The norm is also reinforced through discussion leaders' deployment of a range of subtle, nonverbal behaviors that signify approval or disapproval of participants' efforts to exemplify the norm. Through nods, frowns, eye contact (or the lack of it), sighs of frustration or pity, grunts of agreement, disbelieving intakes of breath at the obvious absurdity of a particular comment, and a wide range of other gestures, discussion leaders communicate to the group when members are close to, or moving away from, the norm. Unless discussion leaders as judges of normality redefine criteria for discussion participation to challenge this norm, learners will work assiduously to gear their behavior toward its realization.

Although we dislike this fact intensely, the reality is that early on in a course students will ascribe to us the role of judge of normality. Given that this will happen whatever we do, how can we (as judges of normality) ensure that this invisible norm of participation is challenged? We have found several things to be useful. The first is to use the syllabus as a way of setting expectations regarding what participation means. Here we advocate specifying nonverbal indicators of effective participation such as bringing in resources for the group not contained in course materials, posting a reflective comment in the course chat room that moves the conversation in a fruitful new direction, or making a comment on the CIQ that indicates how discussion participants either avoid or misunderstand a contentious issue. The opening speech we describe in Chapter Four can also be used to stress that participation means showing appreciation, inviting further elaboration, demonstrating links and connections between previous contributions, and so on. This speech can underscore how being a good discussion participant involves making the kinds of moves described in "Conversational Moves" (Chapter Five), none of which emphasize erudition for the sake of erudition, or frequency of participation for frequency's sake. An early use of the "Conversational Moves" exercise in the course can be a good teaching tool in this regard.

Another way to challenge the norm of participation for the sake of participation (rather than for the sake of learning) is to use the kinds of reflective pauses we advocate in Chapter Nine in our section titled "What Do We Do When Students Talk Too Much?" Calling for regular interludes of reflective silence during which participants note down contradictions or important points that have been made, or future questions they wish to pursue, emphasizes that silence is as much part of conversational rhythm as is speech. The teacher can explain that these mandatory silences are called for not only to assist learning but also to challenge the mistaken notion that good participation should be interpreted as meaning frequency of speech. There is also the possibility of the teacher adding something like the three-person rule to any ground rules the class evolves. The three-person rule holds that once a participant has made a contribution she should hold off making another interjection until at least three other people have spoken. The only time this rule can be broken is if another student asks the speaker to expand on her initial comment. Finally, when students do dominate the conversation this fact will almost always be recorded on that week's CIQs by a majority of students in the class. As we state in Chapter Nine, mentions by a majority of students that certain people are talking too much allow you to reemphasize the importance of nonverbal indicators of participation to the whole class and also to have a confidential word with verbose students about how they might alter their conversational behaviors.

Repressive Tolerance

Repressive tolerance is a theoretical concept drawn from critical theory that is particularly problematic for teachers who use discussion. This concept is associated with Herbert Marcuse, the highly influential philosopher and public intellectual of the 1960s. Marcuse argued that teachers' willingness to run discussions in which a variety of perspectives are present is much less innocent than it appears. On the face of it this practice hardly seems like a problem. A broadening of discussion to include diverse ideas seems an important and obvious part of building a critical practice of education. In one of his most famous essays, however, Marcuse (1965) argues that an emphasis on including a diversity of views and intellectual or racial traditions in discussion is often repressive, not liberating. When they experience *repressive tolerance* (which is the term Marcuse uses to describe this situation) people mistakenly believe they are participating in discussions characterized by freedom of speech and an inclusive emphasis on diverse ideas, when in fact those same discussions actually reinforce dominant ideology.

Repressive tolerance is a tolerance for just enough challenge to an unjust system to convince people that they live in a truly open society in which dissenting voices are expressed and heard. As long as people believe this they will lose the energy to try to change the system, even though in reality nothing has altered. This kind of tolerance functions as a pressure cooker letting off enough steam to prevent the whole pot from boiling over. When repressive tolerance is in place the apparent acceptance of all viewpoints only serves to reinforce an unfair status quo. This is because when an alternative idea is included alongside a mainstream one, people's prior familiarity with the mainstream ensures that the alternative, oppositional perspective is inevitably seen as an exotic option rather than a plausible viewpoint around which a new worldview can be constructed. In classroom discussions repressive tolerance allows, and even encourages, participants to express the widest possible range of views. In the manner of this apparently free expression of views, however, certain centrist ideas are always given greater credence. They are subtly favored, presented by both participants and leader as more "reasonable" or "balanced." So while alternative interpretations and opinions are pursued, the fact that they are framed as alternatives only serves to support the implicit legitimacy of the center.

One way to illustrate this is to think about what happens when those teachers who can afford it travel abroad. Typically, when you get to a foreign country you are enraptured with the different aspects of the culture—the cuisine, the music, the clothing, the street rhythms, the language, and so on. You sample the food, go enthusiastically to street festivals, dress like a local—all the time reveling in celebrating the exotic diversity you are experiencing. But your enjoyment comes from precisely the awareness that this is not "normal," not "reality." You know you are on a temporary excursion into another perspective and that lurking behind your engagement is the "real" life you inhabit. So the engagement is not with a truly viable alternative that might displace the center, but a temporary flirtation with an exotic diversion. In this way celebrating the diversity of your experience serves only to reinforce the enduring legitimacy of your "normal" way of life. In much the same way inserting the discussion of an alternative idea, concept, or text into the consideration of familiar, mainstream materials serves only to emphasize the alternatives as exotic others and to underscore the normality of the center. Students see their engagement with a new idea as a temporary flirtation with an exotic intellectual (rather than tourist) locale, an enjoyable diversion before returning to the security of mainstream thought.

Repressive tolerance masks its repression behind the façade of open, even-handedness. Alternative ideas are not banned in discussions. Critical texts are published that are read in preparation for classroom discussions and critical messages circulated in those same discussions. The defenders of the status quo can point to the existence of dissenting voices (such as Marcuse's) as evidence of the open society we inhabit, and the active tolerance of a wide spectrum of ideologies. However, the power of radical texts is often diluted by the fact that the texts themselves are hard to get or incredibly expensive. In addition, the radical meanings these texts contain are neutered in any discussion of them because they are framed as the expressions of obviously weird minority opinion.

A crucial component of repressive tolerance is the meta-narrative of democratic tolerance. This narrative is ideologically embedded in the way educators think of democratic discussion, where the intent is to honor and respect each learner's voice. But the implicit assumption that all contributions to a discussion carry equal weight can easily lead to a flattening of conversation. A discussion leader's concern to dignify each student's contribution can result in an unwillingness to point out the ideologically distorted or misguided nature of a particular comment, let alone saying someone is actually wrong. In Marcuse's view, the ideology of democratic tolerance in discussion groups means that "the stupid opinion is treated with the same respect as the intelligent one, the misinformed may talk as long as the informed, and propaganda rides along with falsehood. This pure tolerance of sense and nonsense is justified by the democratic argument that nobody, neither group nor individual, is in possession of the truth and capable of defining what is right and wrong, good and bad" (p. 94). Heretically (at least to many educators), Marcuse even suggests that with some people discussion is a waste of time. In his view "there are in fact large groups in the population with whom discussion is hopeless" (1970, p. 102) owing to the rigidity of their opinions. So the best thing to do, in Marcuse's opinion, is avoid talking to them.

An interesting case study of repressive tolerance in action is Cale's analysis of his attempt to work critically and democratically in a freshman composition class by teaching writing through the analysis of race, class, and gender in contemporary America (Cale, 2001; Cale and Huber, 2001). Cale and his sometime coauthor Huber draw on Marcuse to illustrate the danger of providing an array of philosophical and ideological perspectives and assuming that these have rough parity in students' eyes. Despite his giving lectures critiquing the concept of meritocracy and outlining capitalism's deliberate creation of an underclass, Cale notes that "once I allowed the 'common sense' of the dominant ideology to be voiced, nothing could disarm it" (Cale and Huber, 2001, p. 16). It did not matter that a disproportionately large amount of time was spent in criticism of this ideology. As long as Cale allowed his white students (the majority in the class) to voice their own opinions regarding racism—opinions based on their own experiences—the focus was continually shifted away from white privilege and toward discussions of reverse discrimination and black "problems." Cale refreshingly and courageously admits that his past efforts to work democratically by respecting all voices and encouraging the equal participation of all learners "has in many cases actually helped to silence some of my students, to reinforce the dominance of the status quo, and to diminish my own ability to combat racism, sexism, and classism" (Cale, 2001). He concludes that his use of "democratic" discussion achieved little effect other than to provide "opportunities for students to attack and silence oppositional thinkers, including myself" (Cale, 2001, p. 17).

Cale's experience is very predictable in Marcuse's view. For him providing a smorgasbord of alternative perspectives in discussion in the name of a pluralist tolerance of diversity only ensures that the radical ones are marginalized by the dominant consciousness. The only way to break with this kind of spurious impartiality is to immerse learners fully and exclusively in a radically different perspective that challenges mainstream ideology and confronts the learner with "information slanted in the opposite direction" (Marcuse, 1965, p. 99). After all, "unless the student learns to think in the opposite direction, he will be inclined to place the facts into the predominant framework of values" (p. 113). True diversity, in Marcuse's view, requires the suppression of familiar, mainstream views and the deliberate foregrounding only of dissenting analyses.

Here Marcuse is proposing a kind of intellectual affirmative action in classroom discussions in favor of leftist perspectives. For him a "withdrawal of tolerance from regressive movements, and discriminating tolerance in favor of progressive tendencies would be tantamount to the 'official' promotion of subversion" (p. 107). Marcuse believed that giving learners' access to objective, liberatory truth justified censoring dominant, mainstream ideas and discriminating in favor of outlawed knowledge. Realizing the objective of truly liberating tolerance calls "for intolerance toward prevailing policies, attitudes, opinions, and the extension of tolerance to policies, attitudes, and opinions which are outlawed or suppressed" (Marcuse, 1965, p. 81).

How can the emergence of repressive tolerance be countered? How can we stop the consideration of alternative ideas and concepts being taken less seriously than the consideration of more familiar, mainstream perspectives? One approach we have found useful is to tell students at the start of a particular class that we will be saving five to ten minutes toward the end of that day's discussion period to give some of our own reflections on the discussion. We view this as keeping a "discussion inventory" that will be unpacked just before students leave the class. The inventory is essentially a list of the things we want to make sure students are exposed to before they exit the room that day. It is blank at the start of the discussion but fills up as we jot down errors we hear, perspectives that we feel are glossed over or ignored, and important oppositional views that we think are too easily rushed past. A good time to unpack this inventory is just before the CIQ is completed at the end of the class.

In the five-minute inventory time we provide information about perspectives that were missed during the discussion and we offer alternative interpretations that students did not wish to consider. This is also an excellent time for us to draw students' attention to what we consider to be major errors of understanding we have noticed being expressed during the conversation. Sometimes in the middle of a discussion that is going well someone makes a statement that shows a complete misunderstanding of a concept, or is clearly factually wrong, but we feel uncomfortable interrupting the flow of talk at that particular time and singling that contributor out as somehow lacking. When that erroneous statement is made we jot down a note on our inventory pad to make sure we address it in the time we've reserved for ourselves toward the end of the class that day. So the discussion inventory allows us to correct mistakes and to tackle repressive tolerance by making sure participants do not leave the room without being exposed to a perspective we feel it is necessary for them to encounter.

We have also found the "Critical Debate" exercise, and the conversational role of devil's advocate (both described in Chapter Four) to be useful hedges against repressive tolerance. Both exercises require students to engage, at least temporarily, with perspectives that they either fundamentally disagree with (as in critical debate) or that oppose the consensus view (as in the devil's advocate role). The "Methodological Belief" approach described in Chapter Seven can also be used to combat repressive tolerance. In this exercise the teacher asks students to spend five minutes considering what the world would look like if an alternative viewpoint they strongly disagree with were true. We have found these three exercises work quite well with resistant students because in each of them the student knows the engagement is temporary, even playful. They are being asked to participate in a fixed-time consideration of an alternative view after which they are assured they can go back to their own perspective if they choose. Students know that you as the teacher are not asking them to "convert" to a view they profoundly dislike or disagree with, but only to play at considering it for a brief amount of time. This tends to reduce their resistance while providing an opening for exposure to a potentially unsettling viewpoint.

In addition, when we are generating questions for discussion, or deciding on texts to be addressed during discussion, we sometimes negotiate with the students what these texts and questions might be. A rough and ready rule one of us has used is that teachers choose 30 percent of the texts or questions, students choose 30 percent of the texts or questions, and 40 percent are negotiated between faculty and students. If this process is followed the teacher can use her 30 percent to emphasize perspectives and materials that are dramatically different from the mainstream consensus items likely to be suggested by the students.

The teacher can also play a role in combating repressive tolerance by being explicit about this tendency in the syllabus and by describing how she will take steps to counter this. For example, she can set out in her syllabus for the course, or in her expectations for a particular discussion, that she sees one of her teaching tasks as being to combat repressive tolerance. She can let students know in advance that her role is to present important alternative views that students are not willing to explore of their own volition, perhaps by assigning herself the devil's advocate conversational role explained in Chapter Four. Teachers can also say that for part of a particular discussion session, or part of a course, they are going to expose students only to an alternative view and to allow consideration of that view only on its own terms. In a course on adult education, for example, Stephen Brookfield would feel fine saying that for a particular period only an Africentric paradigm, or Islamic paradigm, or Marxist paradigm on adult education will be considered, knowing full well that Eurocentric humanist, behavioral, and human capital paradigms will swarm around students as soon as they exit the classroom walls. Of course the objection can be raised that once the class, or the course, is over students will fall back into familiar, comfortable patterns of thought. One obvious way around this is to construct a whole college curriculum that focuses only on marginalized ideas.

Finally, we are struck by the practice of the People's Institute for Survival and Beyond of New Orleans, an organization dedicated to anti-racist education. The institute advocates what is in effect an extended, workshop-long commitment to the kind of methodological belief described in Chapter Seven. Chisom and Washington (1997) emphasize how institute workshops insist that certain assumptions will not be debated. Examples of these would be that white supremacy prevails, that such supremacy is the basis of all other inequalities, and that attempts to overcome other oppressions must begin with anti-racist efforts. Why can't these assumptions be debated? Partly, because if debate of these is allowed valuable time for anti-racist work will be lost. But, chiefly, because if these assumptions are debated the previous ideological conditioning of participants (which says race is no longer an issue since the civil rights movement, and that affirmative action now discriminates unfairly against white males) will cause the workshop's central assumptions to be marginalized and obfuscated.

CONCLUSION

As this chapter shows, apparently unequivocal and innocent discussion practices can, depending on the theoretical position you hold, be seen to contain multitudes of problematic realities. The three theoretical positions we have chosen to highlight in this chapter deliberately challenge the dominant, almost relentless, optimism we see informing teachers' discourse surrounding discussion practices. Although we share the belief that discussion is generally "a good thing" we are also aware of the pitfalls of an uncritical optimism concerning its effects. Too uncritical a belief in the benefits of discussion participation makes it harder to survive the inevitable moments of student dissatisfaction, frustration, and hostility. It is very hard to be told that your attempt to respect a minority view has only served to marginalize it even further. It is profoundly upsetting to see your supposedly emancipatory interventions work to undercut the serious consideration of alternative perspectives and bolster the authority of frequently voiced mainstream ideas. And it is deeply unnerving to discover that in students' eyes the use of classroom discussion has undermined the very democratic, inclusive practices you were seeking to foster and has strengthened the position and behavior of bigots. But if we are familiar with the theoretical analyses explored in this chapter we stand a greater chance of keeping their destructive effects in check. However, because of the undeniable strength of the wider social forces explored in this analysis we need to be realistic about what we can accomplish as discussion leaders. The suggestions we make should not be viewed as fault-free recipes for success. They're just the best that two struggling teachers can come up with at the present time.

CHAPTER FOURTEEN

DISCUSSION GROUPS AS DEMOCRATIC LEARNING LABORATORIES

One of the strongest claims we make for discussion is that, properly conducted, it is inherently democratic; indeed, the subtitle of this book makes this preference quite explicit. Few writers have advanced this claim more determinedly than the German critical theorist Jurgen Habermas. Over the past five decades Habermas has produced a constant stream of texts that, in their different ways, examine the connections between learning discussion behaviors and practicing democracy. In this chapter we navigate this stream and explore those eddies that represent some of his chief preoccupations.

Habermas believes that postindustrial society has seen the decline of the public sphere (the civic space or commons in which people come together to discuss and decide their response to shared issues and problems) and the weakening of civil society. We review his contention that the key to reversing these negative trends is understanding how people learn communicative action and how they apply that learning in democratic conversation. For us, Habermas is a theorist of democracy who believes that a society is more or less democratic according to the discussion processes its members use to come to decisions about matters that affect their lives. As societies democratize its citizens have fuller access to information and endure progressively fewer distortions to constrain discussion. Truly democratic discussion represents the freest, least restricted communication possible. In Habermas's view the greater the freedom of discussion that people enjoy, the higher the chance that true critical reason—reason employed to create a just, humane democracy—will emerge.

THE DECLINE OF THE PUBLIC SPHERE

The public sphere is like an enormous discussion arena. Think of an outdoor café full of people talking about concerns they share in common, or an internet chat room in which people log on to register and exchange their views about something. As people talk with varying degrees of informality about issues that affect them, viewpoints emerge that represent the chief clusters of their opinions. These are the viewpoints that are noticed by politicians, government officials, pollsters, media workers, and so on. As a result the opinions developed informally in the public sphere come to affect how more formal political and legislative deliberations are conducted. In this way the public sphere is "an intermediary between the political system, on the one hand, and the private sectors of the lifeworld and functional systems, on the other" (Habermas, 1996, p. 373).

In *The Structural Transformation of the Public Sphere* (1989b), first published in German in 1962, Habermas painstakingly traces how, as society becomes ever larger and more differentiated into complex subsystems, "the communicative network of a public made up of rationally debating private citizens has collapsed" (p. 247). The town meeting, village green gathering, or tribal circle cannot provide effective forums for the kind of public discussion of community concerns that lies at the heart of democracy. Yet democracy cannot exist without a public sphere that allows people to talk out their feelings and opinions and gather their political energies behind a particular movement for change. If there is no arena in which adults can come together to debate and engage in political will formation (the development of strands of opinion and the decision to act on these that sometimes comes after prolonged discussion), we cannot accurately talk about public opinion. This lack of a public sphere is a boon to governments that seek to steamroller a vision of the world they wish people to accept as self-evident. For example, a public sphere that debates long and hard about the morality of invading another country that poses no imminent threat is extremely inconvenient for a regime obsessed with damping down public criticism of its policies.

What are some of the other consequences of the decline of the public sphere? One is the growth of a destructive privatism, a focus on the self. When people have no way to influence discussion and decisions in the wider society they decide to pursue private goals without regard to the effects this pursuit has on others. In such a situation what Habermas calls civic privatism—"political abstinence combined with an orientation to career, leisure and consumption" (Habermas, 1975, p. 37)—is bound to flourish. The diminution of the public sphere also neutralizes intellectual challenges to the dominant order. When intellectuals act as social critics to reveal and uncover the existence of social inequities they need a public to receive, consider, and then sometimes act on such critiques. With no public to debate the arguments and evidence they offer, no philosophical commons in which their analyses can be heard, intellectuals are rendered impotent. By definition, intellectual work is premised on the existence of a public sphere to receive and respond to it. This sphere can only exist when supported by constitutional safeguards that ensure and encourage the free expression of critical opinion. In order to perform their proper critical function intellectuals therefore "rely on a half way constitutional state" and on "a democracy that for its part survives only by virtue of the involvement of citizens who are as suspicious as they are combative" (Habermas, 1989a, p. 73).

REVITALIZING THE PUBLIC SPHERE THROUGH COMMUNICATIVE ACTION

Although the decline of the public sphere is a disturbing trend, Habermas is hopeful it can be countered. In his view communicative action—people learning to understand each other's viewpoint so as to come to an agreement—is both a ubiquitous dimension of human existence and a crucial hedge against the total collapse of the public sphere. Habermas argues that if enough people in society are intentional about their engagement in communicative action then the public sphere can be revitalized.

What exactly is communicative action? In Volume 1 of his massive *The Theory of Communicative Action* (1984), Habermas says such action happens when attempts by people to communicate "are coordinated not through egocentric calculations of success but through acts of reaching understanding" (p. 286). When we act communicatively we try to step out of our normal frames of reference to see the world as someone else sees it. We make this effort because we live in a world full of different cultures, agendas, and ideologies. In a sense living with others continually forces perspective-taking upon us. Life keeps presenting situations to us in which we need to understand others' desires and reach compromises with them. Sometimes we also need to live with the realization that compromise is impossible. The communicative action such compromises and containments call for requires a good faith effort to try and understand another's point of view.

This communicative disposition is fostered through several of the practices described in this book. "Methodological belief" in Chapter Seven explicitly requires us to put our prejudices aside and try to accept (if only temporarily) a worldview with which we are unfamiliar and perhaps disagree. The same logic informs the practice of "Critical Debate" (Chapter Five). The "Circle of Voices" and "Circular Response" described in Chapter Four both have as an important task the attempt to express one's comments within the context of another's perspective. The role of designated listener in Chapter Five requires the student to understand comments from the perspective of the speaker as does the paired listening exercise in the same chapter.

Habermas believes that in social living communicative action is unavoidable. He declares in a 1994 interview, "I never say that people *want* to act communicatively but that they *have to*" (Habermas, 1994, p. 111). As long as we live in association with others, and as long as we accept that our lives are better without constant conflicts and disputes, then communicative action is required. This is because there are basic social tasks that can only be accomplished through communicative action. Rearing children, cooperative action of any kind, solving problems peacefully all require us to balance personal preferences with the collective good. Developing the ability to put aside egocentric calculations of success in a society run by money and power is a daunting prospect. Indeed, in Habermas's view learning to do this is *the* adult learning task, made doubly difficult by the existence of schooling systems run according to the competitive ethic and by the spread of civic privatism.

When we learn to come to agreement we are, in Habermas's view, engaged in an inherently democratic process, since true agreement springs from the freely given assent of the parties concerned. Hence, "a communicatively achieved agreement . . . cannot be imposed by either party (whether instrumentally via intervention or strategically via undue influence)" (1984, p. 287). Embedded in any authentic agreement are certain democratic norms. First, the agreement must not be coerced. Those involved must feel that the understanding has been reached of their unforced volition. Second, coming to an understanding must be based on the truthful giving of reasons for various actions. Third, an agreement between people is based on the assumption that the views of others involved in the agreement have some validity. We can see the intentional creation of these kind of democratic speech norms exemplified at different points in this book. For example, the effort to create discussion ground rules described in Chapter Three focuses on the norms just discussed. In addition, use of the CIQ referred to throughout the book will often necessarily lead into the kind of communicative action Habermas refers to. Whenever the CIQ reveals a dynamic in class that involves different subgroups of learners displaying markedly different preferences (for example one groups wants only lectures, one group wants only small group projects, one group wishes to hold most of the class online, and so on), we have to hold discussions that work to resolve these different agendas to the point where all can live with what is arranged.

THE VALIDITY CLAIMS OF DISCUSSION

Habermas contends that raising validity claims is intrinsic to every human conversation and, by implication, to every educational discussion. Validity claims are the basic conditions of speech that people strive to practice when they attempt to communicate in good faith with each other. If I struggle to understand what you're saying and try to make my comments to you as comprehensible as possible in return, then I am communicating in good faith. If I then try to connect to, build on, and take account of what you have said as I respond to you, I am likewise sincerely trying to build some shared understandings. What Habermas calls communicative action—two or more people trying to come to an understanding or agreement—is premised on their effort to speak in the most truthful, best informed way they can. Hence, "whenever we mean what we say, we raise the claim that what is said is true, or right, or truthful" (Habermas, 1994, p. 102).

Throughout the book we employ exercises that attempt to implement the kinds of validity claims Habermas describes. "Circle of Voices" (Chapter Four), "Circular Response" (Chapter Four), "Conversational Moves" (Chapter Five), and the "Reflective Analyst" conversational role (Chapter Five) all involve participants struggling to understand what others are saying and then to respond to them on the basis of this understanding. In Chapter Five our section on responding to discussion by affirming, clarifying, and inviting further elaboration is based on the idea that good teachers strive to understand what students are saying and to be as clear as possible in their own comments. Indeed, one could argue that the attempt to use lectures to model democratic talk (Chapter Three) and the giving of individualized feedback (Chapter Fifteen) are two activities that require us to take account of Habermas's validity claims as we try to make transparent our explanations and assessments. Whenever students ask questions of us we try to accomplish what Habermas claims is a central task of valid communication; that is, to do our best to understand what the question is and why it is important to the student, and then to give the clearest response we can that takes account of what we know about the student's experience, culture, race, learning style, and so on.

Clearly, not all discussion interactions are examples of communicative action. Indeed, in a society dominated by money and power, a great deal of conversation will be the exact opposite of this kind of talk. People will speak for the purpose of exploiting or dominating others in discussion groups or to justify and support conversational rules that legitimize this domination. The true, fully realized communicative action so valued by Habermas is a rarity in life, something that always needs fostering. For Habermas it is the most endangered human resource on the planet. This is why the role of education, particularly the actions of discussion leaders, is important.

It is striking how Habermas's unabashed hope in the possibility of two or more people coming to understand each other's views and then agreeing on a common course of action stands firmly against postmodernism. From a postmodern perspective Habermas is engaged in something of a fool's errand. If postmodernism teaches us anything (and teaching us something is too directive an activity for many in this orientation), it is that language can never be trusted. Logocentrism—the assumption that a central, unequivocal discoverable meaning exists at the core of speech and writing—is completely rejected. Words are viewed instead as slippery, opaque, and contextual. From a postmodern perspective the thoughts we have can never be expressed in words in exactly the way we think them. Furthermore, despite our best intentions to craft words that convey our meanings as transparently and accurately as possible, the meanings that others take from them will never be exactly what we intend. People's experiences and history will always skew how others understand the words we use and ensure that they invest them with connotations and meanings we never intended. Hence, postmodernism views comprehensibility, rightness, and authenticity as meaningless criteria in a world of fractured discourses and local meanings.

Despite the postmodern critique of his theory of communicative action, Habermas steadfastly refuses to ditch modernity's dream of using human reason to create a more humane world. Part of that dream is clearly bound up with the possibility of people learning to speak to each other in honest and informed ways so that they can hold democratic conversations about important issues in a revived public sphere. Since, to Habermas, learning to talk in this way is the best hope we have for creating a just society, there could hardly be anything more important in social life than education, and no more significant educational activity than discussion.

PRACTICING THE VALIDITY CLAIMS OF DISCUSSION

What are the validity claims Habermas is seeking to practice through discussion? The first is "the comprehensibility of the utterance" (1973, p. 18) in which we ask how clear and understandable are the words participants are using. This claim of *comprehensibility* requires speakers to strive to use language that stands the best chance of being understood by hearers. When we hear a sentence we also try to gauge "the truth of its propositional component" (1973, p. 18); that is, whether or not the words being voiced accurately represent some state of affairs in the wider world. This is the second claim of *truth*. Is the speaker doing her best to give us the fullest possible information about the matter under consideration? The extent to which the speaker sticks to the rules of talk that prevail in our discussion community is a third feature we pay attention to. This is the claim of *rightness*. A sentence is judged partly according to "the correctness and appropriateness of its performatory component" (1973, p. 18); that is, whether or not it is stated in a form that is familiar and likely to be understood the way it is intended. Communication is impossible without people observing the intuitively understood norms and rules governing speech, the sort of broadly accepted road map of talk. Finally, we need to know that the people speaking to us are sincerely interested in reaching understanding. This is the claim of *authenticity*, particularly "the authenticity of the speaking subject" (1973, p. 18). We must be able to trust that others in conversation sincerely wish to make themselves understandable and to understand us in return.

Learning to recognize when, or how far, these validity claims are being met is an unending learning project, one crucial to democratic discussion. If we haven't learned to distinguish between propogandizing and a genuine statement of deeply held views, or to discern those times when apparent truthfulness masks coercive intent, then our ability to defeat subtle demagoguery within the public sphere is severely curtailed. It is in everyday communicative action that people learn to recognize the manipulation of speech that, on a larger scale, diminishes the public sphere. The chair of a community gathering who, in giving the "sense of the meeting" carefully slants his summary to highlight his preferred view; the facilitator who sums up the main points of a discussion and gives an account that some in the room barely recognize; the spouse or lover in a supposedly open conversation who skillfully manipulates the outcome so that the blame for any marital stress or interpersonal tension always rests on the other's shoulders—all these communicative actions are violating one or other of the validity claims Habermas emphasizes. In learning how to detect when these violations are happening, and how to bring these to people's attention, citizens prepare themselves for discussions in the public sphere. They show that they are learning communicative competence.

One of Habermas's ideas that is most relevant for the conduct of discussion (and that has also drawn considerable criticism) is his stress on the giving of reasons as a universal feature of speech. To him "even the most fleeting speech act offers, the most conventional yes/no responses, *rely on* potential reasons" (1996, p. 19). If asked, we could supply the reasons we believe something, propose something, or respond to another's ideas in the ways we do. Reasons, therefore, "are the primary currency used in a discursive exchange that redeems criticizable validity claims" (1996, p. 35). The reasons given for various proposals or assertions can, of course, be false, wrong, exploitative, or immoral. But the giving of reasons is universal. We may appeal to authority (do this because I tell you to) or supernatural powers (do this because the rain God will be displeased if you don't). We may cite experience as the reason for our beliefs or actions, or we may appeal to formal rules of logic. Sometimes we go back to dogma or text and cite that as the reason for a decision. At other times our reason is that "it's just common sense." The point for Habermas is that we always cite reasons to justify our beliefs or actions to ourselves and to others.

Nowhere is this giving of reasons more important than in discussions within a democratic public sphere. Habermas believes that when a speech community functions as it should it is also a democratic community. Hence, the rules that govern communicative action (such as the giving of ideas for the viewpoints and ideas we hold) are the same as those informing the democratic process. If learning to participate in communicative action is a universal learning project, then learning democratic process is its political counterpart. When we learn to give reasons fully and honestly for our conduct, and to talk to each other in ways that are comprehensible, truthful, appropriate, and authentic, we are learning democracy. This is because the standards and rules we use to judge the rightness of our participation in a discussion are the same as those we adopt when assessing the legitimacy of a democratic decision.

A Discourse Theory of Democracy

As indicated, Habermas consistently argues that the rules of discussion suggested by communicative action are also the basis of democratic process. Readers may well recognize that something like these rules informs the conduct of many of their discussion groups. The rules Habermas specifies are "that (a) all relevant voices are heard, (b) the best of all available arguments, given the present state of our knowledge are accepted, and (c) only the non-coercive coercion of the better argument determines the affirmations and negations of the participants" (Habermas, 1992, p. 260). In other words, good discussion, and therefore good democratic process, depends on everyone contributing, on everyone having the fullest possible knowledge of different perspectives, and on everyone being ready to give up their position if a better argument is presented to them. Taken together, these rules constitute an ideal that citizens can use to judge the effectiveness of political deliberations, and educators can use to judge the validity of education programs and learning activities. Habermas calls this the "ideal speech situation."

Of course the problem with this ideal is that judgments as to which voices are relevant, how relevance itself is to be determined, how we decide which are the best arguments, and who estimates exactly what is the present state of our knowledge, are both highly subjective and contentious. If we're not careful we end up asking those in authority to decide these things and privileging the very experts Habermas is trying to restrain. Not surprising, Habermas is quick to recognize this danger. In an interview in *Justifications and Applications* (1993), he voices his regret at coining the term "ideal speech situation," calling it "a term whose concretistic connotations are misleading" (p. 164). However, Habermas does not believe that these drawbacks inevitably render rules of discourse as useless. To reject these rules because they can be co-opted and manipulated by dominant groups is to throw the baby of communicative reason out with the bath water of potentially distorted communication. For Habermas the ideal rules of discourse—participants striving to understand others' perspectives, being open to all views, and being prepared to change their minds based on new evidence or better arguments—offer the best hope of keeping democratic forces alive. We can use these rules to determine whether a speech community (of, say, elected representatives) is reaching its decisions in a fair and morally defensible way.

Suggestions for implementing these rules have been made throughout this book. We have tried to emphasize discussion exercises (such as "Circle of Voices, "Hatful of Quotes", and "Circular Response") that ensure genuine equity of participation. The creation of ground rules for discussion outlined in Chapter Three represents a particular opportunity for focusing students' (and teachers') minds on how we should talk to each other. Exercises such as "Methodological Belief" and "Critical Debate" emphasize intentional perspective-taking in which students are asked to see the world through an alternative set of eyes. This can also be accomplished by requiring students to engage with texts and perspectives that are unfamiliar or uncongenial to them (as described in our response to Marcuse's analysis of repressive tolerance in the previous chapter). Discussing the evidence and perspectives emerging from the results of the Critical Incident Questionnaire (CIQ) also allows a speech community to change its processes. In particular it provides the teacher with a crucial opportunity to model a willingness to change her mind (about classroom assignments, teaching activities, evaluative criteria, deadlines, curriculum and so forth) based on new evidence or better arguments reported on the CIQ.

In addition, one of the conversational roles not mentioned in Chapter Seven that we have added to our own practices is that of *textual focuser*. This role involves requesting participants to specify precisely where in the text is expressed the particular viewpoint they claim it contains. Doing this prevents learners making claims for authors and books that are really only students' own opinions. We have also emphasized to students that one of the foundations of academic discourse, and one of our most important responsibilities as teachers, is constantly to ask students, colleagues, and published "experts" for the evidence that supports their particular analyses. One thing you can do early in a discussion is to make it clear to participants that your role that day will be that of *evidential inquirer* and that you will perform that role by asking students to give evidential support for any and all of their general contentions. You can ask students to hold you to the same standard and request that you give evidence for your own general assertions.

Indeed, early on in a course you might specify this as a prime indicator of good student participation (a situation that puts students who are used to earning approval by flattering the teacher in a productively unsettling double bind). The role of *evidential assessor* can also be added to the conversation roles discussed in Chapter Seven.

In situations where ground rules for discussion have been generated by students, the teacher can also announce that one of her responsibilities that day will be to check whether or not these rules are being followed. Alternatively, different students can be asked to assume this role in different class meetings. Early on in a course, or with learners to whom the idea of ground rules for discussions comes as a surprise (which is the case for the majority of groups we've worked with), we believe the teacher has a special responsibility to take on this role. Our general assumption is that teachers have greater experience of discussion process, and certainly the necessary positional authority, to be the best monitor of discussion ground rules in the first weeks of a class.

Teachers can also tell students that as a way of ensuring that rules of discourse are followed they (the teachers) will keep introducing unfamiliar or rarely articulated perspectives that they wish students to review. This reinforces being open to all perspectives that Habermas emphasizes as such an important rule of democratic discourse. Teachers themselves can model this openness by engaging with an unfamiliar text or idea in front of the students. This is most effective if students themselves are asked to bring in to class books, articles, online chat excerpts, Web site addresses, and so on that contain information that challenges the teacher's arguments. When students do take this opportunity (and they will have to be very sure you can be trusted not to punish them for seeming to challenge your authority in class) the effects can be very dramatic. It strongly affirms the notion that effective participation in discussion entails the deliberate engagement with contrary perspectives.

CONCLUSION

Throughout this book we have enumerated the many reasons we teach through discussion. Undoubtedly, discussion opens students to alternative perspectives, increases their tolerance for ambiguity, makes them aware of the value of peer learning, and strengthens their emotional engagement with abstract subject matter. But out of all the reasons we commonly give for teaching through discussion it is the fostering of democratic habits we find the most compelling. We endorse Habermas's contention that discussion groups are ideal laboratories in which students can learn democracy. We believe that discussion-based classrooms offer appropriate environments for the practice of democracy and for a relatively safe exposure to its contradictory and complex dynamics. Discussion as a way of teaching is, for us, the best pedagogy to prepare learners to participate actively, critically, transparently, and hopefully in realizing at least some of democracy's untapped promise.

CHAPTER FIFTEEN

EVALUATING DISCUSSION

As a way of bringing our book to a close, we want to say a few words regarding the evaluation of discussions. Our commentary will be brief, however, because we don't believe there really are any standardized protocols or universal measures we can apply to assessing a discussion leader's competence or the value of students' contributions. If our advice has a central theme, it is that any evaluative approaches or judgments must be grounded in students' subjectivity. We are aware of the flaws associated with self-reporting, but we believe that discussion is such an elusive and idiosyncratically experienced phenomenon that no other method is likely to yield much meaningful information. Furthermore, when students regularly document their perceptions of the contributions they are making to the ongoing exchange of ideas, they can learn an enormous amount about the conditions and behaviors that make discussion successful. So the evaluative processes that we suggest (like all good educational evaluation) emphasize learning as much as assessment.

Because most higher educational institutions mandate annual assessments of faculty's pedagogic proficiency, we know that lecturers and professors regularly have to demonstrate that they are effective teachers. If they use discussion, this will involve them in documenting their own capabilities as discussion leaders as well as their students' learning. But doing this is problematic. Discussion is an infinitely varied and multifaceted reality experienced by students in multiple ways. We wish we could say that an instrument were available that could record accurately your own proficiency as a discussion leader and your students' achievements. We cannot. To spend ten chapters insisting on the complex subjectivity of discussion and then to propose a form of standardized, supposedly objective measurement in the final chapter would be the ultimate irony!

The problem is that most evaluative systems work in a positivist way. First, an ideal type or exemplar of how an educational process should look is established. The standard of what counts as a proper demonstration of the process is usually determined by polling experts in the field and then translating theoretical tenets into practical terms. Then, whether or not an activity is judged to be done well or poorly is determined by how closely it reproduces these exemplary characteristics. But discussion cannot be judged by how closely it approximates a decontextualized ideal. Discussions are like marriages—no two are alike, and no one on the outside can ever really understand what's going on inside. Because discussions are always contextual—always shaped by the cultural backgrounds, social classes, genders, experiences, and personalities of its participants—they can only be evaluated from the inside. So we generally advocate that teachers work from students' own testimony regarding the nature of their discussion experience.

However, we do acknowledge that even the most phenomenologically inclined teachers have to survive in a system that often puts them through positivist paces. Few of us have the luxury of rejecting standardized evaluative formats, no matter how misconceived we might judge them to be. So let's begin by examining an evaluative approach that at least gives the appearance of being grounded in clear and unequivocal criteria. This approach involves assessing how well students have observed the rules of conduct they have evolved to govern the discussion process. If the class has created guidelines for democratic discussion in which several specific behaviors are proposed, evaluating students' participation becomes a matter of working with them to assess how often these were exhibited. Students could keep a weekly audit of their participation in class discussions and then summarize and analyze their entries in an end-of-semester learning portfolio. Here's an example of a discussion audit used in a course where getting students to think critically was a prime objective.

Discussion Audit Instructions

Please write down anything that occurs to you about your contributions to the discussions we've had in class this week and anything you may have learned from those discussions. You may record your thoughts in a free-flowing way. If you prefer more structure, it might be helpful to consider the following questions.

Don't feel that you have to answer every one or even any of them—they're just here to help your reflections.

List the assumptions that you held about the topic of the discussions this week that were uncovered or clarified for you.

Of all these assumptions, which did you feel were accurate and valid? Try to write down what was said during the discussion that confirmed the accuracy of your assumptions.

Of all these assumptions, which did you feel were most challenged by the discussion? Try to write down what was said during the discussion that challenged the accuracy of your assumptions.

What different perspectives on the topics were suggested for you by our discussions?

What's the most important learning you've taken from this week's discussions?

What's the most pressing question you're left with about the topic as a result of this week's discussions?

In what ways did you, and other group members, observe and implement the class rules for discussion?

In what ways did you, and other group members, contradict the class rules for discussion?

After your experience this week, which of these class rules should be amended or abandoned? And what new rules would you like to propose?

Midway through the semester and again at the end, you will be asked to read what you've written each week about your discussion experiences. You will be expected to prepare a summary in which you identify patterns, similarities, contradictions, discrepancies, and surprises. This summary (not the individual weekly entries) will be a part of your learning portfolio for the course.

Another way to evaluate discussions is to generate evaluative criteria that are organized around the fifteen claims for discussion outlined in Chapter Two. Through this approach, students have the task at the end of the semester (perhaps as part of their course portfolio) of documenting the extent to which their experience increased their tolerance for ambiguity and complexity, helped them investigate their own assumptions, increased their appreciation for differences, and so on. They would be asked to document how they tried to affirm and show respect for other participants' experiences, to engage in active listening, to ensure that a diversity of perspectives was considered, to increase their ability to communicate ideas clearly, and to develop the skills of synthesis and integration.

Incorporating instructions like the following into the section of the course syllabus dealing with evaluation will help communicate to students the criteria against which their participation is going to be judged.

Course Portfolio: Instructions for Evaluating Your Discussion Participation

Participating in class discussion is an important part of this course. However, what participation means and how it can be observed are open questions. In this course both you and your instructor will judge your participation in discussion according to how seriously you try to live out the conditions of critical conversation.

Below are listed fifteen purposes for discussion. Each week I want you to write about the extent to which you think each of these purposes was accomplished. Give as many examples of your own discussion behaviors as you can.

1. *Becoming aware of diversity:* Were a variety of perspectives explored in the discussion this week? What views from outside the mainstream did you or others try to bring into the group? What questions, issues, or perspectives did you think the group was trying to avoid during the discussion, and how did you or others try to bring these to the attention of group members? Did the students who spoke in discussion include at least some representatives from subgroups demarcated by gender, race, class, occupation, ideology, and so on?

2. *Appreciating ambiguity and complexity:* Was the discussion open-ended, and did the participants show respect for the complexity of the issues discussed? What were some of the questions raised for you this week as a result of your participating in class? Were as many questions raised as were answered during the discussion? Did the teacher guide the discussion toward a predetermined end point, or did the discussion conclude more ambiguously, stimulating further inquiry and reflection?

3. *Hunting assumptions:* Were there opportunities in the discussion this week for you to increase your awareness of the assumptions you hold and

to critique these? What assumptions about the topic did you uncover or clarify? Of these assumptions, which did you challenge, and how?

4. *Listening attentively and respectfully:* To what extent was the behavior of discussion participants respectful? What did you do in discussion to show others that you were listening attentively? What signals did you receive from others to show that they were or were not listening attentively?

5. *Acknowledging continuing differences:* Were there open and frank disagreements in discussion? If so, was there a willingness on the part of those who disagreed to acknowledge and respect differing viewpoints?

6. *Increasing intellectual agility:* As each week passes, are you finding it increasingly easier to express yourself in discussion? Are you able to respond to unexpected comments with more sureness and confidence? Do the other members of the group appear to understand your comments more clearly?

7. *Seeing connections:* How did the discussion this week connect to your life? What ideas surfaced that had implications for how you'll think and act in the future?

8. *Respecting experience:* What relevance, if any, did the discussion this week have to your own experiences? How did others affirm the value of your experiences? How did you affirm the experience of others? In what ways were these experiences respectfully subjected to critical analysis?

9. *Practicing democratic habits:* Were there frequent opportunities this week for many students to voice concerns and formulate ideas? Were there frequent opportunities to affirm and question one another? Were there opportunities to reach small group consensus through collaborative, deliberative processes? Was dissent also encouraged and honored?

10. *Creating knowledge together:* Did you feel that your ideas were valued as much as anyone else's, including the teacher's? Were there times this week when you thought your comments advanced the understanding of the group? Did the comments of others help you understand an issue or idea better?

11. *Communicating clearly:* How could you tell that your ideas were or were not being clearly communicated to others? What were you and others doing to communicate more clearly across cultural, racial, gender, class, and ideological differences?

12. *Learning collaboratively:* Were there opportunities this week for you to work closely with others? If so, did this work increase your understanding of collaboration or enhance your sensitivity to it? Did your peers display collaborative work habits?

13. *Broadening understanding and empathy:* To what extent did the discussion this week broaden your understanding of an issue or idea? Were you better able to understand and articulate the perspectives of others?

14. *Synthesizing and integrating:* How were you able to connect your contributions to the contributions of others? In what ways did the discussion lead you to a deeper understanding of an idea or issue? How did it give you a new appreciation of the topic's complexity?

15. *Transforming ideas and actions:* In what ways did the discussion this week cause you to consider acting differently outside the classroom?

At the middle and end of the semester, please write interim and final summaries of your main contributions toward realizing the fifteen claims for discussion. You don't need to produce your weekly logs. In fact, you don't need to mention any specific examples if you feel it would violate your own or someone else's privacy.

An option that is less time-consuming than the portfolio is to ask students to keep a short discussion log. A discussion log is a set of brief responses to three questions. Unlike the portfolio (which deals with the full gamut of discussion behaviors and dispositions), the log concentrates on what students think they have learned.

Discussion Log

At the end of our discussion today, please take the time to write a few sentences in response to the following three questions:

1. What do you know as a result of participating in this discussion that you didn't know last week?

2. What can you do as a result of participating in this discussion that you couldn't do last week?

3. What could you teach someone to know or do as a result of participating in this discussion that you couldn't teach them last week?

The information in this log can be used in two possible ways. Students can submit their responses to you once a week, and you can start the next class by summarizing these. This is the CIQ approach. As with that instrument, it is crucial that students know their anonymity is assured. No names are allowed on the logs that are handed in. Or, taking a more longitudinal approach, students can use these logs as primary data for a report on their discussion learning that they will include in their portfolios.

For teachers who deal with a heavy workload involving a large number of students, the time needed to read and evaluate students' audits, logs, and portfolios may simply not be available. All these teachers have time to do is read an end-of-course evaluation form once a semester. We think that such a summative approach to evaluating learning and practice is of limited value. For one thing, waiting until the end of a course to find out how it's going denies you the chance to improve it as it's happening. But we know too that some of us have little option but to work within these constraints. For teachers in this position, we propose the following end-of-course evaluation form.

Note that this form doesn't mention discussion (or any other teaching approach) by name. This is deliberate. The form is open-ended and focuses on learning. It starts and ends with students' experiences as learners. Teaching is the secondary concept, learning the primary one. According to this form, good teaching is determined by how and what students are learning, not by whether or not they display predetermined competencies. Whether or not teachers are working well becomes a matter of judging the extent to which they are helping learning. The form helps us decide if particular teaching behaviors are good or bad, helpful or unproductive, by reading how students write about them. If participating in discussions is what helps students learn, this will come through loud and clear in their responses to the instrument. If, by contrast, students' responses make little or no mention of discussions, something is seriously amiss. Although teachers may ask students to spend a lot of time in discussion, there is no necessary correlation between talking and learning. The form will help teachers determine the extent to which participating in discussion is helping students learn.

COURSE EVALUATION FORM

Course _____

Instructor _____

Semester _____

This form is designed to help your teachers gain a better understanding of how they are assisting your learning and how they might improve their teaching. Please answer each item as candidly as possible. Your anonymity is assured.

Please complete the following statements.

1. What most helped my learning in this course was . . .
2. What most hindered my learning in this course was . . .
3. What most helped me to take responsibility for my own learning in this class was . . .
4. What most prevented me from taking responsibility for my own learning in this class was . . .
5. This class revealed to me that the area for my development as a learner that I need to work on most is . . .

Please respond by circling one of the responses and adding some personal comment:

6. In this course I found that different teaching approaches were used *(circle one)* often / sometimes / rarely. What are your reactions to the teaching approaches used?
7. In this course I found that the instructor was responsive to students' concerns *(circle one)* consistently/ occasionally/rarely. What are your feelings about this level of responsiveness?
8. In this course I found that the teacher tried to get students to participate *(circle one)* frequently / occasionally / rarely. What are your feelings about the amount of participation by students in this course?
9. In this course I found that I received information about my learning *(circle one)* regularly / occasionally / rarely. What is your opinion about the frequency with which you received information about your learning and the quality of that information?

10. In this course I found that democratic habits of including all students' voices, creating equal time for all to speak, and allowing students to disagree with the teacher and each other were practiced *(circle one)* regularly / occasionally / rarely. What are your feelings about the level of democracy in this class?

11. In this course I found that I was exposed to a variety of perspectives, opinions, voices, and views *(circle one)* regularly / occasionally / rarely. What are your feelings about the level of your exposure to diverse perspectives in this class?

12. In this course, to what extent was the instructor . . . *(please circle one response for each question)*

    Knowledgeable about the subject?   very/somewhat/not at all

    Able to communicate that
    knowledge well?   very/somewhat/not at all

    Clear about why the course was
    organized as it was?   very/somewhat/not at all

    Courteous and respectful to
    students?   very/somewhat/not at all

What would you most like to say about the instructor's effectiveness as a teacher?

Please complete the following statements.

13. Overall, the moments in the course when I was most engaged, excited, and involved as a learner were when . . .

14. Overall, the moments in the course when I was most distanced, disengaged, and uninvolved as a learner were when . . .

Please respond to each question.

15. What would you most like to say about your experiences as a student in this course?

16. What piece of advice would you most like to give the instructor on how to teach the course in the future?

17. Is there anything else you'd like to say about the experience of being a student in this class that you haven't already said in response to previous items? If so, please note it here.

Like it or not (and as a rule we don't), reward systems drive many students' behaviors. Students will do whatever they feel will help them earn a good grade. So in setting evaluative criteria, it's very important that at the first class meeting you try to break one of the most prominent and unquestioned assumptions they bring to discussion: that the best students are those who speak the most. Unless this assumption is challenged directly, repeatedly, and early, a pattern of interaction will quickly emerge. By the third or fourth meeting, a small group of particularly confident students (usually 20 to 25 percent of the group) will create a pecking order of contributors that is only very occasionally broken by a comment from someone outside this "in" group.

If you say that a part of the course grade will be awarded for participation in discussion, you need to help students realize that participation can be accomplished silently. You can provide examples at the first few class meetings of what silent and productive participation looks like. A student may discover independently some provocative material that's not provided as part of the course reading. If the student photocopies this material and distributes it to classmates, this should be considered an important contribution to the quality of conversation. The contributed material could add neglected but important perspectives, provide counterbalancing information, challenge an emerging consensus, or provide new avenues for consideration.

A student could also make a significant nonspeaking contribution by circulating (on paper or via e-mail) an extract from her learning log that points out how the group starts to move toward discussing certain contentious issues and then at the last moment veers away. She could point out that a form of unchallenged groupthink is emerging. Or she could add an insight about the discussion that occurred to her after the class had finished. If all a student does is to say, "I think we need to be quiet for a while now so that we can think a bit more about what we've just said," this should be acknowledged as a crucial contribution to the quality of the conversation.

EVALUATION AS APPRECIATION

A major element in evaluation should be appreciation. After all, any truly evaluative judgment involves positive as well as negative appraisal. We think that important moments in a discussion group's life are when its members show their appreciation of each other's efforts. At the outset of this book we argued that discussion is based on mutuality and reciprocity—that without others' participation, none of us can learn. In a very real sense, discussion group members need and depend on each other for their own learning. Because this is so, members need to acknowledge how others' efforts have been crucial to their own learning and how much they depend on others' contributions for their future development. Teachers can create regular moments when group members have a chance to recognize each other for the particular contributions they have made to an individual's understanding or the group's development. This can be done informally, by using perhaps ten minutes of the last class of the week for students to express appreciations of each other, verbally or in writing. Or it can be done as part of reporting on the CIQ, particularly when reporting comments to the class regarding question 3 on that form (the actions taken by others in the room that students have found particularly helpful or affirming).

A more ceremonial approach that might be appropriate to a last class or end-of-course meeting is the stone of gratitude. The teacher hands a stone to a student and asks him to give it to another member of the group. The student reflects, chooses a peer, and passes the stone to her. As he gives the stone to her, he states publicly in what particular way the student who is receiving the stone has been helpful for his learning. The student who receives the stone then chooses another student and passes the stone along, expressing gratitude for a particular insight, comment, or personal quality that she has appreciated from that third student. The exercise continues this way for as long as people wish to express appreciation. The stone can visit the same group member several times, and the teacher can also be included. When we have seen this exercise used (it was introduced to one of us by Randee Lawrence of National Louis University), we are struck by how many times students preface their choice of a peer by saying, "Of course, I want to give this to all of you" or "How can I possibly choose one person when all of you have been so important to me?" So although the exercise seems focused on expressing appreciation for individuals, it actually ends up affirming the importance of the whole group as a crucible for learning.

CONCLUSION

How shall we end this book? We could conclude with a rhetorically rousing call to arms intended to inspire teachers to use discussion more regularly. We could recap the benefits we think discussion brings—how it trains us in democratic discourse, challenges our easy assumptions, and opens us to diverse views and voices. Or we could reprise our airing in the Preface of the most frequent objections faculty make to using discussion (that the process takes time away from content, that it's unrealistic to use in large lecture courses, that it's unsuited to the natural sciences, and so on) and summarize our responses.

But we want to finish instead on a personal note. We love discussion. We think that participating in discussion is its own reward, an experience so intrinsically satisfying that we can't get along without it. Though we never get it exactly right and though we invariably fall short of our ideals, we enjoy its sheer unpredictability. We luxuriate in its open-endedness, in the feeling that there is always another perspective to be expressed, another understanding to be gained. The sense of multiple and infinite possibilities waiting in the future is the joyful essence of teaching and learning through discussion.

So we use discussion for selfish reasons. We find that not knowing how the conversation will proceed, where we'll end up when the class is over, or what we'll learn along the way is wonderfully intriguing. The uncertainty of it keeps us alive and alert. We feel that predictability is the enemy of engagement, and the one thing we desire above all else is to be engaged in our practice. Discussion does this for us. It serves constantly to renew our commitment to and enthusiasm for teaching. It constitutes a source of methodological pleasure we crave and an experience of learning we celebrate.

REFERENCES

Althusser, L. *Lenin and Philosophy*. New York: Monthly Review Press, 1971.

Aragon, S. R. "Creating Social Presence in Online Environments." In S. R. Aragon (ed.). *Facilitating Learning in Online Environments* (pp. 57-68). New Directions for Adult and Continuing Education, no. 100. San Francisco: Jossey-Bass, 2003.

Aronson, E. *The Jigsaw Classroom*. Thousand Oaks, Calif.: Sage, 1978.

Ayers, W. *To Teach: The Journey of a Teacher*. New York: Teachers College Press, 1993.

Barber, B. *Strong Democracy*. Berkeley: University of California Press, 1984.

Barber, B. "Neither Leaders nor Followers." In B. Barber and R. Battistoni (eds.), *Education for Democracy*. Dubuque, Iowa: Kendall/Hunt, 1993.

Barber, B. *An Aristocracy of Everyone*. New York: Ballantine, 1994.

Barth, R. S. *Learning by Heart*. San Francisco: Jossey-Bass, 2001.

Basseches, M. *Dialectical Thinking and Adult Development*. Norwood, N.J.: Ablex, 1984.

Bateman, W. L. *Open to Question: The Art of Teaching and Learning by Inquiry*. San Francisco: Jossey-Bass, 1990.

Bean, J. C., and Peterson, D. "Grading Classroom Participation." In R. S. Anderson and B. W. Speck (eds.), *Changing the Way We Grade Student Performance: Classroom Assessment and the New Learning Paradigm*. New Directions for Teaching and Learning, no. 74. San Francisco: Jossey-Bass, 1998.

Belenky, M. F., Clinchy, B. M., Goldberger, N. R., and Tarule, J. M. *Women's Ways of Knowing: The Development of Self, Voice, and Mind*. New York: Basic Books, 1986.

Bell, D. *Faces at the Bottom of the Well*. New York: Basic Books, 1985.

Bellah, R., Madsen, R., Sullivan, W., Swidler, A., and Tipton, S. *The Good Society*. New York: Knopf, 1991.

Bender, T. *Discussion-based Online Teaching to Enhance Student Learning*. Sterling, VA: Stylus, 2003.

Berge, Z. L. "Components of the Online Classroom." In R. E. Weiss, D. S. Knowlton, and B. W. Speck (eds.), *Principles of Effective Teaching in the Online Classroom* (pp. 23-28). New Directions for Teaching and Learning, no. 84. San Francisco: Jossey-Bass, 2000.

Bernstein, B. *Class, Codes, and Control, Vol. 3.* New York: Routledge, 1977.

Bernstein, B. "On Pedagogic Discourse." In J. G. Richardson (ed.), *Handbook of Theory and Research for the Sociology of Education.* Westport, Conn.: Greenwood Press, 1986.

Bernstein, B. *The Structuring of Pedagogic Discourse: Class, Codes, and Control, Vol. 4.* New York: Routledge, 1990.

Bernstein, R. "Metaphysics, Critique, and Utopia." *Review of Metaphysics,* 1988, *42,* 255–273.

Bernstein, R. *The New Constellation: The Ethical-Political Horizons of Modernity/Postmodernity.* Cambridge, Mass.: MIT Press, 1992.

Boal, A. *Games for Actors and Non-Actors.* New York: Routledge, 1992.

Bourdieu, P. "Forms of Capital." In J. G. Richardson (ed.), *Handbook of Theory and Research for the Sociology of Education.* Westport, Conn.: Greenwood Press, 1986.

Bowles, S., and Gintis, H. *Schooling in Capitalist America.* New York: Basic Books, 1974.

Boyte, H. *Commonwealth: A Return to Citizen Politics.* New York: Free Press, 1989.

Bridges, D. *Education, Democracy, and Discussion.* Lanham, Md.: University Press of America, 1988.

Britzman, D. *Practice Makes Practice: A Critical Study of Learning to Teach.* Albany: State University of New York Press, 1991.

Brookfield, S. D. *The Skillful Teacher: On Technique, Trust, and Responsiveness in the Classroom.* San Francisco: Jossey-Bass, 1990.

Brookfield, S. D. *Becoming a Critically Reflective Teacher.* San Francisco: Jossey-Bass, 1995.

Bruffee, K. A. *Collaborative Learning: Higher Education, Interdependence, and the Authority of Knowledge.* Baltimore: Johns Hopkins University Press, 1993.

Bruner, J. *The Culture of Education.* Cambridge, Mass.: Harvard University Press, 1996.

Burbules, N. *Dialogue in Teaching.* New York: Teachers College Press, 1993.

Cale, G. *When Resistance Becomes Reproduction: A Critical Action Research Study.* Proceedings of the 42nd Adult Education Research Conference. East Lansing: Michigan State University, 2001.

Cale, G., and Huber, C. "Teaching the Oppressor to Be Silent: Conflicts in the 'Democratic' Classroom." In *The Changing Face of Adult Learning.* Proceedings of the 21st Annual Alliance/ACE Conference. Austin, TX, 2001.

Carnoy, M., and Levin, H. *Schooling and Work in the Democratic State.* Stanford, CA: Stanford University Press, 1985.

Chisom, R., and Washington, M. *Undoing Racism: A Philosophy of International Social Change.* (2nd ed.). New Orleans: The People's Institute Press, 1997.

Christensen, C. "The Discussion Leader in Action: Questioning, Listening, and Response." In C. Christensen, D. Garvin, and A. Sweet (eds.), *Education for Judgment: The Artistry of Discussion Leadership*. Boston: Harvard Business School Press, 1991a.

Christensen, C. "Every Student Teaches and Every Student Learns: The Reciprocal Gift of Discussion Teaching." In C. Christensen, D. Garvin, and A. Sweet (eds.), *Education for Judgment: The Artistry of Discussion Leadership*. Boston: Harvard Business School, 1991b.

Collins, M. *Adult Education as Vocation: A Critical Role for the Adult Educator.* New York: Routledge, 1991.

Crawford, M. *Talking Difference: On Gender and Language.* Thousand Oaks, Calif.: Sage, 1995.

Damrosch, D. *We Scholars: Changing the Culture of the University.* Cambridge, Mass.: Harvard University Press, 1995.

Davis, B. G., and Sumara, D. J. "Cognition, Complexity, and Teacher Education." *Harvard Educational Review,* 1997, *67,* 105–125.

Delpit, L. *Other People's Children: Cultural Conflicts in the Classroom.* New York: New Press, 1995.

Dewey, J. *Democracy and Education.* Old Tappan, N.J.: Macmillan, 1916.

Dewey, J. "Creative Democracy: The Task Before Us." In I. Edman (ed.), *John Dewey: His Contribution to the American Tradition.* Indianapolis: Bobbs Merrill, 1955.

Dewey, J. "Democracy and Educational Administration." In J. A. Boydston (ed.), *Late Works, 1925–1953.* Carbondale: Southern Illinois University Press, 1991.

Dews, C.L.B., and Law, C. L. (eds.). *This Fine Place So Far from Home: Voices of Academics from the Working Class.* Philadelphia: Temple University Press, 1995.

Digby, T. (ed). *Men Doing Feminism.* New York: Routledge, 1998.

Diller, A., Houston, B., Morgan, K. P., and Ayim, M. (eds.). *The Gender Question in Education: Theory, Pedagogy, and Politics.* Boulder, Colo.: Westview Press, 1996.

Dillon, J. *Using Discussion in Classrooms.* Buckingham, England: Open University Press, 1994.

Duckworth, E. *"The Having of Wonderful Ideas": And Other Essays on Teaching and Learning.* New York: Teachers College Press, 1996.

Elbow, P. *Embracing Contraries.* New York: Oxford University Press, 1986.

Ellsworth, E. "Why Doesn't This Feel Empowering? Working Through the Repressive Myths of Critical Pedagogy." *Harvard Educational Review,* 1989, 59, 297–324.

Fein, A. D., and Logan, M. C. "Preparing Instructors for Online Instruction." In S. R. Aragon (ed.), *Facilitating Learning in Online Environments* (pp. 45-55). New Directions for Adult and Continuing Education, no. 100. San Francisco: Jossey-Bass, 2003.

Ferrier, B., Marrin, M., and Seidman, J. "Student Autonomy in Learning Medicine: Some Participants' Experiences." In D. Boud (ed.), *Developing Student Autonomy in Learning*. New York: Nichols, 1988.

Finkel, D. L. *Teaching with Your Mouth Shut*. Portsmouth, N.H.: Heinemann, 2000.

Fishkin, J. *The Voice of the People*. New Haven, Conn.: Yale University Press, 1995.

Foucault, M. *Power/Knowledge: Selected Interviews and Other Writings, 1972-1977*. New York: Pantheon Books, 1980.

Frederick, P. "The Dreaded Discussion: Ten Ways to Start." In D. Bligh (ed.), *Teach Thinking by Discussion*. Guildford, England: Society for Research into Higher Education/National Foundation for Educational Research–Nelson, 1986.

Freire, P. *Pedagogy of the Oppressed*. New York: Continuum, 1993.

Freire, P. *Pedagogy of Hope*. New York: Continuum, 1994.

Fromm, E. *Escape from Freedom*. New York: Holt, Rinehart and Winston, 1941.

Fromm, E. *The Sane Society*. London: Routledge, Kegan and Paul, 1956.

Fromm, E. *The Revolution of Hope: Toward a Humanized Technology*. New York: Harper and Row, 1968.

Gadamer, H. G. *Truth and Method*. New York: Crossroad, 1989.

Gastil, J. *Democracy in Small Groups*. Philadelphia: New Society, 1993.

Gawalek, M. A., Mulqueen, M., and Tarule, J. M. "Woman to Women: Understanding the Needs of Our Female Students." In S. M. Deats and L. T. Lenker (eds.), *Gender and Academe: Feminist Pedagogy and Politics*. Lanham, Md.: Rowman & Littlefield, 1994.

Gilligan, C. *In a Different Voice: Psychological Theory and Women's Development*. Cambridge, Mass.: Harvard University Press, 1982.

Giroux, H. "Citizenship, Public Philosophy, and the Struggle for Democracy." *Educational Theory*, 1987, *37*, 103–120.

Giroux, H. *Schooling and the Struggle for Public Life*. Minneapolis: University of Minnesota Press, 1988.

Glickman, C. D. *Revolutionizing America's Schools*. San Francisco: Jossey-Bass, 1997.

Gordon, T. *Leader Effectiveness Training*. New York: Bantam Books, 1977.

Gore, J. M. *The Struggle for Pedagogies: Critical and Feminist Discourses as Regimes of Truth*. New York: Routledge, 1993.

Great Books Foundation. *An Introduction to Shared Inquiry*. (2nd ed.) Chicago: Great Books Foundation, 1991.

Gudykunst, W. B. *Bridging Differences: Effective Intergroup Communication*. Thousand Oaks, Calif.: Sage, 1994.

Gunawardena, C. N. "Social Presence Theory and Implications for Interaction and Collaborative Learning in Computer Conferences." *International Journal of Educational Telecommunications 1*(2), 147-166, 1995.

Gunawardena, C. N., and Zittle, F. J. "Social Presence as a Predictor of Satisfaction Within a Computer-Mediated Conferencing Environment." *American Journal of Distance Education, 11*(3), 8-26, 1997.

Gyant, L. "Alain Leroy Locke: More Than an Adult Educator." In E. A. Peterson (ed.), *Freedom Road: Adult Education of African Americans.* Malabar, Fla.: Krieger, 1996.

Habermas, J. *Theory and Practice.* Boston: Beacon Press, 1973.

Habermas, J. *Legitimation Crisis.* Boston: Beacon Press, 1975.

Habermas, J. *The Theory of Communicative Action, Vol. 1: Reason and the Rationalization of Society.* Boston: Beacon Press, 1984.

Habermas, J. *The Theory of Communicative Action, Vol. 2: Life World and System: A Critique of Functionalist Reason.* Boston: Beacon Press, 1987.

Habermas, J. *The New Conservatism: Cultural Criticism and the Historians' Debate.* Cambridge, Mass.: MIT Press, 1989a.

Habermas, J. *The Structural Transformation of the Public Sphere: An Inquiry into a Category of Bourgeois Society.* Cambridge, Mass.: MIT Press, 1989b.

Habermas, J. *Autonomy and Solidarity: Interviews with Jurgen Habermas.* London: Verso, 1992 (revised ed.).

Habermas, J. *Justification and Application: Remarks on Discourse Ethics.* Cambridge, Mass.: MIT Press, 1993.

Habermas, J. *The Past as Future.* Lincoln, Neb.: University of Nebraska Press, 1994.

Habermas, J. *Between Facts and Norms: Contributions to a Discourse Theory of Democracy.* Cambridge, Mass.: MIT Press, 1996.

Hale, J. E. *Unbank the Fire: Visions for the Education of African American Children.* Baltimore: Johns Hopkins University Press, 1994.

Harbour, P. M. *Spiritual, Moral, and Cultural Dimensions of Cultural Diversity.* Kalamazoo, Mich.: Fetzer Institute, 1996.

Hook, S. *Education for Modern Man.* New York: Dial Press, 1946.

hooks, b. *Teaching to Transgress: Education as the Practice of Freedom.* New York: Routledge, 1994.

Horton, M. *The Long Haul.* New York: Doubleday, 1990.

Horton, M., and Freire, P. *We Make the Road by Walking.* Philadelphia: Temple University Press, 1990.

Isaacs, W. *Dialogue and the Art of Thinking Together: A Pioneering Approach to Communicating in Business and in Life.* New York: Currency, 1999.

Jacobson, R. "Asking Questions Is the Key Skill Needed for Discussion." *Chronicle of Higher Education,* July 25, 1984, p. 20.

Jacques, D. *Learning in Groups.* (2nd ed.) Houston: Gulf, 1992.

James, D., and Clarke, S. "Women, Men, and Interruptions: A Critical Review." In D. Tannen (ed.), *Gender and Conversational Interaction.* New York: Oxford University Press, 1983.

James, D., and Drakich, J. "Understanding Gender Differences in the Amount of Talk: A Critical Review of Research." In D. Tannen (ed.), *Gender and Conversational Interaction.* New York: Oxford University Press, 1983.

Johnson, S. D., and Aragon, S. R. "An Instructional Strategy Framework for Online Learning Environments." In S. R. Aragon (ed.), *Facilitating Learning in Online Environments* (pp. 31-43). New Directions for Adult and Continuing Education, no. 100. San Francisco: Jossey-Bass, 2003.

Johnson, D. W., Johnson, R. T., and Smith, K. *Active Learning: Cooperation in the College Classroom.* Edina, Minn.: Interaction, 1991a.

Johnson, D. W., Johnson, R. T., and Smith, K. *Cooperative Learning: Increasing College Faculty Instructional Productivity.* Edina, Minn.: Interaction, 1991b.

Kingwell, M. *A Civil Tongue.* University Park: Pennsylvania State University, 1995.

Lather, P. *Getting Smart: Feminist Research and Pedagogy with/in the Postmodern.* New York: Routledge, 1991.

Leonard, H. "With Open Ears: Listening and the Art of Discussion Leading." In C. Christensen, D. Garvin, and A. Sweet (eds.), *Education for Judgment: The Artistry of Discussion Leadership.* Boston: Harvard Business School Press, 1991.

Lindeman, E. C. "Adult Education and the Democratic Discipline." *Adult Education,* 1947, *6*(3), 112–115.

Lindeman, E. C. "Proposition 2: Ideals Can Never Be More Than Partially Realized." In T. V. Smith and E. C. Lindeman (eds.), *The Democratic Way of Life.* New York: Mentor Books, 1951.

Lindeman, E. C. "Democratic Discussion and the People's Voice." In S. D. Brookfield (ed.), *Learning Democracy: Eduard Lindeman on Adult Education and Social Change.* London: Croom Helm, 1987.

Lipman, M. *Thinking in Education.* Cambridge: Cambridge University Press, 1991.

Luke, C., and Gore, J. M. (eds.). *Feminisms and Critical Pedagogy.* New York: Routledge, 1992.

Maher, F. "Classroom Pedagogy and the New Scholarship on Women." In M. Culley and C. Portuges (eds.), *Gendered Subjects: The Dynamics of Feminist Teaching.* New York: Routledge, 1985.

Maher, F., and Tetreault, M.K.T. *The Feminist Classroom: An Inside Look at How Professors and Students Are Transforming Higher Education for a Diverse Society.* New York: Basic Books, 1994.

Marcuse, H. "Repressive Tolerance." In R. P. Wolff, B. Moore, and H. Marcuse. A *Critique of Pure Tolerance*. Boston: Beacon Press, 1965.

Marcuse, H. *Five Lectures*. Boston: Beacon Press, 1970.

Mattingly, C. "Valuing the Personal: Feminist Concerns for the Writing Classroom." In S. M. Deats and L. T. Lenker (eds.), *Gender and Academe: Feminist Pedagogy and Politics*. Lanham, Md.: Rowman & Littlefield, 1994.

McKeachie, W. J. Teaching Tips: *A Guidebook for Beginning College Teachers*. (7th ed.) Lexington, Mass.: Heath, 1978.

McLaren, P. *Life in Schools: An Introduction to Critical Pedagogy in the Foundations of Education*. (2nd ed.) New York: Longman, 1989.

McWilliam, E. *In Broken Images: Feminist Tales for a Different Teacher Education*. New York: Teachers College Press, 1994.

Mills, C. W. *The Sociological Imagination*. New York: Oxford University Press, 1959.

Murray, D. *Shoptalk: Learning to Write with Writers*. Portsmouth, N.H.: Boynton/Cook, 1990.

Naake, J. "Stand Where You Stand." 1996. Classroom handout.

Nieto, S., Ramos-Zayas, A., Pantoja, A., and Associates. *Colonialism and Working-Class Resistance: Puerto-Rican Education in the United States*. Cambridge, Mass.: Harvard Education Publishing Group, 1998.

Noddings, N. *Caring*. Berkeley: University of California Press, 1984.

Oakeshott, M. *Rationalism in Politics*. London: Methuen, 1962.

Orwell, G. "Politics and the English Language." In *A Collection of Essays*. New York: Doubleday, 1946.

Osborne, M. "Teaching Through Conversation: Making the Hidden Curriculum Part of the Overt Curriculum." In S. Feiman-Nemser and H. Featherstone (eds.), *Exploring Teaching: Reinventing an Introductory Course*. New York: Teachers College Press, 1992.

Palloff, R. M., and Pratt, K. *Building Learning Communities in Cyberspace: Strategies for the Online Classroom*. San Francisco: Jossey-Bass, 1999.

Palloff, R. M., and Pratt, K. *The Virtual Student: A Profile and Guide to Working with Online Learners*. San Francisco: Jossey-Bass, 2003.

Palmer, P. J. *To Know as We Are Known*. San Francisco: HarperSanFrancisco, 1993.

Palmer, P. J. *The Courage to Teach: Exploring the Inner Landscape of a Teacher's Life*. San Francisco: Jossey-Bass, 1998.

Parsley, B., and others. "Celebrating American Indian Culture and Education in Montana." *Montana Schools*, 1993, *36*(5), 6–10.

Pateman, C. *Democracy and Participation*. Cambridge: Cambridge University Press, 1970.

Paterson, R.W.K. "The Concept of Discussion: A Philosophical Approach." *Studies in Adult Education*, 1970, 2(1), 28–50.

Roffman, E. "The Personal Is Professional Is Political: Feminist Praxis in a Graduate School Counselor Training Program." In S. M. Deats and L. T. Lenker (eds.), *Gender and Academe: Feminist Pedagogy and Politics*. Lanham, Md.: Rowman & Littlefield, 1994.

Rorty, R. *Philosophy and the Mirror of Nature*. Princeton, N.J.: Princeton University Press, 1979.

Rorty, R. *Contingency, Irony and Solidarity*. Cambridge: Cambridge University Press, 1989.

Rose, M. *Lives on the Boundary*. New York: Penguin Books, 1990.

Rubin, L. B. *Worlds of Pain: Life in the Working Class Family*. New York: Basic Books, 1976.

Russell, M. "Black-Eyed Blues Connections: Teaching Black Women." In M. Culley and C. Portuges (eds.), *Gendered Subjects: The Dynamics of Feminist Teaching*. New York: Routledge, 1985.

Ryan, J., and Sackrey, C. *Strangers in Paradise: Academics from the Working Class*. Boston: South End Press, 1984.

Sattler, C. E. *Talking About a Revolution: The Politics and Practice of Feminist Teaching*. Creskill, N.J.: Hampton Press, 1997.

Sennett, R., and Cobb, J. *The Hidden Injuries of Class*. New York: Vintage Books, 1973.

Shor, I. *Critical Teaching and Everyday Life*. Chicago: University of Chicago Press, 1987.

Shor, I. *Empowering Education: Critical Teaching for Social Change*. Chicago: University of Chicago Press, 1992.

Shor, I. *When Students Have Power: Negotiating Authority in a Critical Pedagogy*. Chicago: University of Chicago Press, 1996.

Shor, I., and Freire, P. *A Pedagogy for Liberation: Dialogues on Transforming Education*. Westport, Conn.: Bergin and Garvey, 1987.

Slavin, R. *Cooperative Learning: Theory, Research, and Practice*. Upper Saddle River, N.J.: Prentice Hall, 1990.

Spender, D. Man Made Language. New York: Routledge, 1980.

Spring, J. *Deculturization and the Struggle for Equality: A Brief History of the Education of Dominated Cultures in the United States* (4th ed.) New York: McGraw-Hill, 2003.

Stanton, A. "Reconfiguring Teaching and Knowing in the College Classroom." In N. R. Goldberger, J. M. Tarule, B. M. Clinchy, and M. F. Belenky (eds.), *Knowledge, Difference, and Power: Essays Inspired by Women's Ways of Knowing*. New York: Basic Books, 1996.

Stewart, D. *Adult Learning in America: Eduard Lindeman and His Agenda for Lifelong Education*. Malabar, Fla.: Krieger, 1987.

Swisher, K., and Deyhle, D. "Adapting Instruction to Culture." In J. Reyhner (ed.), *Teaching American Indian Students*. Norman: University of Oklahoma Press, 1992.

Tannen, D. *You Just Don't Understand: Women and Men in Conversation.* New York: Morrow, 1990.

Tarule, J. M. "Voices in Dialogue: Collaborative Ways of Knowing." In N. R. Goldberger, J. M. Tarule, B. M. Clinchy, and M. F. Belenky (eds.), *Knowledge, Difference, and Power: Essays Inspired by Women's Ways of Knowing.* New York: Basic Books, 1996.

Usher, R., and Edwards, R. *Postmodernism and Education.* New York: Routledge, 1994.

Van Ments, M. *Active Talk: The Effective Use of Discussion in Learning.* New York: St. Martin's Press, 1990.

Vella, J. *Training Through Dialogue: Promoting Effective Learning and Change with Adults.* San Francisco: Jossey-Bass, 1995.

Viadero, D. "Culture Clash." *Teacher,* 1996, *7,* 14–17.

Wah, L. M. *The Color of Fear.* Oakland, Calif.: Stir Fry Productions, 1994. Film.

Walden, P. "Journal Writing: A Powerful Tool for Developing Women as Knowers." In K. Taylor and C. Marienau (eds.), *Learning Environments for Women's Adult Development: Bridges Toward Change.* New Directions for Adult and Continuing Education, no. 65. San Francisco: Jossey-Bass, 1995.

Weiler, K. *Women Teaching for Change: Gender, Class, and Power.* New York: Bergin & Garvey, 1988.

Welty, W. "Discussion Method Teaching." *Change,* 1989, *21*(4), 41–49.

West, C. *Race Matters.* New York: Vintage Books, 1993.

White, J. J. "Involving Different Social and Cultural Groups in Discussion." In W. W. Wilen (ed.), *Teaching and Learning Through Discussion: The Theory, Research, and Practice of the Discussion Method.* Springfield, Ill.: Thomas, 1990.

Willis, P. *Learning to Labor: How Working Class Kids Get Working Class Jobs.* Westmead, England: Gower, 1977.

Wiseman, F. *High School II: A Documentary by Frederick Wiseman.* Cambridge, Mass.: Zipporah Films, 1995.

Woodbridge, L. "The Centrifugal Classroom." In S. M. Deats and L. T. Lenker (eds.), *Gender and Academe: Feminist Pedagogy and Politics.* Lanham, Md.: Rowman and Littlefield, 1994.

INDEX

Discussion circles. *See* Circles

Discussion inventory, 259

Discussion leaders, *See also* Teachers: as judges of normality, 252–253; mistakes to avoid as, 63–65; talking too little, 200–203; talking too much, 193–195, 235

Discussion logs, 281–282

Dissenting views, 46–47

Diversity. *See* Cultural diversity; Pluralism

Drakich, J., 152

Dramatizing discussions, 119–120, 250

Drawing discussion, 121–122, 250

Duckworth, E., 236

E

E-mail discussions, 68, 122–123

Education: economic socialization and, 248–249; ensuring dominant ideology with, 249; knowing purpose of, 196–197, 202–203; structuralist analysis theories of, 248–249

Edwards, R., 78

Elaborated codes of speech, 249–250

Elbow, P., 135

Ellsworth, E., 19, 126, 132–133

Emotions: dealing with, 19; expressing appreciation, 15–16, 285–286; gender and expression of, 155; ground rules accounting for, 38–39; increasing student empathy, 34–35; providing outlet for anger and grief, 136–138; responding with silence, 98–99; working-class speech norms and, 142

Empathy: developing with methodological belief, 134–135, 259, 266; increasing student, 34–35

End-of-course evaluation form, 282–284

Engaged pluralism, 17–18

Escape from Freedom (Fromm), 232–233

Evaluating discussion: appreciation and, 285–286; discussion logs, 281–282; end-of-course form for, 282–284; flaws of evaluation systems, 276–277; including instructions in syllabus, 279–281; weekly student audits, 277–278

Evaluation system flaws, 276–277

Evidential assessor role, 274

Expectations: clarifying in course syllabus, 59–61; combating repressive tolerance via, 260; failure and unrealistic, 37–38, 41; online course, 242–243; succumbing to others', 197–198; teachers' failing to model, 202

Experience: disclosing personal, 160–161; discussions based on, 29–30; recalling memorable, 73–75; reviewing text based on, 57–58; traumatic discussion, 180, 187–188

F

Face-to-face classes, 219, 229

Faculty, *See also* Professional colleagues: demonstrating norms of participation, 51–52; presenting dissenting views in lectures, 46–47

Failures in discussion: lack of ground rules, 38–39; reward systems for discussion and, 39–40; student unpreparedness, 38; teacher and, 40–41; unrealistic expectations and, 37–38, 41

Fear of looking stupid, 179–180, 184–185

Feeling unprepared, 180, 185

Feeling unwelcome, 180, 186–187

Fein, A. D., 223–224

Female speech, 149, 154–155, *See also* Gender; Women

Feminist approach to pedagogy, 156–157

Fetzer Institute of San Francisco, 130

Finkel, D. L., 235

Fishkin, J., 13–14

Five-minute inventory, 258–259

Five-minute rule, 135–136

Foucault, M., 248, 252

Frankfurt School of critical social theory, 7

Frederick, P., 68, 71, 72

LINEBERGER
MEMORIAL LIBRARY
LUTHERAN THEOLOGICAL
SOUTHERN SEMINARY
COLUMBIA, SOUTH CAROLINA 29203

DEMCO